UNDERSTANDING
INDIAN POLITICS

UNDERSTANDING
INDIAN POLITICS

Sheikh Javaid Ayub

PARTRIDGE

A Penguin Random House Company

Print information available on the last page.

To order additional copies of this book, contact
Partridge India
000 800 10062 62
orders.india@partridgepublishing.com

www.partridgepublishing.com/india

CONTENTS

FOREWORD

More than two millennia ago Aristotle said that man was a social being. His gregariousness was greatly responsible to make him live as a part of society. And this society once politically organized, geographically demarcated with a sovereign decision-making agency (government) it took the form of modern state. Whatever the forms of government and whatever way the government operates every individual's life is directly or indirectly impacted. Now when the population of states runs in hundreds of millions and when the functions of state have multiplied manifold an individual cannot remain unconcerned with the affairs of state, plain and simple. In these times the elementary knowledge about the basic elements of state, different organs of government and other agencies and institutions is simply essential.

This book is the culmination of sincere efforts of the author to lucidly elaborate major themes in the Indian political system. The contents of the book are targeted for a wider readership. It will benefit under-graduate, post-graduate and students aspiring to appear in different Union and State level competitive examinations. The contents of the book are presented in an attractive and imaginative way. In discussing the Indian political system an attempt has been made by the author to make suitable comparisons with the other political systems of the world as well. This enables a comparison of different political systems to find out the outstanding similarities and dissimilarities between them. The theoretical components of the subject are made more relevant by incorporating tables. Various debates have been added on the burning issues concerned with the subject matter at proper places which only add to the beauty of the book.

In the present age of knowledge convergence and high political activism, a study of the Indian political system becomes highly imperative. The book will make a reader feel the political history of India in the immediate aftermath of Indian partition when existing constitution of the country was being debated in the Constituent Assembly to the present times when the constitution stands amended more than hundred times. In these six decades after independence all major challenges in the way of nation-building are adequately covered in the book. The book sets to socialize the younger generations in the spirit of secularism, democracy, liberalism and brotherhood, which are must for evolution of an informed and participant citizenry. The author has throughout tried to view the changes in the Indian political system over the decades from an egalitarian and social democratic prism.

The expectations of 125 crore Indians from the political system have increased partly due to increase in literacy rate, globalization and widening of democratic space. There is a tendency among these people to learn about their political system quite closely. This book fits to that requirement as well.

The author has made a serious attempt to throw light upon the popular jargons making rounds in media and academic circles, inter alia, Khilafat, Islam and politics, etc. Besides, the book in your hands gives adequate space to the understanding of political institutions and process in the state of Jammu and Kashmir. This makes the book a novel read indeed.

Ibrahim Khaja
Assistant Professor Degree Collage Sopore
Jammu and Kashmir

December 05, 2014

ACKNOWLEDGEMENTS

I owe gratitude and more to:

Ibrahim Khaja, greatest of friends, for not only writing the foreword of the book but also for going through the book page by page, line by line, and for providing some valid insights and guidances that helped to make the book more comprehensive.

Bilkeesa Jan, my cousin, whose support and meticulous feedback came when I needed it the most.

Mohammad Ayub, my father, Qulsooma, my mother whose abundance of love, bundles of praise, make me feel proud.

Bilkeesa, my wife-the book, and life, might not have been possible if she hadn't arrived on the scene. Her love and patience make work easier and charming.

Tawseef, my brother, Rukhsana and Swaiza, my sisters-their supportive role was vital for completion of the book.

Wajeeha (Sunat), my daughter, Abu Hayan, my son for complaisant nature, their beautiful smiles and warm hugs rejuvenated me whenever I felt tired or bored.

Manzoor Ahmad Mir, my childhood friend and companion, for patiently doing the proof reading of the book.

Reyaz Ahmad Sheikh, my uncle, who gladly typed the major portion of the manuscript.

Partridge Publishing House, without them the book would never have come to light.

And

To all those who encouraged me to write this book.

Dedicated to my beloved children
Wajeeha (Sunat) and Abu Hayan

INTRODUCTION

Since the dawn of political thought 'who should rule' has been a recurrent issue of agreement and debate. Since the twentieth century, however, the question has tended to elicit a single and almost universally accepted response that people should govern. Perhaps no other political idea is accorded the unquestioning approval currently enjoyed by democracy. Whether they are, Liberals, Conservatives, Socialists, Communists etc. politicians everywhere are eager to proclaim their democratic credentials and to commit themselves to the democratic ideals.

Democracy functions on the principle of 'rule of law' and 'supremacy of law'. Thus constitutions hold a significant place in democratic governments. India is regarded as the largest democracy of the world, thus understanding the constitution of a country like India is a must.

This book 'Understanding Indian Politics' is culmination of a desire to make the working of Indian Constitution easier for students to grasp. The book is written in a fashion to create an appetite for more information about Indian government and politics. There is no doubt in the statement that the study of the working of the Indian Constitution is a gateway to understand politics in India.

Written in a lively and engaging style, the book provides a clear and highly accessible introduction to the Constitution of India, its functioning and various issues that confront its application. Each chapter discusses a cluster of interrelated terms and concepts. The book is designed systematically to build understanding not only of the making of the Indian Constitution but also different issues that emerged in its working.

We know that the independence of India came along with a partition. The partition and the problems it unfolded made nation building a challenge for the Indian leaders. The most daunting challenge was to frame a constitution that will accommodate different diversities, and will inculcate among Indian people a spirit of nationalism, secularism and democracy. The challenge was boldly accepted by the Constituent Assembly of India when it met for the first time on 29th December, 1946. To build a democratic and civil libertarian society among an illiterate people is an accomplishment the Constituent Assembly must be praised for.

The first chapter of the book discusses the origin, composition and working of the Constituent Assembly. The sources of the Indian constitution and the salient features are also part of the first chapter.

Constitutions have their guiding philosophies and for Indian Constitution the philosophy is embedded in the Preamble of the Constitution. The words of the preamble are so noble and eloquent that Professor Barker made it the preface of his famous book 'Principles of Social and Political Theory'. The second chapter discusses the philosophy underlying the Indian Constitution.

Individual has been accorded a privileged place in the Constitution. His development and welfare is what the state exists for. Part third of the Constitution contains Fundamental Rights which are essential for the development of individual personality. Therefore, it is no coincidence that the third chapter of the book contains rights and duties of the Indian citizens.

One of the important rights citizens of India enjoy is right to participate in government formation. This right is enjoyed through voting and every citizen above 18 years is entitled to vote. Elections are seen nothing less than democracy in practice. Election process, methods of election with their advantages and disadvantages are discussed in the fourth chapter of the book. Election Commission is the 'vanguard' of whole electoral process, so its role is due to be highlighted. Further, the chapter contains a commentary on the most recent efforts of judiciary to de—criminalize elections in India.

The three organs of the government – Executive, Legislature and Judiciary function on the theory of separation of powers. Montesquieu propounded the doctrine of separation of powers. To him when the legislative power is united with the executive power in the same person or legislative and judicial power is not separated, there is no liberty, because in the first case, he will make tyrannical laws and execute them tyrannically and in latter case, the power over the life and liberty of citizens would be arbitrary, because the judge will be the legislature. Chapter five, six and seven are devoted to the structure and functions of the government.

Right from the first day of independence it was realized by the Indian leaders that the most important task was to preserve, consolidate and strengthen India's unity, to push forward the process of national integration. Indian unity, it was realized, was not to be taken for granted. It had to be strengthened by recognizing and accepting India's immense regional, linguistic, ethnic and religious diversity. A federal form of government, although a made in India federalism, became an unavoidable choice. Indian federalism has changed from cooperative federalism to bargaining federalism. Collapse of Congress system and emergence of coalition politics changed the face of Indian federalism. Chapter eight debates Indian federalism and highlights some challenges Indian federalism faces with special focus on Jammu and Kashmir.

It is an established fact that a sound party system is indispensable to democracy. It is important to visualize a health polity without a vigorous party system. Indian party system has evolved since ages. From one party dominance to the era of coalitions, the Indian party system has shown tremendous dynamism. Chapter nine of the book deals with party system in India.

Indian nation dreams development; development demands decentralization and a bottom top approach of power. 73rd and 74th Amendment Acts are worthy to be mentioned in this direction. These amendments act as milestones in bringing a second democratic upsurge in India by granting Panchayat institutions a constitutional status. Local self institutions represent the ethos of democracy and act as the institutions for political socialization. Panchayati raj system is discussed in the ninth chapter of the book with special space provided to the Panchayat Raj system of Jammu and Kashmir.

The Constitution of India has undergone many a changes since its formation. Change is the law of nature. New situations demand either a change in the existing legal apparatus or altogether new laws. And constitutions that discourage change face the wrath of the time. The makers of the Indian Constitution, while holding the sacredness of the constitution intact, empowered the Parliament to amend the constitution. The constitution at present stands amended almost hundred times. Some of the Amendments are explained in between the chapters to make readers feel the flexibility of the Indian Constitution and the dynamism of the political system.

The last chapter discusses some of the important challenges Indian democracy confronts with. Maoism is one such challenge which needs a special mention along with communalism and regionalism.

Sheikh Javaid Ayub

21 December, 2014

CHAPTER 1

MAKING OF THE INDIAN CONSTITUTION

'Government without a Constitution is Power without Right'
Thomas Paine

Constitutionalism, in a narrow sense, is the practice of limited government ensured by the existence of constitution. Thus constitutionalism can, in this sense, be said to exist when government institutions and political processes are effectively constrained by constitutional rules. More broadly, constitutionalism is a set of political values and aspirations that reflect the desire to protect liberty through the establishment of internal and external checks on governmental power. In this sense constitutionalism is a species of political liberalism. It is typically expressed in the form of support for constitutional provisions that achieve the goal: for example a codified constitution, a bill of rights, a separation of powers, bicameralism, and federalism or decentralization. It stands for the supremacy of law and not of the individuals. **Aristotle** was the champion of rule of law.

A constitution may be said to be a set of rules, written or unwritten, that seek to establish the duties, powers and functions of the various institutions of government, regulate the relationships between them, and define the relationship between the state and the individual. It lays down a procedure according to which the powers of the government, the rights of the governed and the relations between the two are adjusted.

Constitution of a country lays down the basic structure of the political system under which its people are to be governed. It establishes the main organs of the state, i.e. the legislature, the executive and the judiciary, defines their powers, demarcates their responsibilities and regulates their relationships with each other and with the people. A constitution not only specifies who has the power to take the decisions in the society but also clarifies in whose interest these decisions should be made. Thus constitutions are essentially based on a two-fold relationship. One, between the government and the citizens and the other relationship is between one authority and another within the government structure. Constitutions check the illegal use of political power, hence are based upon a common belief in limited government. The age of constitutions was initiated by the enactment of the first written constitution: the US Constitution in 1787 and the French Declaration of Rights of Man and the Citizen in 1789.

> **Aristotle:** Aristotle (384- 322 BC) is regarded as the father of Political Science. He joined Plato's Academy at the age of 17 and remained there for next twenty years, first as a student and then as a member of the faculty. His most influencing work *Politics* is a masterpiece in the subject of Political Science.

Classifying Constitutions

The tradition of classifying Constitutions is as old as Political Science itself. **Plato** and Aristotle started the tradition. Aristotle had classified constitutions on two important bases, the number of persons who rule and secondly in whose interest they rule. Aristotle has given a six-fold classification of governments.

Number of persons who rule	Good Governments	Bad Form
Rule of one	Monarchy	Tyranny
Rule of few	Aristocracy	Oligarchy
Rule of many	Polity	Democracy

In the modern sense constitutions can be classified in many different ways. These include the following:

1. **Written and unwritten constitutions:** In simple terms, a written constitution is one whose provisions are written in detail and an unwritten constitution is one whose provisions are very brief and most of the rules of the constitution exist in the form of usage and customs. Written constitutions are created by human beings themselves at a given period of time while as unwritten constitutions are organic entities that have evolved through history. Only three liberal democracies (Israel, New Zealand, and UK) continue to have unwritten constitutions together with a handful of non-democratic states such as Bhutan, Saudi Arabia and Oman.

> **Plato**
>
> *Plato (428/27 - 347) was born in Athens in Greece. His real name was Aristocles, which meant 'best and renowned'. A great philosopher, Plato was the student of Socrates. In 386 Plato established his school known as Academy. Plato taught that the material world consists of imperfect copies of abstract and eternal 'ideas'. His political philosophy, expounded in* The Republic and The Laws, is an attempt to describe the Ideal State in terms of the theory of justice.

2. **Flexible and Rigid:** Constitutions are usually classified as 'flexible' or 'rigid', depending upon the process through which they can be amended. Prof. A.V. Dicey defines two types of Constitutions—the flexible as *'one under which every law of every description can legally be changed with the same ease and in the*

3

same manner by one and the same body', and the rigid as 'one *under which certain laws generally known as constitutional or fundamental laws, cannot be changed in the same manner as ordinary laws'*. Simply stating, if the process of amendment is very simple and convenient, the constitution is flexible and if the process of amendment is quite difficult, the constitution is rigid. Written constitutions are generally rigid and unwritten constitutions generally flexible. Under the rigid constitutions a special procedure i.e. 2/3 majority is required to amend the constitution, while for the amendment of a flexible constitution a simple majority is required. The constitutions of USA, Switzerland, France and Australia are rigid and the constitutions of Israel, New Zealand, and UK are flexible. Indian constitution is a mixture of both rigidity and flexibility.

Explaining why it was necessary to introduce an element of flexibility in the Constitution, **Pundit Jawaharlal Nehru** observed in the Constituent Assembly:

While we want this Constitution to be as solid and as permanent a structure as we can make it, nevertheless there is no permanence in Constitutions. There should be certain flexibility. If you make anything rigid and permanent, you stop a nation's growth, the growth of a living, vital, organic people. Therefore, it has to be flexible.... In any event, we should not make a

Pundit Jawaharlal Nehru

Jawaharlal Nehru (1889 - 1964) was one among the great leaders of India. He was born on 14th November 1889 in Allahabad, India to Motilal Nehru. The Nehru family was originally from Kashmir. He joined Indian National Congress in 1919 and became a prominent figure in the freedom struggle of India. Once India achieved Independence in 1947 he became the first Prime Minister of Independent India. He was a prominent architect of modern Indian political thought. His books include: Discovery of India, Glimpses on World History.

Constitution, such as some other great countries have, which are so rigid that they do not and cannot be adapted easily to changing conditions. Today especially, when the world is in turmoil and we are passing through a very swift period of transition, what we may do today may not be wholly applicable tomorrow. Therefore, while we make a Constitution which is sound and as basic as we can, it should also be flexible.

3. **Effective, Nominal or Façade Constitutions:** A third system of classification takes account of the relationship between constitutional rules and principles on one hand and the practice of government (the 'working' constitution) on the other. An effective constitution is one that fulfills two criteria. First, in major respects at least, the practical affairs of government correspond to the provisions of the constitution. Second, this occurs because the constitution has the capacity, through whatever means, to limit governmental behavior. An effective constitution therefore requires not merely the existence of constitutional rules, but also the capacity of those rules to constrain government and establish constitutionalism. But all constitutions are violated to a greater or lesser extent; the real issue is thus the significance and regularity of such violations. Some constitutions can be classified as nominal, in that their texts or principles may accurately describe governmental behavior but fail to limit it. Sham or façade constitutions differ substantially from political practice and tend to fulfill, only a propaganda role. This is particularly the case in dictatorial or authoritarian states, where commitment to individual rights and liberties extends little further than the content of the state's constitutional document.

4. **Monarchical or Republican, Unitary or Federal, Parliamentary or Presidential:** Constitutions have also been classified in terms of their content and, specially, by the institutional structure they underpin. This enables a number of distinctions to be made. For example, constitutions have traditionally been categorized as either monarchical or republican. In theory, the former invests

constitutional supremacy in a dynastic ruler, while in the latter the political authority is derived from the people. Another category is made between unitary and federal. In a unitary constitution, all powers are vested in the central government to which the authorities in the units are subordinate and function as the agents of the government at the centre and exercise authority to be delegated from the centre. In a federal polity, usually, there must be a rigid, written constitution, it must be supreme and it must specifically divide powers between the centre and the units. Yet another approach is to differentiate between a parliamentary system of government and a presidential system of government. In parliamentary systems the legislature and executive branches of the government are fused together and the executive is derived from and accountable to the legislature. But the presidential system of governments work on separation of powers and the two branches of government function independently.

The Purpose of a constitution

In present times constitutions have acquired greater significance. Not only do the vast majority of states have constitutions, but also most institutions and organized groups have rules that have some kind of constitutional effect. This applies in the case of international bodies such as United Nations, European Union, ASEAN and the like. The popularity of these constitutional rules draws attention to the fact that constitutions somehow play a very important role in our organized life. Can states and other organizations function without constitutions? The answer is 'No', but why? Because the constitutions play a number of vital functions which are as under:

1. The first function of a constitution is to provide a set of basic rules that allow for minimal coordination amongst members of a society.

2. The second function of a constitution is to specify who has the power to make decisions in a society. It decides how the government will be constituted.

3. The third function of the constitution is to set some limits on the government power so as to protect the freedom of individuals. These limits are fundamental in the sense that government may never trespass them.

4. The fourth function of a constitution is to enable the government to fulfill the aspirations of a society and create conditions for a just society.

5. The fifth function of a constitution is that it establishes values and goals for the society or state. Besides laying down a framework for government, constitutions invariably embody a broader set of political values, ideals and goals. These ideals are mostly enshrined in the preamble of the constitution and can vary from a commitment to democracy, freedom or welfare state to a belief in socialism, federalism or Islam.

6. Lastly and most importantly constitutions express the fundamental identity of the people.

CONSTITUENT ASSEMBLY

The Constitution of every country has a distinctive colour of its own. Just as each country has a culture and language; it has a constitution that represents its ethos. Some constitutions, like the Constitution of France and the Constitution of the USA are the products of political revolution. The British Constitution is a gradual evolution of many centuries. Indian constitution is not the product of a political revolution, but is the result of deep deliberations of a body called as the Constituent Assembly. A constituent Assembly is a democratic device for formulating or bringing about some fundamental changes in the existing constitution.

Mahatma Gandhi
Mohandas Karamchand Gandhi (1869- 1948) is regarded as the father of Indian Nation. Popularly known as Mahatma Gandhi, he developed the philosophy of Non-violence and Truth which became potent weapons to fight against a mighty colonial power. His famous autobiography is titled as 'My Experiments with Truth.'

The idea of a Constituent Assembly, where by Indians themselves might frame a constitution for their country, was for the first time given by **Mahatma Gandhi** in 1922 when he said, "Swaraj will not be a free gift of the British Parliament, it will be a declaration of India's full self – expression." The adoption of the famous Motilal Nehru demand was a historic event in as much as the central legislature had, for the first time, lent its support to the growing demand that the future constitution of India should be framed by Indians themselves.

Nevertheless, it was not until 1935 that the idea was officially and seriously put forward by the Indian National Congress. Jawaharlal Nehru wrote in January 1938, that Indian National Congress stands for independence and a democratic state. It has proposed that constitution of a free India must be framed without outside interference, by a Constituent Assembly elected on the basis of adult franchise.

Till the World War II, the British Government resisted India's demand for a Constituent Assembly. But the war and the international situation created circumstances, which opened the eyes of the Churchill Government. The British Government showed some favours in the form of '**August Offer'** and **Cripps Mission** but were rejected by Congress.

A definite advance in this direction was made with the arrival of the Cabinet Mission in India on 24th March 1946 and acceptance of the Cabinet Mission plan by the British Parliament which gave the outline of a 389 member Constituent Assembly. The Cabinet Mission, however, used the term, 'constitution making body' instead of Constituent Assembly.

The Cabinet Mission realized that the most satisfactory method to constitute a constitutional making – body would have been by election based on adult franchise, but that would have caused "a wholly unacceptable delay" in the formulation of the new constitution. So the constitution makers focused on utilizing the recently elected provincial legislative assemblies as electing bodies. So, the members were indirectly elected by a system of proportional representation from the provincial legislature which themselves had been constituted on the basis of restricted franchise-about 25 percent of the adult population. Hence the method of election was not perfectly democratic, and it is not to deny that the constituent assembly was not largely a representative body. Looking at the composition of the constituent assembly (82 percent were Congress

August Offer: Lord Linlithgo on 8 August 1940 made a statement in which he explained the new constitutional policy for India. The main features of August Plan were: The Indians were to frame a constitution for India which was to be drafted after World War II by the Constituent Assembly.

Cripps Mission: The Crips Proposal envisaged complete transfer of power to Indians after the war, and partial transfer during the war. In return of this, Britain wanted the Indian leaders to support and wholeheartedly for the prosecution of the war.

members), Granville Auston has rightly pointed out that Constituent Assembly was the Congress and the Indian National Congress was India.

We know that India was divided under the Indian Independence Act of 1947. The important characteristic of this act was that from the 15th August 1947, there would setup two independent Dominions, to be known as India and Pakistan and the Constituent Assembly of each Dominion was to have unlimited power to frame and adopt any constitution. As a result of Partition, a separate Constituent Assembly was set up for Pakistan. The representatives of Bengal, Punjab, Sindh, North Western Frontier Provence, Baluchistan and the Sylhet district of Assam joined Pakistan by a referendum and thus ceased to be members of the Constituent Assembly of India. The partition made Congress the sole maker of the Constitution for India and Muslim League that of Pakistan.

Dr. Rajender Prasad

Dr. Rajendra Prasad (1884-1963) was the first President of Independent India. He was elected as the President of the Constituent Assembly of India in 1947 and when Indian became a Republic in 1950, Prasad was elected its first President.

In the first session of the sovereign constituent assembly of India, **Dr. Rajender Prasad** said that it was to be cooperative common wealth and the making of its constitution was the supreme task of the assembly. The foundation of its constitutional structure was laid by the **Objective Resolution** moved by Jawaharlal Nehru on 13 December 1946. The drafting committee changed the draft from Sovereign, Independent, Republic to Sovereign, Democrat, Republic and added one new clause of 'Fraternity' which was not mentioned in the Objective Resolution.

Framing of the Constitution: The Constituent Assembly held its 1st meeting on 9th December, 1946 under the temporary chairmanship of Dr. Sachidanand Sinha. On 11th December 1946, the Constituent Assembly elected Dr. Rajendra Prashad as its permanent President. Speaking in the momentous session of the Constituent Assembly on 15 August 1947 as the President, Dr. Rajendra Prasad spelled out the vision and appealed to the members of the Constituent Assembly to build the free India of their dreams. He said:

"Let us resolve to create conditions in this country, When every individual will be free and provided with the wherewithal to develop and rise to his fullest stature, When poverty and squalor and ignorance and ill health will have vanished, When the distinction between high and low, between rich and poor, will have disappeared, When religion will not only be professed and preached and practiced freely but will have become a cementing force for binding man and man and not serve as a disturbing and disrupting force dividing and separating, When untouchability will have been forgotten like an unpleasant dream, When exploitation of man by man will have ceased......."

This vision is reflected in the Preamble to the Constitution of India, providing the machinery to realize it through the principles fundamental in governance contained in the Directive Principles of State Policy, assuring the dignity of the individual and the guarantee of Fundamental Rights.

> **Objective Resolution:** The Objective Resolution was adopted by the Constituent Assembly on 22nd of January 1947. This Resolution was circulated by Jawaharlal Nehru and it contains objectives which the constitution of India has to achieve. It specified the objectives of making India a Sovereign Independent Republic based on principle of popular sovereignty, and committed to secure social, economic and political justice for all. The resolution put a great emphasis on making India a secular polity which will secure the interests of the minorities. The constitution fully upholds the philosophy and ideas of the objective resolution.

The major task before the Constituent Assembly was indeed the making of a constitution of India and just after four days of its inaugural meeting, the first step was taken towards this goal when Pundit Jawaharlal Nehru introduced the objective resolution in it and described it as a solemn pledge of the people.

For conducting its work in a systematic and efficient manner, the Constituent Assembly constituted several committees which were to report on the subjects assigned to them. Some of these committees were Committees on Procedural matters and some were Committees on Substantive matters. In the first category came, Rules of Procedure Committee, Finance and Staff Committee, Credential Committee, Urdu Translation Committee, Press Gallery Committee, House Committee and Committee on Independence Act. The substantive matters committee included: Union Power Committee, Union Constitution Committee, Provisional Constitution Committee, Advisory Committee on Minorities and Fundamental Rights and Committee on Financial Rights between the Union and the States. The reports of these committees provided the bricks for the formulation of the constitution of India.

B.R. Ambedkar

Dr. Bhimrao Ramji Ambedkar (1891-1956) popularly known as Babasaheb, was an Indian jurist, politician and social reformer who was born in a lower caste Mahar family in Madhya Pradesh India. He fought for the rights of deprived classes and socially backward castes. Popularly known as the father of Indian Constitution, he acted as the chairman of the Drafting Committee. In 1990, Ambedkar was posthumously conferred with the Bharat Ratna, India's highest civilian award.

The most important committee, among all was the Drafting Committee. This committee played a very important and valuable role in the making of the constitution. This committee was constituted on 29th August 1947 with **Dr. B.R. Ambedkar** as its chairman. The drafting committee submitted its report (draft) to the Constituent Assembly on 21 February 1948 and the Constituent Assembly held debate on it. On the basis of these discussions, a new draft was prepared and submitted to the Assembly on 4th November 1948. The first debate on this draft was held from 4th to 9th November 1948. Thereafter, from 15th November 1948 to 17th October 1949, each clause of the draft was thoroughly debated upon and passed. In all, 7635 amendments were proposed, out of which 2473 amendments were discussed. From 14th November 1949 to 26th November 1949 final debates were held on the draft. On 26th November

1949, the constitution was finally adopted and enacted when it was signed by the President of the Constitution Assembly. The final session of the Constituent Assembly was held on 24 January 1950. It unanimously elected Dr Rajeder Prashad as the first President of the Republic of India. At the concluding session of the Constituent Assembly, both, Dr. B. R. Ambedkar and Dr. Rajendra Prasad, struck a note of caution:

Dr. B. R. Ambedkar said, '*I feel, however good a constitution may be, it is sure to turn over bad because those who are called to work it happen to be a bad lot. However bad a constitution may be, it may turn out to be good if those who are called upon to work it happen to be a good lot. The working of a constitution does not depend wholly upon the nature of the constitution..........*"

The Constituent Assembly was able to conclude its labor within a period of less than three years-2 years 11 months and 17 days to be exact. According to Subash C Kashyap, "It was no mean achievements that within a period of less than three years, the founding fathers succeeded in evolving a constitution acceptable throughout the length and breadth of this vast country and one capable of salvaging and strengthening the threads of national unity in the midst of the multiplicity of religions, races, language and all the variants of diversity". On 26th November, 1949 the Constituent Assembly could proudly declare on behalf of the people of India that "we do here by adopt, enact and give to ourselves this constitution". Even after its commencement on 26 January 1950, the constitution of India was being further made through its actual working, judicial interpretation and constitutional amendments. The constitution kept growing for better or worse and acquired newer and newer meanings by the manner in which and the men by whom it was worked from time to time.

Whatever the constitution may or may not provide, the welfare of the country will depend upon the way in which the country is administered. That will depend upon the men who administer it. If the people who are elected are capable and men of character and integrity, they would be able to make the best even of a defective constitution. If they are lacking in these, the constitution cannot help the country. After all, a constitution like a machine is a lifeless thing. It acquires life because of the men who control it, operate it. Criminalization of politics and politicization of crimes has fueled the caste colour differences, regional and religious differences and so on. India needs today nothing more than a set of honest men who will have the interest of the country before them and be men of vision, men who will not sacrifice the interest of the country for petty political interests or group interests. Well known is the saying that 'India is not underdeveloped but under administered'.

	Important Communities of the Constituent Assembly	Chairman
1	The committee on rules of procedure	Chairman of the constituent assembly
2	The negotiating committee	Jawaharlal Nehru
3	The strength committee	Chairman of the constituent
4	The business committee	assembly
5	Fundamental Rights sub-committee	K.M Munshi J B Kriplani
6	The minorities sub-committee	H. C Mukhirjee
7	Union power committee	Jawaharlal Nehru
8	The union constitution committee	Jawaharlal Nehru
9	The provincial constitution committee	Sardar Vallabh Bhai Patel
10	The drafting committee	Dr B.R Ambeedkar
11	The export committee on the financial provisions of the union constitution	N.R Sarkar
12	The linguistic provinces committee	S.K Dahar

Dr B.R Ambeedkar (the father of the Indian constitution) said, "People always keep on saying to me, 'Oh you are the maker of the constitution' My answer is I was a hulk, whatever I was asked to do, I did much against my will. I have made the constitution, but I am quite prepared to say that I shall be the first person to burn it on. It does not suit anybody".

SOURCES OF THE CONSTITUTION

Indian constitution is the unique constitution not only for being the constitution of world's largest democracy but also for embodying the best features of a number of constitutions of the word. The sources of the constitution of India are diverse and many. They are both indigenous and foreign. In framing the constitution of India the founding fathers kept before them ideals and values of the national movement as well as they depended upon several world constitutions, their own preparations and value and the views of the experts. Even after its commencement on 26 January 1950, the constitution of India was being further made through amendments, decisions of the Supreme Court and several conventions. Its interpretation by constitutional experts had also helped it to grow. All these are then the sources of the Indian constitution.

The founding fathers took a conscious decision not to make a complete departure from the past, but to build on the existing structure and experience of institutions already established. The Indian constitution makers tried to adopt the best features from the important constitutions of the world. Mainly, they borrowed features of the constitution of UK, USA, Canada, Ireland, Germany and USSR. But borrowing these ideas was not a slavish imitation. Far from it, each provision of the constitution had to be defended on grounds that it was suited to Indian problems and aspirations. India was extremely lucky to have an assembly that, instead of being parochial in its outlook, could take the best available everywhere in the world and make it their own. The opening and closing words of the preamble, *"We the people of India ....adopt, enact and give to ourselves this constitution"* conveys that the real sources of the constitution of India are people themselves; in other words, it can be said that the people of India are the real sources of the constitution and it is they who hold the sovereign power. However, the framers borrowed essentially from three sources: 1. The Government of India Act, 1935 which was a foundation document, 2. the Objective Resolution adopted during the December

1964 Assembly Session. 3. Along with these the framers of the constitution drew widely upon the mature experience of democratic countries.

1. **GOVERNMENT OF INDIA ACT, 1935**

The 1935 Act for the first time provided for a federal system for India taking the provinces and the Indian states as units. As we know that after the rejection of the demand for a Dominion Status, the 1929 Lahore Session of the Congress adopted a resolution on Purna Swaraj. A Civil Disobedience Movement began with a call to break the Salt Tax Law. The Government decided to hold a Round Table Conference in London in November 1930 to consider constitutional reforms. After three Round Table conferences, the British Parliament passed the Government of India Act, 1935. The most remarkable feature of the Act was that it prescribed, for the first time, a federation for India. The Government of India Act 1935 was a detailed and complicated document consisting of 321 sections and 10 schedules.

The Act constitutes the next milestone in the journey of constitutional development in India. Some of the important features of the Act are:

1. The Act provided for the establishment of a federal form of government in place of the prevailing unitary one. The proposed federation was to consist of the British Indian Provinces and the Princely States. Though the scheme consisted of some of the essential features of a federation like a written constitution, a scheme for the distribution of powers between the federal government and units, a federal court to settle the disputes between the Centre and the States, it had certain peculiar features which made it a unique one among the federations. A. B. Keith condemned the federal scheme as "bastard federation'.

2. Just as the Act of 1935 made the division of powers between the centre and the states through three lists, the Constitution

of India also provides for three lists_ the Union List, the State List and the Concurrent List for effecting a division of powers.

3. The Act introduced the system of diarchy at the Centre. It divided the federal subjects into two categories, *viz.*, reserved and transferred. The reserved subjects (like defense, external affairs, and ecclesiastical affairs) were to be administered by the Governor-General in his discretion with the help of Councilors appointed by him. The transferred subjects on the other hand were to be administered by the Governor-General on the advice of the Council of Ministers, which was responsible to the Legislature. However, the Governor-General could act contrary to the advice of the Ministers, if he thought it necessary to do so.

4. Provincial autonomy was the most important feature of the Act. It divided the legislative powers between the provincial and central legislatures and provinces were to be treated as autonomous units of administration rather than as delegates of the central government. The executive authority of the province was henceforth to be exercised by the Governor on behalf of the Crown and not as a subordinate of the Governor-General. The Governor was expected to act on the advice of the ministers who were responsible to the legislature.

5. The Act introduced a bicameral legislature in the Centre. It consisted of two houses, namely, Federal Assembly and Council of States. The Federal Assembly was to consist of 375 and the Council of States was to consist of 260 members. The two Houses were given co-equal powers even though the money bills could originate only in Federal Assembly. The Upper House could amend or reject a money bill. The Governor-General could veto measures passed by the federal legislature.

6. The Act conferred a plenitude of powers on the Governor-General. Unlike the King of Britain and the President of USA, he both reigned and ruled. His special powers and responsibilities gave him immense authority over the elected legislatures. He was given almost dictatorial powers. So much to that Sir Winston Churchill remarked, "The Viceroy or the Governor-General was armed with all the powers of a Hitler or Mussolini." Prof. Lowell observed that, The Governor-General or the Viceroy of India and the Czar of Russia are sometimes said to be the two great autocrats of the modern world."

7. The Act provided for a Federal Court consisting of a Chief Justice and six other judges. The Court was given original *as* well as appellate jurisdiction. However the Court was not supreme in so far as appeals against its decisions could be taken to the Judicial Committee of the Privy Council.

8. Indian Council was abolished and instead Secretary of State could appoint not less than 3 and not more than 6 members for advice.

9. The Act separated Burma from India and two new provinces Orissa and Sind were created.

10. The Act retained separate electorates to provide representation to special interests and communities in the Federal and Provincial Legislatures! Separate electorates were extended to also cover the labour class and women voters.

11. The Act also provided for a Public Service Commission for the Federal Government and one for each province.

The Government of India Act 1935 holds a significant place in the evolution of the Constitution of India. The Act was first of its kind which endeavored to give a written constitution to India. The Constituent Assembly heavily derived from the insights the Act provided. Besides all its importance and position the Act was bitterly criticised by various sections of Indian society. Jawaharlal Nehru described it as 'a new charter of bondage'. **M.A. Jinnah** of

Muslim League, described it as 'thoroughly rotten, fundamentally bad and totally unacceptable.

2. **The Objective Resolution:** The foundation of the Constitutional structure was laid by the Objective Resolution moved by Jawaharlal Nehru on 13th of December 1946. It said:

i. The Constituent Assembly declares its firm solemn resolve to proclaim India as an Independent Sovereign Republic and to draw up for her future governance a constitution.

ii. Wherein the territories that now comprise British India, the territories that now form the Indian states and such parts of India as are outside British India and the states as well as such other territories as are willing to be constituted into the independent sovereign India, shall be a union of them all;

iii. Wherein the said territories, whether with therein present boundaries or with such others as may be determined by the Constituent Assembly and thereafter according to the Law of the Constitution, shall possess and retain the status of autonomous units, together with residuary powers, and exercise all powers and questions of government and

M.A. Jinnah

Mohammad Ali Jinnah (1876-1948) was a lawyer, politician and the founder of Pakistan. He became the first Governor-General of Pakistan and is revered in Pakistan as Quaid-i-Azam (Great Leader) and Baba-i- Azam (Father of the Nation. Jinnah started his political career as a nationalist and became the member of Indian National Congress in 1906 but by 1940, he had come to believe that the Indian Muslims should have their own state. In that year, Muslim League, led by Jinnah, passed the famous Lahore Resolution, demanding a separate nation. This led to the partition of British India and the creation of Pakistan in 1947.

administration, save and except such powers and functions as are vested in or assigned to the union, or as are inherent or implied in the union or resulting there from; and

iv. Wherein all powers and authority of sovereign Independent India, its constituent parts and organs of Government, are derived from the people; and

v. Wherein shall be guaranteed and secured to all the people of India justice, social, economic and political; equality of status, of opportunity, and before the law; freedom of thought, expression, belief, faith, worship, vocation, association, subject to law and public morality; and

vi. Wherein adequate safeguards shall be provided for minorities, backward and tribal areas, and depressed and other backward classes; and

vii. Wherein shall be maintained the integrity of the territory of the Republic and its sovereign rights on local, seas and air according to justice and the law of civilized nations; and

viii. This ancient land attains its rightful and honoured place in the world and marks its full and willing contribution to the promotion of world peace and the Welfare of mankind.

The Objective Resolution was unanimously passed by the Constituent Assembly on 22 January 1947.

3. **Other Constitutions:**

The British Constitution: The following features have been borrowed from the constitution of U.K.

a. The adoption of parliamentary form of government with bi-cameral legislature is based on British parliamentary model.

b. The office of the President of India is based upon the British monarch who is a nominal head of the state.

c. The office of the prime minister in India is also a replica of the British prime minister.

d. The cabinet system in India is also in the same fashion as the British Cabinet.
e. The office of the Speaker of Indian Lok-Sabha also resembles the office of Speakers of British House of Commons. Some of his powers also resemble the powers of the Speaker in England.
f. In its rules and procedures, the Indian Parliament follows the rules and procedures of the British Parliament.

The American Constitution: In the following respects the constitution of India stands influenced by the constitution of the USA.

a. Indian constitution is a written constitution like that of the USA.
b. The preamble to the American constitution reads: "we *the people of the United State do ordain and establish this constitution for the USA*." The Indian preamble also runs like that, "*we the people of India ....do here by .... adopt, enact and give to ourselves this constitution*".
c. The fundamental rights in the Indian constitution are inspired by the American Constitution.
d. The nature and functions of the Supreme Court of India are comparable to those of the American constitution.
e. Just like the Senate of the USA the Rajya Sabah in India also represents the states.
f. The functions of the vice- President of India have been similar to those assigned to the vice- President of the U.S.A.

The constitution of Canada: The following features of the Indian constitution reflect the Canadian influence.

a. India has borrowed the scheme of federation from Canada.
b. The name 'Union' of Indian Republic' has got its sources in the Canadian constitution.

c. Like the Canadian, the Indian constitution vests residuary power in the hands of the centre.

The constitution of Ireland: From the constitution of Ireland the founding fathers of the Indian constitution have borrowed the concept of Directive principles of the State policy.

The South African constitution: Indian adopted the indirect method of election for Rajya Saba members' from the South African constitution.

The 'borrowing' exercise of the constitution makers has earned a lot of criticism from the critics. Some critics hold that Indian constitution is a 'bag of borrowing' while others call it a 'patchwork'.

SALIENT FEATURES OF THE CONSTITUTION

The constitution of India is remarkable for many outstanding features which distinguish it from other constitutions of the world. It is unique in many ways. The main features of the constitution are as:

1. **Largest, Lengthiest and Bulkiest Constitution:** The constitution of India has the distinction of being the most lengthy and detailed constitutional document the world has so far produced. As originally passed, it contained 395 Articles (divided into 22 parts) and eight schedules. At present the constitution is divided into 24 chapters or parts and twelve schedules. Numerous factors have helped the Indian constitution to be the lengthiest one: considerable numbers of amendments have added more than seventy articles, Three Parts: Part (IV) (deals with fundamental duties), Part IXA (deals with local self government in urban areas) and Part XIVA (deals with administrative tribunals) and four schedules 9th, 10th, 11th and 12th. The US constitution has only 07 Articles, while as Chinese constitution has 138 Articles. The present French Constitution has 92 Articles and the German constitution has 146 Articles.

2. **Partly Rigid and Partly Flexible:** Indian Constitution may be said to be combination of rigidity and flexibility in as much as certain provisions of the constitution can be amended through simple majority of the two Houses of the Parliament. Articles 2, 3, 4, 169 etc can be amended by simple majority in the Parliament. Other provisions which can be amended under Article 368 by a special majority of the members present at voting and a majority of the membership in each House. While there are certain provisions whose amendment requires not only special majority in the Parliament but also ratification by at least one half of the state legislatures. The fact that during the last 66 years there were as

many as 98 amendments, disproves the charge of the rigidity of the Indian constitution.

3. **Partly Unitary and Partly Federal:** The Indian constitution provides for a federation with a strong centre. It is noteworthy that the constitution has not used the word "federation' anywhere, and has described India as a 'Union of States'. India's constitution has been variously described as *Quasi-federal*, federal in character and unitary in spirit, federal in normal times but with possibilities of being converted into a purely Unitary one during Emergency, etc. The fact is that it is difficult to put Indian constitution in any strict mould of a federal or unitary type; it has features of both.

4. **Parliamentary Type of Government:** The Indian constitution established in India a Parliamentary type of government on the British model, but has not adopted the British model in toto. There are several fundamental differences and departures. To name a few; The British Constitution is still largely federal. The British is a **monarchy** with a hereditary King

> **Monarchy:** Monarchy originally meant 'the rule of one', though the word has now come to be attached to the constitution of kingship and queenship that is considered as hereditary.
> In absolute monarchies the monarch claims the, if seldom exercises, monopoly of political power (examples being Saudi Arabia, Morocco). In constitutional monarchies the monarch fulfills an essentially ceremonial function largely devoid of political significance (examples Spain, UK).

while India is a republic with an elected President. The founding fathers preferred the Parliamentary form because they had some experience of operating it and there were advantages in continuing established institutions. In a highly pluralistic society with India's size and diversity and with many pulls and pressures of various kinds, they believed that the parliamentary form was the most suited for accommodating a variety of interests and building a united India. In support of the Parliamentary form of government **K.M. Munshi** put the argument more candidly when he said:

'*We must not forget a very important fact that during the last hundred years, Indian public life has largely drawn upon the traditions of British constitutional law. Most of us have looked up to the British model as the best. For the last thirty or forty years, some kind of responsibility has been introduced in the governance of this country. India's constitutional traditions have become parliamentary. After this experience why should we go back upon the tradition that has been built for over a hundred years and by a novel experience?'*

> **K.M. Munshi** *Kanaiyalal Maneklal Munshi (1887-1971) popularly known as Kulpati Dr. K. M. Munshi, was an Indian Independence Movement activist politician, writer and an educationist from Gujarat state. He believed in the theory of Akhand Bharat and for this he established the Hindu Nationalist organization Vishva Hindu Parishad in 1964.*

Explaining the rationale in choosing Parliamentary system, Jawaharlal Nehru had stated in the Lok Sabha on March 28, 1957, "We choose the system of parliamentary democracy deliberately; We choose it not only because, to some extent, we had always thought on those lines previously, but because we thought it is, keeping with our own old traditions; not the old traditions as they were, but adjusted to the new conditions and new surroundings. We choose it - let us give credit where the credit is due- because we approved of its functioning in other countries, more especially in the United Kingdom."

5. **Compromise between Judicial Sovereignty and Parliamentary Supremacy:** In India, the constitution has arrived at a middle course and a compromise between the British Sovereignty of the Parliament and American Judicial supremacy. Since India has a

written constitution and the powers and functions of every organ are delimited by the constitution, there is no question of any organ being sovereign. Both the Parliament and the Supreme Court are sovereign in their respective spheres. While the Supreme Court may declare a law passed by the Parliament ultra virus or unconstitutional as being violative of the constitution, the Parliament may within certain restrictions amend most parts of the constitution. The theory underlying the Indian constitution in this respect can hardly be better expressed than in the words of Pundit Nehru:

"No Supreme Court, no judiciary, can stand in judgment over the sovereign will of the Parliament, representing the will of the entire country. It can pull up that sovereign will if it goes wrong, but in the ultimate analysis, where the future of the community is concerned, no judiciary can come in the way .... Ultimately, the fact remains that the legislature must be supreme and must not be interfered with by the courts of law in such measures as social reform".

6. **Presence of both Justifiable and Non-justifiable Rights:** The Indian constitution does not only contain a charter on Fundamental Rights (Part III) but also contains a part (Part IV) on Directive Principles of the state Policy which are non – justifiable but are nevertheless to be regarded as fundamental in the governance of the country. They are in the nature of 'Ideals' set by the founding fathers before the state and all the organs of the state must strive to achieve them. The Directive Principles of the State Policy have increasingly assumed greater relevance and importance not only for the legislatures but also in the eyes of the courts.

By the 42nd Constitutional Amendment a noble addition has been made in Part IV, i.e. one new part (Part IV A) was inserted which contains a chapter on Fundamental Duties of citizens. Although these Fundamental Duties are non- justifiable, they have now to be read along with Fundamental Rights.

7. **Single Citizenship:** In keeping with their aim of building an integrated Indian fraternity and a united nation, the founding

fathers provided for a single citizenship despite the federal structure. But the Citizenship (Amendment) Ordinance, 2005 was promulgated, paving the way for dual citizenship by amending the citizenship Act of 1955. It will bestow eligibility for registration as Oversea Citizens of Indian (OCI) on persons of Indian origin, who or whose parents/grandparents migrated from India after January 26, 1950 or were eligible to become Indian citizens on January 26, 1950 or belonged to a territory that became part of India after August 15, 1947 and their minor child, who is the national of a country that allows dual citizenship in some form or the other. Dual citizens do not have voting rights. Neither can they be elected to public office. As per the amended law, persons of Indian origin who were citizens of Australia, Canada, Finland, France, Greece, Ireland, Israel, Italy, Netherlands, New Zeeland, Portugal, Cyprus, Sweden, Switzerland, United Kingdom and the United states were eligible to apply for dual citizenship.

8. **Adult Franchise:** The Indian constitution has introduced the principle of Universal Adult Franchise and has abolished the old system of communal electorates. Dr. Ambedkar said in the Constituent Assembly that, by Parliamentary democracy we mean one person, one vote, one vote one value. Till 1989, an adult Indian meant an Indian citizen above the age of 21 years. But the Sixty – first Amendment to the constitution in 1989, reduced the voting age from 21 years to 18 years. Adult franchise is consistent with the principle of equality and non-discrimination. Adult Franchise was adopted by the constitution makers because they believed it was particularly remarkable in the context of the vast poverty and illiteracy of the Indian populace.

9. **Independent Judiciary:** The integrated and independent judiciary is yet another feature of the Indian constitution. The constitution of India establishes an independent judiciary with powers of judicial review. The High Courts and the Supreme Court form a single integrated judicial structure with jurisdiction over all laws – Union, State, Civil, Criminal or Constitutional.

The Supreme Court is the custodian of the constitution, of the federal system, and of the rights of the people. It is the highest court in the sense that it exercises supervisory and appellate jurisdiction over the courts below it. It interprets both the constitution as well as the law. Though the Supreme Court of India is not as powerful as the Supreme Court of America, it does have jurisdiction of giving advisory opinion; a power not exercised by the American Supreme Court. The role of the Supreme Court of India is evolving gradually. The 'Basic Structure Doctrine' struck by the Supreme Court of India in the Kesavananda Bharati Case has been, indeed significant.

Conclusion: The comparative study of any constitution will reveal that it has certain prominent features which distinguish it from other constitutions. The constitution of India is the most comprehensive document. It is unique in many ways. It is a mixture of unitary and federal features, rigid and flexible features, and President and parliamentary features. It attempts a balance between Fundamental Rights of the individual on the one hand and the socio – economic interests of the people and security of the state on the other.

Indian Constitution at a Glance

List of Chapters or Parts	List of Schedules
Part 1 (Article 1-4): Deals with the territory of India, admission or establishment of new states, formation of new states and alteration of areas, boundaries or names of existing states. **Part II (5-11):** Deals with citizenship at the commencement of the constitution.	**Schedule 1:** Deals with the territories of 28 states and 7 union territories of the Indian Union.

Part III (12-35): Deals with the fundamental Rights of Indian citizens. Originally there were seven Fundamental Rights guarantee by the constitution but abolition of Article 31 has reduced the number of fundamental rights to six.

Part Iv (36-51): Deals with the Directive Principles of the State policy which aim at making India` a welfare state.

Part IV A (51 A): Article 51 A was added by the 42nd Amendment in 1976. It outlines fundamental duties of the citizen of India.

Part V (52-151): Deals with the government at the union level. Article 52-73 deal with the President and vice - President, Article 74-75 deal with Council of Ministers and the Prime Minister of India, Article 79 – 122 relate to Indian Parliament, its composition and working, Article 148-151 deal with comptroller and Auditor general of India.

Part VI (152-237): Deals with the government at the state level.

Part Vii (238): Deals with states in part B of the First Schedule was replaced in 1956 by the seventh Amendment.

Schedule 2: Deals with the salaries, allowances, etc. of the President, Vice President, and Speaker, Judges of the Supreme Court and High Courts, the Comptroller and Auditor General etc.

Schedule 3: Prescribes the various forms of oath or affirmation which various incumbents have to take before assuming a public office.

Schedule 4: Deals with the seats allotted to various states and union territories in Rajya Sabha.

Schedule 5: Deals with the administration and control of the scheduled areas and scheduled Tribes.

Schedule 6: Deals with provision regarding administration of tribal Areas in the states of Assam, Meghalaya and Mizoram.

Part VIII (239 – 241): The administration of union Territories.

Part IX: Related to territories in Part D of the first schedule and other Territories was replaced in 1956. A new part IX was added to the constitution by 73rd Amendment Act, 1992. It comprises of 16 articles and a new schedule 'Eleven'. A new part IX-A to the constitution was added by the 74th Amendment Act, 1992. It consists of 18 articles and a new schedule Twelve.

Part X (244, 244A): Deals with the Scheduled and Tribal areas.

Part XI (245 – 263): Deals with the relations between the union and states. Article 245 – 255 deal with the legislative relations, Article 256 – 263 deal with administrative relations.

Part XII (264-300A): Deals with finance, property, contracts and suits. Articles 268-300A deal with the distribution of revenue between the union and states, appointment of finance provisions, borrowing by the Government of India and states Property, Contracts, rights, liabilities and obligations etc.

Schedule 7: Details the subjects contained in the three lists i.e. union list, state list and concurrent list.

Schedule 8:- Gives the list of 22 regional languages recognized by the centre.

Schedule 9: Contains certain acts and regulations of the state legislature dealing with land reforms and abolition of the Zamindari System. These acts and regulations are protected from judicial scrutiny. At present this schedule contains 284 such acts.

Schedule 10: This Schedule contains provisions containing disqualifications on the grounds of defection.

Schedule 11: It lists 29 subjects under the powers of Panchayats.

Schedule 12: It lists 18 subjects under the authority of Municipalities.

Part XIII (301-307): Relates to trade commerce and intercourse within the territory of India.

Part XIV (308 – 323): Relates to services under the union and states. Articles 315-323 relate to union Public service commission and public service commission and public service commission in the states.

Part XIV-A (323 A, 323 B): Inserted by the 42nd Amendment in 1976 contains only Article 323 A – 323 B which deal with the administrative Tribunals which may be set up by the Parliament to hear disputes and complaints regarding union, state or local government employees as well as for other matters.

Part XV (324 – 329): Deals with the elections and election commission of India.

Part XVI (330 – 342): Concerns special provision relating to certain classes such as reservation of seats of seats for schedule castes and schedule Tribes in Lok Sabha and State Assemblies; representation of Anglo – Indian Community in Lok Sabha and Legislative Assemblies; Claims of Schedule Casts and Schedule Tribes to services and posts etc.

Part XVII (343-351): Relates to official languages.

Part XVIII (352-360): Deals with emergency provisions. The President of India is vested with three emergency powers __ National Emergency under Article 352, Constitutional Emergency under Article 356, and Financial Emergency under Article 360.

Part XIX (361-367): Contains miscellaneous provisions, regarding exemption of the President and governors from criminal proceedings for their official acts; immunity from court proceedings for publication of their report of proceedings of the Parliament and state legislature and so on.

Part XXI (369-392): Contains temporary, transitional and special provisions. Article 370 provides special status to Jammu and Kashmir. Article 371A, 371B, 371C, 371D, 371E, 371F, 371G, 371H and 371I relate to special provisions for Maharastra, Nagaland, Assam, Manipur, Andhra Pradesh, Sikkim Mizoram, Arunachal Pradesh and Goa.

Part XXII (392 – 395):-Concerns the short title; Commencement and repeal of the Constitution.

CHAPTER 2

THE PREAMBLE

The Philosophy Underlying the Indian Constitution:

> *"The preamble to a constitution is expected to embody the fundamental values and the philosophy on which the constitution is based and the aims and objectives which the founding fathers enjoined the polity to strive to achieve."*
>
> Subash C. Kashyap

The constitution of every country has a guiding philosophy which is usually described in the Preamble to that constitution. The American constitution of 1784, The Chinese Constitution of 1954, the constitution of Bangladesh 1973, all begin with the Preamble. For the Philosophy underlying the Indian constitution we must look back into the historic Objective Resolution of Pundit Nehru which was adopted by the Constituent Assembly on January 22, 1947, and which inspired the shaping of the constitution through all its subsequent stages.

Meaning of the Preamble: The Preamble means a preliminary or introductory statement in speech or writing. Simply stating, the Preamble is the starting point of a constitution. According to K.M. Munshi, "The Preamble is the political horoscope of the constitution", meaning thereby that the Preamble lists the basic features of the constitution, its basic philosophy and the nature of Indian state. N.A. Phalkiwala defined the Preamble as the identity card of the constitution. Pundit Thakurdas Bhargave observed, "The Preamble is the most precious part of the constitution. It is the soul of the constitution. It is a key to the constitution." It normally expresses the political, moral and religious values which the constitution is intended to promote.

The preamble is the quaint essence of the Indian polity as it embodies the basic philosophy and throws light on its structure. It is a combination of the Philosophy of two revolutions, The Russian and the French. The concept of social justice has been taken from **Russian Revolution**[1] and the concepts of Liberty, Equality and Fraternity have been taken from the **French Revolution**[2].

The Preamble of the Indian constitution: The Preamble of the Indian constitution reads as:

"We, THE PEOPLE OF INDIA" having solemnly resolved to constitute India into a SOVEREIGN, SOCIALIST, SECULAR, DEMOCRATIC REPUBLIC and to secure to all citizens:

JUSTICE, social economic and political;

LIBERTY of thought, expression, belief, faith and worship.

EQUALITY of status and opportunity; and to promote among them all;

FRATERNITY assuring the dignity of the individual and unity and integrity of the nation;

In our Constituent Assembly this twenty-sixth day of November, 1949, do hereby; Adopt, Enact and give to ourselves this constitution."

---

[1] Russian Revolution of 1917 came by the writings of Karl Marx, a German Philosopher who gave the concept of social and economic justice in a classless and stateless society; what he called as Communist State.

[2] Rousseau is regarded as the god-father of French Revolution. The French Revolution of 1789 is regarded as the first modern revolution because it changed the structure of the society from feudalism to liberalism. The slogan of French Revolution was: Liberty, Equality and Fraternity.

Note: By the 42ⁿᵈ Constitutional Amendment Act the words, socialist, secular and integrity were added to the Preamble.

The words used in the Preamble of the Indian constitution are some of the noblest. They embody the highest values that human ingenuity and experience have been able to devise thus far. The Oxford University Political Science Professor Sir Ernest Barker was so moved by the text that he quoted it as a preface to his book, *"Principles of social and Political theory."*

The Preamble can be understood by dividing it in three main parts.

1. **Declaratory Part**: This part contains the belief that the source of the Indian constitution is people themselves. It is general will of the people of India which has been translated into the Indian constitution. The opening and closing words of the permeable, "We the people of India, adopt, enact and give to ourselves this constitution" convey that the constitution emanated from the people and the sovereignty under the constitution is vested in the people. B.R. Ambedkar said on the floor of the Constituent Assembly in 1949, "I say that this the Preamble embodies what is the desire of every member of the House, that this constitution should have its roots, its authority, its sovereignty from the people".

   In the Constituent Assembly some members objected to the use of the term "We the people" Moulana Hasrat Mohani objected to the use of these words on the ground that since the Constituent Assembly was elected by a small electorate and that too on the basis of communal electorates, it was not fully representative and hence not competent to use these words. However, this view was rejected by the Constituent Assembly and as such, the Preamble adopted by it, begins with the words' we the people." The fact is that such a declaration was essential after the end of the sovereignty of British Crown over India on 15ᵗʰ August 1947 and after the rise of India as a Sovereign Democratic Republic.

2. **Obligatory Part:** This part contains the goals which the state has to achieve, the type of polity assured to the people of India by the constitution. This part refers to the five cordial features of India as a state. It declares India to be a Sovereign, Socialist, Secular, Democratic, Republic. Originally the Preamble did not contain the terms 'Socialist' and 'Secular'. These were added to it by the 42nd Amendment.

Sovereignty: Sovereignty means the independent authority of a state. It means that it has a power to legislate on any subject; and that it is not subject to the control of any other state or external power. In the Kesavananda Bharti case Justice Mathew said that the Republic of India was "Sovereign" because it could make or unmake any decision with respect to itself without any interference from outside. The Preamble proclaims that India is a sovereign state. Such a proclamation was essential to denote the end of British rule over India.

The constitution of India does not contain any specific provision in regard to the vesting of sovereign powers. The only place where from the residence of sovereignty and the source of the constitution it can be ascertained is the Preamble. By saying that "We the people of India" "adopt, enact and give to ourselves this constitution," the founding fathers solemnly affirmed that Indians are one people and not people of different states, etc. and that sovereignty belonged to the whole people of India and not to those of separate states and also that the constitution was framed and adopted not by the people of states but by the whole people of India in the collective capacity as one indivisible sovereign.

Globalization and Sovereignty Debate

Conventional theory of sovereignty upholds supreme legal authority of the state in internal as well as external spheres. In recent years this theory was challenged from both sides i.e. from inside as well as from outside. Internal challenges to sovereignty came from the growing authority of various groups and associations who claimed allegiance from their members within the state. This was brought out by pluralistic theory of sovereignty. External challenges to sovereignty came from the external environment which threatened autonomy of the nation – state. The process of globalization further aggravated the situation. The most significant threat to the state sovereignty is the process of globalization. The state has lost its control on various fronts. In the economic realm there are forces that actually undermine the power and scope of nation states. In the context of world markets, role of multinational corporations, increased social and workforce mobility and the decisive role of technology and communications have surely undermined state sovereignty to a large extent. Internationalization of production has evaded the state's capacity to control its own economic future. The recent global economic recession can be cited as the best example for inability of the states to control their economies.

Till the Second World War the state was the primary military actor which, however, got undermined with the emergence of power blocs, i.e. the US led NATO and the Russia led Warsaw pact. After the fall of the USSR, the US emerged as the sole super power but its dominance within the NATO has diminished, primarily due to the rise of European Union. The proliferation of regional and international organization has also modulated the idea of state sovereignty. International law and international norms have also become constraints on the state sovereignty. International law subjects individuals, governments and non – governmental organizations to a new set of regulations. The International tribunal at Nuremberg laid down for the first time in the history, that when international rules that protect basic humanitarian values are in conflict with state laws, every individual must transgress the state laws.

The concept of sovereignty remains the most important distinguishing mark of the state even today. The process of globalization, the operation of international law during both peace and war, the international organizations and non – governmental organizations redefine its meaning by making it more legitimate and accountable without, however, replacing it. The nation state still plays the role of both *de jure* and *de fecto* sovereign and the citizens identity is linked with it.

Socialism: The word 'Socialist' added by the 42nd Amendment is intended to bring out that Indian state is a socialist state which aims to secure to its people 'Justice __ Social, economic and political. It has been inserted to spell out expressly the high ideals of socialism. It is to be noted, however, that the 'Socialism' envisaged by the Indian constitution is not the usual scheme of state socialism which involves nationalization of all means of production, and the abolition of private property. **Indira Gandhi** explained it as, "We have always said that we have our own brand of socialism. We will nationalize the sectors where we feel the necessity. Just nationalism is not our type of socialism". An effort was made by the Janata Party to define' Socialist Republic' as a republic in which there is freedom from all forms of exploitation, social, political or economic. But because of the opposition of the Rajya Sabha, this definition had to be deleted. The expression 'Socialist' thus remained undefined.

> **Indira Gandhi**
>
> *Indira Priyadarshini Gandhi (1917-1984) was the daughter of Jawaharlal Nehru. She became the first lady Prime Minister of India in 1966. She is known for centralization of power. Her role was instrumental in the creation of Bangladesh in 1971. She presided over a state of emergency from 1975 to 1977 during which time some lasting changes in the Constitution of India were made. She was assassinated by her own Sikh body guards in the aftermath of Operation Blue Star on Golden Temple, Amritsar Punjab.*

Looking at the miseries which a common Indian faces, the goal of a 'Socialist Pattern of Society' or 'Socialist State' seems ages far. Especially after the adoption of the new economic policy of Liberalization, Privatization and Globalization (LPG) along with disinvestment in public sector undertakings, India can hardly be considered socialistic by any definition.

Has Indian Socialism worked?

Indian concept of Socialism seems to have failed to deliver the goods as India still is a home for largest number of poor, illiterate, malnutritioned, unhygienic people. These downtrodden people are the assets for politicians who grab their votes by playing opportunistic politics, sometimes in the name of 'India Shining' (NDA) and some times in the name of 'Aam Admi' (UPA). These hefty slogans clearly demonstrate the division between two Indias one the rich and modern and the second one poor and wrecked. There is no doubt in the two fundamental aspects of Indian economy; one Indian economy is growing at a faster rate and, second inequality among people too is growing, indicating that the booming effect has not trickled down to the common masses who constitute the major chunk of Indian population. Although we have lowered the number of people below poverty line (BPL), (thanks to drawing of poverty line really very low), adequate and more concrete measures are yet to be taken. Despite high growth, more than three fourths of Indians are poor and vulnerable with a level of consumption not more than twice the official poverty line. Four groups of people i.e. extremely poor, poor, marginal and vulnerable constituted about 77 percent of the population in 2004-05. The SC/ST constitutes the bottom layer followed by Muslims, OBC and others. These groups experience worst human sufferings, low education level, low income, absence of work and health care and security – all have made them victims of the growing economic boom. Besides this there is also evidence to suggest that inequality is growing not only between the common man and the better-off sections of the society, but also among different regions, creating uneven regional growth and development.

Economic growth alone, however, cannot ensure the removal of poverty, unless supplemented by other policies and complementary measures targeted directly at promoting the welfare of the masses. Economy is booming but also has created a wide gulf between haves and have-nots. This uneven and disproportionate growth has not evenly trickled down_ resulting in a kind of growth without development.

One can easily see India at the top of the ladder in the list of highest number of dollar billionaires and lags far behind in the field of Human Development. The data from National Sample Survey (NSS) organizations, 61st round for 2004-05, presented in the report of National Commission for Enterprises in the Unorganized Sector shows that 77 percent of the population consumes less than Rs.20 per person per day and 96 percent consumes less than Rs. 48 per person per day. The consumption base is indeed narrow. The Indian situation is that while it has increased the number of billionaires, the poor have become poorer and even the middle class is finding it difficult to make ends meet because of rising prices, especially of food commodities. These can of course become the cause of political instability and upset the aggregate growth scenario. The leadership seems to have developed a vested interest in keeping the people poor, illiterate and backward and is quite good at the art of redistributing just enough crumbs to the toiling masses to keep insurgency at bay.

To sum we may conclude that there are two broad opinions about the LPG model; one highlights its success in creating economic boom. The most important success has been, increase in investment, savings and growth. This was combined with the diversification of the industrial sector. There is another side of this balance sheet the failure of new development strategy in improving the conditions and the quality of life of common people in both urban and rural sectors. These critics harp on, what they call, a division between India and Bharat; the first a shining and resurgent one and the second, a suffering yet laboring one.

Secularism: The word secular is derived from Latin '*Saecularis*' which meant, among other things, 'that which belongs to this world, non-spiritual, temporal as opposed to spiritual or ecclesiastical things'. It is a term applied in general to the separation of state politics or administration from religious matters, and 'secular education' is a system of training from which religious training is definitely excluded. The term 'Secularism' was coined in 1850 by G.J. Holyoake who saw it as a movement which provided an alternative to theism.

When Jawaharlal Nehru framed the objective Resolution of the constitution, Secularism figured as an important aspect of it. Nehru associated secularism with modernity and considered sentiments based on caste, colour and religion as backward and a relic from the past. He felt that religious tolerance was a characteristic of Indian culture and in a country with different religious groups, it is important to build real nationalism on the basis of secularity. Secularism is essential for the survival of a multi-nation state. To quote Subhash C. Kashyap, "The vision of the founding fathers was that of a nation transcending all diversities of religion, caste and creed. They were not hostile to religion but they hoped that it would be possible to forge political unity and that religious differences would not hamper nation building. The constitution envisaged a new social order free from communal conflicts and based on justice, social, economic and political. It visualized a polity under which laws would not discriminate between citizens on grounds of religion, caste or the like."

There is an inseparable linkage between democracy and secularism in India. In this multi-religious and multi-cultural society democracy cannot function if it propagates any one religion. The people in general will not tolerate discrimination on the part of state on religious matter. Hence, secularism is a compulsion for Indian Democracy. In India secularism has emerged in our struggle for freedom, as a complimentary value of democracy and nationalism. According to **K.M. Panikkar**, a secular state has three essential characteristics:

1. Firstly, the secular state postulates that political institutions must be based on the economic and social interests of the entire community, without reference to religion, race or sect, that all must enjoy equal rights and no privileges.
2. Secondly, it eliminates from the body political ideas of division between individuals and groups on the basis of their faith or racial origin.
3. In the third place, it is obvious that a composite secular state must accept as the basis of its policy what Aristotle termed as 'distributive justice'.

Democracy: According to Bernard Crick, "democracy is perhaps the most promiscuous word in the world of public affairs. A term that can mean anything to anyone is in danger of meaning nothing at all." Democracy is derived from a Greek word 'demos' meant 'the people' and *'Kratos'* meant 'government' or 'rule'. Democracy therefore can be defined as a government by the people as against monarchy, dictatorship or hereditary rule. Abraham Lincoln has defined democracy as "government of the people, by the people and for the people." Democracy is based on the notion of collective good or good for all which gives rise to the concept of welfare politics. In a narrow political sense democracy refers to the form of government, a representative and responsible system under which those who administer the affairs of the state are chosen by the electorate and are accountable to them. But in its broadest sense, it embraces, in addition to political democracy, social and economic democracy also. In the words of Nehru:

'Democracy has been spoken of chiefly in the past, as political democracy, roughly represented by every person having a vote. But a vote by itself does not represent very much to a person who is down and out, to a person, let us say, who is starving or hungry. Political democracy, by itself, is not enough except that it may be used to obtain a gradually increasing measure of economic democracy, equality and spread of good things of life to others and removal of gross inequalities."

In short, the Indian constitution promises not only political but also social democracy, as explained by Dr. Ambedkar in his concluding speech in the constituent Assembly:

"Political democracy cannot last until there lies at the base of it social democracy. What does social democracy mean? It means a way of life which recognizes liberty, equality and fraternity which are not to be treated as separate items in a Trinity. They form a union of trinity in the sense that to divorce one from the other is to defeat the very purpose of democracy."

The state in a democratic society derives its strength from the cooperative and dispassionate will of all its free and equal citizens. Social and economic democracy is the foundation on which political democracy would be a way of life in the Indian Polity.

Republic: The term 'Republic' implies a state whose head is elected by its people for a fixed term. Explaining the meaning of the term 'Republic' as used in the Preamble, D.D.Basu holds that it signifies two things, "For not only shall we have an elected President instead of a hereditary king as the head of our state, but the state will also be characterized by the absence of any ruling or privileged class and all offices from the humblest to the highest (including that of the President) will be open to all citizens without any distinction of caste, creed, religion or sex. Thus, Indian citizens will be subjects and free citizens at the same time." A democratic republic may, therefore, broadly means a state with an elected head and a government by the representatives of the people. According to Madison, "Republic is a government which derives its powers directly or indirectly from the great body of the people, and is administered by persons holding their offices during pleasure, for a limited period, or during good behavior." India meets this standard and hence is a Republic.

3. **Descriptive Part:** In this part, the position of an Indian citizen vis-a-vis state is determined; his rights against the state and the basic obligations of the state are mentioned. This part explains to us the nature of the Indian State, that is, 'India is a welfare State.' The part contains four coordinate objectives which are to be secured for all citizens." These include:

   Justice: Socio – economic and Political;

   Liberty of thought, expression, belief, faith and worship Equality of Status and opportunity;

   Fraternity assuring the dignity of the Individual and the unity and integrity of the Nation.

Social justice means social equality which in turn implies that all citizens are equal tangible units of society and no one is entitled to special privileges. All have an equal opportunity to stand up and develop their personality. It implies absence of distinction in social status of the people because of differences in race, colour, sex, class or caste etc. Social justice demands that there exists no unnecessary social restraint which retards the growth of an individual and the realization of his ambition of a good and happy life. However, viewed in a wider perspective the idea of social justice not only aims at the proper reconciliation of the interest of an individual with the over-all interest of the community, or the prevalence of the latter over the former in the event of any conflict. In India the constitution has taken various steps to provide social justice by breaking the vicious circle of caste and culture. Thus it has incorporated certain provisions in the Chapter of Fundamental Rights and Directive Principles of the State Policy.

Conclusion: The Preamble of the Indian constitution serves two purposes: (a) it indicates the source from which the constitution derives its authority and (b) it also states the objectives which the constitution seeks to establish and promote. According to Subash C. Kashyap, "the noble words of our Preamble represent the quintessence, the Philosophy, the ideals or the soul of the entire constitution of India. Other parts and provisions of the constitution are only an elaboration and an attempt to give concrete shape, content and meaning to the words of the Preamble. No wonder that the Supreme Court found that the Permeable contains some of the basic features of the constitution which could not be altered even by an amendment of the constitution under Article 368.

Relation between Liberty, Equality and Justice

Earnest Barker in his book *"Principles of Social and Political Theory"* has showed that justice represents a synthesis of the principle of liberty, equality and fraternity. Justice is a thread which runs through all these values and makes them parts of an integrated whole. Justice is the basic idea behind all these values. It is our sense of justice that impels us to postulate that human relations in society should be regulated by reason. It demands that each individual should be treated as an end in itself, not a means to any end. They should be treated as equal to each other without discrimination. All individuals are potentially capable of acquiring excellence according to their capacities. Thus they all need equal freedom to personal development in their own right so as to prove their worth in society.

The principle of liberty will not conform to the principle of justice until the benefit of liberty is equally extended to each individual in society. If liberty is defined as the absence of restraint, it cannot become a universal principle unless it is qualified by the principle of equality. This postulates such restraint on liberty that liberty of one does not become a threat to another's equal and similar liberty. On the other hand, the principle of equality does not mean 'absence of discrimination' but social justice demands that deprived and underprivileged sections of society should be given special protection in order to save them from excesses of the dominant sections.

CHAPTER 3

FUNDAMENTAL RIGHTS

"Every State is known by the rights that it maintains. Our method of judging its character lies, above all, in the contribution that it makes to the substance of man's happiness."

H. J. Laski (A Grammar of Politics; 1938)

Fundamental Rights in Indian **Constitution:** The fundamental rights were included in the constitution because they were considered essential for the development of the personality of every individual and to preserve human dignity. The writers of the constitution regarded democracy of no use if civil liberties, like freedom of speech and expression were not recognized and protected by the state. Democracy is, in essence, a government by opinion and therefore, the means of formulating public opinion should be secured to the people of a democratic nation. For this purpose, the constitution guaranteed to all the citizens of India the freedom of speech and expression and various other freedoms in the form of the fundamental rights.

The fundamental rights protect the rights and liberties of the people against encroachment by the government and impose limitation upon all the powers of the legislative as well as executive wings, not withstanding their representative character. The main objective of the inclusion of fundamental rights in the constitution is to establish a government of law and not of man. The importance of fundamental rights was emphasized by justice Bagawati in *Maneka Gandhi VS Union of India* case. Thus, these fundamental rights represent the basic values cherished by the people of this country since the ancient times and they are calculated to protect the dignity of the individual and create conditions in which every human being can develop his personality to the fullest extent. They weave a pattern of guarantee on the basic structure of human rights, and impose negative obligations on the state not to encroach upon individual liberty in its various dimensions.

Fundamental rights for Indians have also been aimed at overturning the inequalities in the existing social system of the nation. Specifically, these rights were used to abolish untouchability and hence prohibited discrimination on the grounds of religion, race, caste, gender or place of birth. They also forbid trafficking of human beings and forced labour.

Bill of rights

A Bill of Rights is a constitutional document that specifies the rights and freedoms of the individual, and so defines the legal extent of civil liberty. Entrenched bills of rights can be distinguished from statutory ones. An entrenched bill of rights is enshrined in higher law and thus provides basis for constitutional judicial review. A statutory bill of rights, or statute of rights, can be amended or replaced through the same procedure as other statute laws. Supporters of bills of rights argue that they are the only effective means of providing citizens with legal and possibly constitutional protection against the state, and that they have an educational value in promoting a 'human rights culture' Opponents point out that they enlarge the authority of judges at the expense of elected politicians; that they are inflexible and artificial, and that they foster a litigious culture.

They also protect cultural and educational rights of ethnic and religious minorities hence cultivate a spirit of multiculturalism and secularism.

The development of constitutionally guaranteed fundamental human rights in India was inspired by historical examples such as England's **Bill of Rights** (1689), The United States Bill of Rights (1787) and French Declaration of the Rights of Man (1789). Under the educational system of British Raj, students were exposed to ideas of democracy, human rights and European political history. The Indian student community in England was further inspired by the working of parliamentary democracy and the system of rule of law.

In 1919, the **Rowlatt Act** gave extensive powers to the British government and police, and allowed indefinite arrest and detention of individuals, warrantless searches and seizures, restrictions on public gatherings, and intensive censorship of media and publications. The public opposition to this act eventually led to mass campaigns throughout the country demanding guaranteed civil freedoms, and limitations on government power.

In 1928, the Nehru commission composing of representatives of Indian political parties proposed constitutional reforms for India that apart from calling for dominion status for India and elections under universal suffrage, would guarantee rights deemed fundamental, representation for religious and ethnic minorities, and limit the powers of the government. In 1931, the Indian National Congress adopted a resolution committing itself to the defense of fundamental civil rights, as well as socio – economic rights.

Rowlatt Act 1919

The act was passed by the Imperial Legislative Council in London on March 10, 1919 on the recommendation of the Rowlatt Committee headed by British judge Sir Sidney Rowlatt. This act effectively authorized the government to imprison any person suspected of terrorism for up to two years without a trial. The act provided for strict control of the press, arrests without warrant, indefinite detention without trial and juryless in camera trials for proscribed political acts. The act was same in nature as the present day acts like TADA, POTA, Public Safety Act or any other Preventative detention act.

When India acquired independence on 15 August 1947, the task of developing a constitution for the nation was undertaken by the constituent assembly of India. The Fundamental Rights Sub- Committee of the constituent assembly was entrusted with the task of framing the Fundamental Rights. It would be worthwhile to recall in this respect that both part III, which contains the fundamental rights, and part IV, which contains directive principles of the state policy, were originally designed and drafted in one united chapter on Fundamental Rights. Taken together, they really proclaim the fundamental values and constitute the foundational principles of the constitution. Thus, the Preambular assurance of the dignity of the individual is sought to be implemented through various provisions of parts III and IV.

Fundamental rights are defined as basic human freedoms which every Indian citizen has the right to enjoy for a proper and harmonious development of personality. These rights are considered essential for the proper, moral and material upliftment of people. These rights universally apply to all citizens, irrespective of race, place of birth, religion, caste, creed, colour or gender.

The rights enshrined in part III of the Indian constitution are 'Fundamental' in the sense that they have been incorporated in the fundamental law of the land, that is, constitution. These are justifiable rights and cannot be amended through the ordinary procedure of the law. They are fundamental in the sense that they are binding on public authorities both at the central level, at the state level and at the local level. The word fundamental also suggests that these rights are so important that the constitution has separately listed them and made special provisions for their protection. The fundamental rights are so important that the constitution itself ensures that they are not violated by the government.

These rights are fundamental in the sense that any law passed by any legislature in the country would be declared as null and void if it is derogatory to the rights guaranteed by the constitution. If any of these rights is violated, the individual affected is entitled to move to the Supreme Court or High Court for the protection and enforcement of his rights.

Fundamental rights are not absolute and are subject to reasonable restrictions as necessary for the protection of national interest. The constitution thus, attempts to strike a balance between individual liberty and state control by making the fundamental rights subject to reasonable restrictions. In the *Kesavananda Bharati Vs State of Kerala case,* the Supreme Court ruled that all provisions of the constitution, including fundamental rights can be amended. However, the Parliament cannot alter the **basic structure**[3] of the constitution. The fundamental rights are among the basic features of the constitution. Therefore, while they may be abridged, the abridgement can not extend to the point of damage to or destruction of their core.

Suspension of fundamental Rights: When the President makes a proclamation of emergency under Article 352, the freedoms guaranteed under Article 19 are automatically suspended. During the proclamation of emergency no law or executive order issued by the state can be challenged on the ground that it is inconsistent with the rights guaranteed by Article 19. The President can suspend other fundamental rights through specific orders, but these orders must be approved by the Parliament. It may be observed that such orders of the President may extend to the whole or

> *Kesavananda Bharati Vs State of Kerala case*
>
> In this case the Court ruled that there is a basic structure of the constitution and anybody _ not even the Parliament (through amendment) _can violate the basic structure. The Court did two more things. First, it said that right to property was not the part of basic structure and therefore could be suitably abridged. Secondly, the Court preserved to itself the right to decide whether various matters are the part of the basic structure of the constitution.

---

[3] There are certain basic features of the constitution which cannot be altered in exercise of the power to amend it, under Article 368. The basic features include: sovereignty and territorial integrity of India, judicial review, the federal system, parliamentary system of government, secularism etc.

any part of the territory of India. The provisions regarding suspension of fundamental rights have been severely criticized by some, but the general view has been that the interests of the country must get precedence over the interests of the individual.

Classification of Fundamental Rights: Originally, the constitution classified the fundamental rights into seven categories, but with the deletion of right to property under Article 31, from the list of fundamental rights by the 44th Constitutional Amendment Act 1978, there are now six categories of rights which are as under:

1. **Right to Equality (Article 14-18):** Equality under Indian constitution is defined under five articles from Article 14 to 18. The constitution holds that all such inequalities are eliminated which are unjust, irrational and hinder the growth of individual personality. Right to equality is the principal foundation of other rights and liberties. It guarantees that every citizen is assured equality before law and equal protection of law within the territory of India. It means that the state cannot discriminate against a citizen on the basis of caste, creed, colour, gender, religion or place of birth. However, the state may make any special provision for the advancement of any socially or educationally backward class. Thus, the concept of equality is used positively as well as negatively. In the positive sense it prohibits discrimination but on the other side it focuses on giving special treatment to the needy. The constitution of India defines equality as :

   1. Equality before law and equal protection of law (Article 14).
   2. Prohibition of discrimination on grounds of religion, race, caste, gender or place of birth (Article 15)
   3. Equality of opportunities in matters of public employment. (Article 16)
   4. Abolition of untouchability. (Article 17)
   5. Abolition of titles. (Article 18).

2. **Right to Freedom (Article 19 to 22):** The demand of liberty includes freedom of the individual to develop all his potentialities as a human being endowed with reason. Equality and liberty are the two rights that are most essential to a democracy. Freedom means – freedom of thought, expression and action. According to M.Y. Pylee, "personal liberty is the fundamental of fundamental rights. Article 19 to 22 deal with the different aspects of this basic right. Taken together, these four articles form a charter of personal liberties, which provides the backbone of the chapter of fundamental rights." Freedom under this 'Right' is not defined negatively, rather, freedom is defined in such a manner that every person will enjoy his freedom without threatening freedom of others or without endangering the law and order situation. Originally there were seven freedoms provided under Article 19 (1), but the freedom to *acquire, hold and dispose of property* was deleted by 44th Constitutional Amendment Act in 1978, leaving only six freedoms in that Article. They are:

   1. *Freedom of speech and expression*, which enable an individual to participate in public activities. Freedom of speech and expression implies that the citizens are free to express their views, beliefs and convictions freely through writing, printing, pictures, speeches or any other manner. However, this right is not absolute and reasonable restrictions can be imposed on the exercise of this right in the interest of public order, security of state, decency or morality, defamation, incitement of offence against sovereignty and integrity of the nation.
   2. *Freedom to assemble* gives the citizens the right to assemble peacefully without arms. This also includes the right to hold public meetings and demonstrations and to take out peaceful processions. The only restriction on the assembly is that it must be peaceful and without arms. However, the state can impose reasonable restrictions in the interest of public order and the sovereignty and integrity of India.

3. *Freedom to form associations* or unions on which the state can impose reasonable restrictions in the interest of public order, morality and the sovereignty and integrity of India.

4 and 5: *Freedom of movement and residence* implies that the citizens are free to move throughout the territory of India and to reside and settle in any part of the territory of India. However, the state can impose restrictions on this freedom in the interests of general public or for the protection of the interests of any Scheduled Tribe.

6. *Freedom of Profession and Trade* assures all citizens the right to practice any legal profession or to carry on any occupation, trade or business. The state may impose reasonable restrictions on this freedom in the interest of general public. Thus, the state may deny to a citizen the freedom to carry on trade or business in noxious, hazardous or dangerous goods like intoxicating drugs or liquors or to indulge in trafficking in women and children.

Protection in Respect of the Conviction for Offences (Article 20): The constitution also guarantees the right to life and personal liberty, which in turn cites specific provisions in which these rights are applied and enforced. The constitution guards the citizens' right to freedom by providing under Article 20 protection in respect of conviction for offence which means that:

a) No person shall be convicted of an offence except for the violation of law in force at the time of the commission of the act charged as an offence. In this sense, Article 20 prohibits retrospective criminal legislation, commonly known as *ex post facto* legislation.

b) No person shall be punished for the same offence more than once, and in other words it prohibits double jeopardy.

c) No person shall be compelled to be a witness against himself. Thus, compulsion to give self-incriminating evidence is prohibited. "Compulsion" in this Article refers to what in Law is called "Duress," meaning injury, beating, or unlawful imprisonment to make a person do something that he does not want to do.

Protection of life and personal liberty (Article 21):- Citizens are assured protection against arrest and detention. Article 21 declares that no citizen can be denied his life and liberty except by law. This means that a person's life and personal liberty can only be disputed if that person has committed a crime. However, the right to life does not include right to die, and hence, suicide or an attempt thereof, is an offence. Personal freedom includes all the freedoms which are mentioned under Article 19 (1) plus some more freedoms. Right to life has acquired broader meanings by the judicial decisions. The 'Life' in Article 21 does not mean continuation of mere biological existence but life with a dignity, with clean drinking water, pollution free atmosphere, free and compulsory education etc.

Article 21 A: This Article deals with Right to Free and Compulsory Education for the children from the age of 6 to 14 years. This right is an outcome of the judgment pronounced by Justice Kuldeep Singh and R.M. Sahai in *Miss Mohini Jain VS State of Karnataka case* in which they stated that the right to life and the dignity of an individual cannot be assured unless it is accompanied by the right to education. This right has been granted by the 86th constitutional amendment carried out in 2002. The amendment stipulates that the "government shall provide free and compulsory education to all children from the age of 6 to 14 years in such a manner as the state may by law determine." The act also enjoins upon the parents to send their children to school by including it as a Fundamental Duty under Article 51 A.

Protection against Arrest and Detention (Article 22): Detention of a person without trial was a common feature of the colonial rule and a major issue during the struggle for freedom.

Thus the inclusion of Article 22 in the list of fundamental rights aimed to provide safeguards against arbitrary arrest and detention. The procedural safeguards against arbitrary arrest and detention provided for in clause (1) and (2) of Article 22 are:

a) No person who is arrested shall be detained in custody without being informed, as soon as may be, of the grounds of such arrest.
b) No such person shall be denied the right to consult, and to be defended by a legal practitioner of his choice.
c) Every person who is arrested and detained in custody shall be produced before the nearest Magistrate within a period of twenty four hours and no such person shall be kept or detained in custody beyond the said period without the authority of a magistrate.

Exceptions to Article 22: The safeguards mentioned under Article 22 are not, however, available to:

a) An enemy alien.
b) A person arrested and detained under a law providing for Preventive Detention.

Meaning of Preventive Detention: Preventive detention means detention of a person without trial. It is so called in order to distinguish it from *punitive detention*. The objective of punitive detention is to punish a person for what he has done and after he is tried in the courts for the illegal act committed by him. The object of preventive detention, on the other hand, is to prevent him from doing something and detention in this case takes place on the apprehension or mere suspicion that he is going to do something wrong which comes within grounds specified by the constitution, viz acts prejudicial to the security of the state, public order, defense, foreign affairs or security of India etc. Preventive Detention is something unknown in the United States of America or the United Kingdom, in times of peace. Some acts passed by the Parliament are:

1. The Preventive Detention Act, 1950 which was abandoned in 1969.
2. Maintenance of Internal Security Act 1971 (MISA) which was repealed in 1978.
3. Conservation of Foreign Exchange and Smuggling Activities Act of 1974 (COFEPOSA).
4. National Security Act of 1980.
5. Terrorist and Disruptive Activities Act of 1985 (commonly known as TADA).
6. Prevention of Terrorist Activities Act of 2002 (commonly known as POTA)

3. **Right against Exploitation (Article 23 and 24):** Exploitation means misuse of services of others with the help of force. This right seeks to protect the weaker sections against exploitation by unscrupulous persons or even the state. As we know in India, prior to the promulgation of the constitution, services of backward communities and weaker sections were used without any payment. This was known as the practice of *beggar*. The constitution has therefore, abolished this hated practice. Similarly women from backward areas were and still are purchased and sold elsewhere. Under this right, trafficking in women has been abolished. In the same way, children were employed in hazardous employment to which the constitution has put an end. This right is composed of two articles i.e. Article 23 and Article 24. These articles seek to provide protection against:

i) Exploitation through traffic in human beings,
ii) *Beggar* and other forced labour,
iii) Employment of children in factories.

The constitution also prohibits forced labour of any form which is similar to *beggar*. This right was instrumental in the enactment of the Bounded Labour System (abolition) Act, 1976. In nutshell it can be said that the whole idea is, not to allow the state or anyone to compel a person to work against his will or to misuse the human person in any way.

Trafficking of women: A case study of South Asia:

Human trafficking (according to recent estimates) has now acquired equal second ranking in terms of profit with the trade in illegal armaments. Migration in South Asia has contributed enormously to this illegal trade, as globalization has created dramatic shifts in the world market, and more women are leaving their traditional occupations in search of work. Trafficking is an increasingly growing, transnational problem affecting mainly, though not exclusively, women and girls. It is estimated that 700,000 to four million people are smuggled into foreign countries per annum and that the profits from illegal syndicates total approximately US$ 7 billion. Though trafficking occurs for a variety of reasons (sweatshop labor, illegal adoption of children, forced marriages, domestic work, begging, etc.), trafficking of women and girls for commercial sex work is the fastest growing international business in the world. In fact, many women who are initially trafficked for domestic labor usually end up being sexually exploited as well.

In South Asia, Bangladesh and Nepal are the main originating countries for trafficking, although India and Pakistan are countries of destination or transit to other regions (Middle East, East Asia) and trafficking is ripe in both. The problem of trafficking is particularly acute, with an estimated 150,000 people trafficked annually. Because of the clandestine nature of trafficking, reliable statistics are hard to come by. As Hugles has written, "the trade is secretive, the women are silenced, the traffickers are dangerous.............. and many agencies are counting." However, the available statistics paint a bleak picture. To cite just a few, it is estimated that:

- 100,000 to 200,000 Nepali women have been trafficked and have been forced into prostitution in India and an additional 5,000 to 11,000 Nepali women are trafficked annually.
- Over 200,000 Nepali sex workers are employed in India, 20 percent of whom are under the age of 16.
- 40,000 Bangladeshi children are involved in prostitution in Pakistan and 300,000 in India.
- Estimates suggest the participation of more than 2 million women in commercial sex work in South Asia of whom 25 per cent are below 18 years.

Link between forced labour trafficking and migration of women in South Asian context:

Trafficking in South Asia is inevitably related to global experience. The accent in the past decade has been on hyper-mobility of capital, but the phenomenon often neglected is mobility and sometimes hyper-mobility of people as well, because irregular migration and its anomalies open the door to exploitation and trafficking of women. Yet the work of women migrants contributes enormously to the economies of the countries of the subcontinent, and in the process enriches a whole series of people connected with women's exploitation.

The Feminization of migration has been going on at an increasing rate globally in the 21st century and in the case of South Asia women are also subjected to forced labour (both sexual and non-sexual) and which is often related to the work for which they were trafficked. Bruckert and Parent (2002), have written "it seems to be more economical and quicker to proceed through informal and often illegal channels to obtain regular labour than to pass through legitimate official channels" and because women have fewer resources financially than men in the subcontinent, this term has also been extended to "feminization of poverty".

The poorer the migrants, the more the correlation is with women and, as will be seen, this has implications in terms of trafficking, whether on the subcontinent or globally. Trafficking in Nepalese women and girls has been described by Deepa Mehta in the office of the Director General of Police in Delhi, as "less risky than smuggling narcotics and electronic equipment into India"."The growing demand for cheap labor in high growth countries has given rise to a growing market for irregular migration processes and trafficking as an outcome of this mismatch between demand and supply conditions in the global market".

The trafficking of women is also linked with the domestic problems of women. Her plight as a trafficked person may be less precarious than if she were returned to her previous condition – e,g an abusive family (as in case of Sri Lanka). The human rights and feminist approaches, seek to address what is usually invisible in the equation, "the 'demand' side: the men who buy trafficked women," that is the power relationship between men and women. Except for the women who are in the most desperate of circumstances as a result of their conditions, it suits the interests of all the other parties involved (governments, employers, and families) to ignore the problem.

The global position of women in regard to labour is that they now easily outstrip men as targets for work, because women are prepared or can be made to take on roles men will not, as they are the poorest, least skilled and most vulnerable of migrant workers. The other side of the coin is that women have skills that men do not, or are finding employment or work for which women are preferred – domestic service in particular. In Sri Lanka, for example, women out-migrate men for this latter reason.

In the migration which ends up in sex work, the transitional element can be identified through an analysis of commodification of the process, and this applies both internationally and on the subcontinent. On the one hand women and girls are considered as commodities by the family members; on the other hand the women concerned are put into debt bondages by their smugglers / traffickers, or labour agencies etc., which leads to an ultimate choice to work in the Commercial Sex Industry (CSI).

The nature and face of trafficking is also changing in the light of the IT revolution which has made it quicker, easier and the result is that pornography has assumed a new importance and more women and children are increasingly becoming victims of it. Thus it is clear that the problem of trafficking exists not only in the subcontinent but throughout the world and has a multi layered nature and cannot be addressed in isolation. It is linked intractably with issues of poverty, gender disparity, unsafe migrations and increasingly national security and hence, requires multidimensional solutions for tackling it.

4. **Right to Religion (Articles 25 to 28):** Indian Constitution describes India as a secular country. The opening words of the preamble stress to make India a Sovereign, Socialist, Secular, Democratic Republic. A secular state is defined as a state which observes an attitude of neutrality and impartiality towards all religions. The concept of secularism in the constitution is not that of irreligion or anti religion. It only means that there is no state religion, there is equal respect for and protection of all religions.

    Right to freedom of religion is covered in Articles 25, 26, 27 and 28 which guarantee every citizen to profess, practice and propagate any religion (Article 25). The state can neither patronize any particular religion nor ask any citizen to pay taxes for the promotion of any religion (Article 27). No religious instructions can be imparted in educational institutions maintained by the state or receiving aid from it (Article 28). However, the right to Freedom of Religion is not absolute, as the constitution itself mentions three restrictions to the right, namely Public Order, Morality and Health. For example the government has taken steps banning practices like sati, untouchability, human sacrifice, child marriages etc. Such restrictions cannot be opposed in the name of interference in the right to freedom of religion.

    Propagation Vs Conversion: No doubt the constitution has guaranteed the right to propagate one's religion. This includes persuading people to convert from one religion to another.

However, some people assert that the word 'Propagate' in Article 25 (1) gives them a fundamental right to convert people of other faiths into their own faith, by any means, which surely is not right and goes against Supreme Court's decision pronounced in *stainislaus's vs. state of M.P.* In this case the Supreme Court has held that the right to propagate religion does not include any right to forcible conversions as these may disturb public order. The Supreme Court holds that:

The right to Propagate in Art 25 (1) gives to each member of every religion the right to spread or disseminate the tenants of his religion (say, by advocacy or preaching), but it would not include the right to convert another, because each man has the same freedom of 'Conscience' guaranteed by that very position {Art 25 (1)}

The equal freedom of conscience, belonging to each man, under Article 25 (1), means that he has the freedom to choose and hold any faith of his choice and not to be converted into another religion by means of force, fraud, inducement or allurement. He can, of course, voluntarily adopt another religion, but 'force, fraud, inducement or allurement' takes away the freedom of consent from the would–be convert.

Religious Conversion has become a hot debate in the Indian politics in recent times because of the mass conversion programmes organized by Bajranjdal, Shive Sena, Vishva Hindu Parishad and other Hindu Rightist parties across India. "Ghar Wapsi" (Home Coming) what they call, has acquired much criticism for forcibly converting religious minorities especially Muslims and Christians to Hinduism. The programs of mass conversions started from Agra where hundreds of Muslims were made to covert to Hinduism. Some of the victims blamed that they were promised ration cards and OBC status. Opposition parties raised the issue in the Parliament and demanded a debate in the Parliament about Right to Religion and forceful conversion. Mohan Bhagwat, the chief of the RSS said that India was a Hindu Nation where many Hindus had been forcibly converted to other religions. To him,

Ghar Wapsi aims to bring them back into their original faith to make India a pure Hindu Nation.

Alas! One wonders what can change of religions do to those whose socio-economic positions become more vulnerable by changing their faiths.

DEBATE:

Shall We Switch to Religious Based Education

Nani A. Palkiwala, the eminent constitutional expert observes that, 'I do not think India, in its entire history of five thousand years, has ever reached a lower level of degradation that it has reached now....The picture that emerges is that of a great nation is in a state of moral decay, of which crime, chaos, and corruption are three of the several facets". A crimson wave of crime seems to have blanketed India. Every manner of misdemeanor is on the rise_ from rape to robbery, kidnapping to killings, torturing to acid attacks_ and the common man is under siege, with neither respite nor retreat in sight. It is a disturbing darkness. If the suicides are added to the list, one looks to the heavens for answer of the question, will there be a brighter dawn.

It isn't just the crimes but also the manner in which they happen, have troubled the law enforcing agencies and have thrown common man in a state of anxiety. This crime spike is no overnight phenomenon. National Crime Record Bureau (NCRB) statistics show that incidents and rates of violent crimes_ murder, kidnapping, decoity, robbery, arson, dowry deaths – have gone up dramatically in past five years. In 2006, 205,656 crimes were committed across India. By 2011 the number had gone up to 256,329, a sharp rise of 24.6%.

Across the country, murders have increased by 5.6%, rape by a disturbing 20%; crimes against women too have shot up during the same phase by 8.8%. In 2011, the conviction for violent crimes was a mere 28%; for crime against women, it is even lower: 26.9%. In 2010, 39148 cases of abduction were recorded by NCRB. According to analysts, actual numbers, including unreported cases, may be much more. Arvind Verma, an IPS officer turned professor, says, 'almost 75% of the abductors are males and 67% of them are below 29 years of age.'

Possible Causes: The stories like girl killed by a chaser by, a boy killed by his friend because both were chatting to the same girl on net, or a Would be husband pushes his would be wife into a river, or a frustrated Romeo throws acid on the face of a girl etc. are being re-enacted nearly every day in our mohallas and villages, hostels and universities, young men and women are killing or being killed, committing suicide, going on shooting and stabbing sprees, selling scores online with morphed photos or smear campaigns, abducting and murdering innocents, all with a single minded motive_ revenge or unrequited or unfulfilled love. "It is more about egoism", says sociologist Mala Kapur Shankardas, 'the feeling such people have is, if I cannot have her, no one should get her too'.

Other equally strong reason can be 'frustration aggression syndrome'. Opportunities that have come with so called economic boom and open markets have also brought more job anxiety, higher expectations and more pressures to achieve followed by the dream to live a luxurious life, force one to go for short cut ways and means for earning money. Furthermore, the greater likelihood of disappointments when aspirations that define success and happiness are distorted or unmet by the reality faced by young people in a rapidly changing society. G.S. Bajpai, criminologist and professor of law at National Law University, Delhi says, "What is noticeable is that the violence is taking extreme forms and is not meant to hurt only a little. I call it a 'Subculture of Crime' which is a dangerous development".

The communication revolution, the internet facility and the wide publicity to these crimes have also added to their growing pace. To quote Rousseau 'ignorance is bliss' seems relevant. Furthermore, the crime based TV serials, Bollywood and Hollywood movies portraying crimes have inspired many to crime.

The philosophy of Individualism and negative freedom has uprooted the very basic values of our society. The social fabric, the blood relations, the moral bonds etc. are fast evaporating. This has resulted in, what Robert Putnam calls 'the loss of social capital'. The social traditions and values are fading away, rather disappearing. 'WE' does not seem any more appropriate word; rather, 'I' and 'ME' have gained the ground. Songs like *Ma chahey ye karo Ma chahey Wo karo MERI MARZI best summarizes the story.*

Possible Remedies: No doubt the situation is gloomy but we cannot be pessimistic about the future, as future belongs to us. The situation, at present we are in, reminds us the situation Arabian society was in, before the arrival of Prophet Mohammad SAW. We may sum up the social situation in Arabia by saying the Arabs of the pre-Islamic period were grouping about in the dark and ignorance, entangled in a mesh of superstitions paralyzing their minds and driving them to lead a cattle like existence. The woman was a marketable commodity and regarded as a piece of inanimate property.

Allah sends down Jabreel ASW with a revelation, a master plan to solve the problems, a remedy for all ills- *Read! In the name of Your Lord, who has created (all that exists); He created man from a clot (a piece of thick coagulated blood. Read! And your Lord is the most Generous, who teacheth by pen, Teacheth man that which he knew not (Al Quran, Chapter 96: Verse1-5).* This was the first revelation revealed to Prophet Mohammad SAW. Allah- all knowing explains the importance of education and education system. Any loophole in the system may cause death to the social fabric. To say otherwise, to make society a heaven to live in or at least saving it from becoming hell, what is needed is a better, well knit and goal oriented education system. From the above quoted verses some principles can be deduced:

1. Secular education system has failed to inculcate the much needed values in our young ones. Today we yearn and press for the value based education but separation of knowledge into religious and worldly spheres has dried up the source of values, as the values have no other authentic and acceptable source other than religion. I am aware about a question being asked- in a multi-religious society which religious values shall we incorporate? The answer is let us have an inter-religious dialogue for understanding and realizing which religious values are best problem solving and pass the test of the time. We have given plenty of time to secular system; let us provide one and only one chance to God centric education.

2. Our education system must have a mission. The mission must be, as the Quran mentions, to create *Khalifa*, best humans because great technologies require great humans. Producing best technologies without best humans is as nothing but 'Destructive Development'.

3. Change in the curriculum is much needed to bring a desired change in the educated youth. What Plato has suggested "censorship of literature" may prove handy in inculcating the necessary values to the young ones. Ethical values must become pivot of our curricular.

4. Launching massive programs for the moral upliftment of the people. Increasing policing or making more and more harsh laws may not make a much difference because such measures may make us fearful rather than make us moral. Morality comes from within, so to bring any long lasting change in the society, the change shall come from within.

5. **Cultural and Educational Rights (Articles 29-30):** Indian is a multicultural society, a unity in diversity, a home of many languages, religions and cultures. The constitution has not only recognized these cultures but also provided safeguards for their protection. The constitution permits the minorities to conserve

their language, script, and culture. Any community which has a language and a script of its own has a right to conserve and develop them (Article 29).

Under Article 30, the constitution provides that a minority shall have the right to establish and administer educational institutions. All minorities, religious or linguistic, can set up their own educational institutions in order to preserve and develop their own culture. In granting aid to educational institutions, the state shall not discriminate against any institution maintained by a minority community on the ground that it is administered by a minority community.

The right to administer however does not mean right to maladministration. The right is subject to regulatory power of the state. The state can make laws in the interests of social welfare, industrial relations, academic standards, efficiency, discipline, health, sanitation, public order, morality, reasonable restrictions to prescribe syllabus etc. and making of such laws does not violate the rights granted under Article 30 as long as it does not deprive the minority of its right to manage the institution.

According to D.D. Basu, "The Sum-total of the above provisions make our state more secular than the United States of America."

6. **Right to Property (Article 31):** The constitution originally provided for the right to property under Articles 19 (1) (f) and 31. The constitution originally had a threefold provision for safeguarding the right to property. It not only guaranteed the right of private ownership but also the right to enjoy and dispose of property free from restrictions other than reasonable restrictions. Article 19 (1) (f) guaranteed to all citizens the right to acquire, hold and dispose off property. Article 31 provided that, "no person shall be deprived of his property save by authority of law." It also provided that compensation would be paid to a person whose property has been taken for public purpose.

But this important right was deleted by the 44th Constitutional Amendment Act in 1978. The amendment made two important changes in the fundamental rights:

i) It replaced Article 19(1) (f).
ii) It deleted Art 31 from the list of Fundamental rights and made it a separate Article i.e. 300 A, which is a legal right.

The reasons cited for the deletion of this act were that it created a rift between Judiciary and the Parliament and it acted as a barrier in the sound and effective national planning especially for launching agrarian reforms. As the constitution of India declares India as a Socialist Republic so the deletion of this Article makes for any government to go ahead with its radical program in the socio-economic sphere.

7. **Right to constitutional Remedies:** Abstract declarations of fundamental rights in the constitution are useless, unless there is the means to make them effective. That is why the Constitution of India not only guarantees certain fundamental rights but under Article 32 it also guarantees the right to move to the Supreme Court for the enforcement of the fundamental rights included in part III and the right to bringing such proceeding before the Supreme Court is itself a fundamental right in part III.

Article 32 is thus the cornerstone of the entire edifice set up by the constitution. Dr. B.R. Ambedkar regarded Article 32 as the heart and soul of the Indian constitution. The Article empowers the Supreme Court to issue directions or orders or writs, including writs in the nature *of Habeas Corpus, Mandamus, Prohibition, Quo Warranto* and *Certiorari.*

i) **Habeas Corpus:** The words 'Habeas Corpus' literally mean to have a body. By the writ, therefore, the Court secures the body of a person who has been imprisoned to be brought before itself to obtain knowledge of the reasons why he has been imprisoned and to set him free if there is no lawful justification for the imprisonment.

ii) **Mandamus:** Mandamus literally means a command. This writ is an order by a superior court commanding a person or a body to perform a public or quasi - public legal duty which he has refused to perform and the performance of which cannot be enforced by any other adequate legal remedy.

iii) **Prohibition:** The writ is issued by a Supreme Court or a High Court to an inferior court forbidding it to continue proceedings in a case in excess of its jurisdiction.

iv) **Certiorari:** This writ is issued by a superior court to an inferior court or body exercising judicial or quasi judicial powers, to transfer a matter pending before it to the higher authority or court. The main objective of this writ is to ensure that an inferior court or tribunal does not usurp jurisdiction which it legally does not possess.

v) **Quo Warranto:** This writ is issued by a court to prevent a person from holding an office to which he is not entitled. The writ can only be issued if the office is public.

Enlargement of Fundamental Rights: A commission for review of working of the constitution was established by the NDA government on 22nd February 2002. Popularly known as Vinkatiya Chilia Commission, it submitted its report on 31st March 2002. The Commission felt that after fifty years, time is ripe to review and enlarge suitably the contents of some of the Fundamental Rights which have been judicially deduced. The National Commission to Review the Working of the Constitution in its report advised to specifically Incorporate the following rights in the list of fundamental rights of the constitution.

1. Freedom of the press and Freedom of information.
2. Right against torture and cruel, inhuman or degrading treatment or punishment.

3. Right to travel abroad and return to one's country.
4. Right to compensation for being illegally deprived of one's right to life or liberty.
5. Right to work.
6. Right to privacy.
7. Right to free elementary education up to age of 14.
8. Right to safe drinking water, clean environment, etc.
9. Right to justice and legal aid.

Judiciary and the Fundamental Rights: The Constitution of India provides (under Article 368) legislature power to amend the Constitution. The Constitution also guarantees Judiciary the power of judicial review under Article 13, 32 etc. This brings confrontation between the two organs of the government. To protect the Fundamental Rights and to enhance their meaning the Judiciary has made various landmarks. Under Kesavananda Bharti's Case judiciary came with the 'basic doctrine' theory and limited the power of the Parliament to damage this basic doctrine. Right to life has been widened to include not only the basic necessities of life but also pollution free environment, pure drinking water, education, sanitation etc.

Fundamental Rights and the Civil Liberties Movements:

Social movement according to Paul Wilkinson is a deliberate collective effort to promote change in any direction and by any means into the society. Once the makers of the Constitution incorporated a list of fundamental rights and safeguards for their protection, these movements intensified on Indian soil. Indian society was and still is traditional, unequal and unjust society divided on the basis of caste, language, religion, gender etc. Once the constitution guaranteed Equality, Liberty and Justice, the underprivileged sections started movements for their rights. Ghanshayam Shah in his book *'Social Movements in India'* has classified social movements in India into eight categories on the basis of their socio-economic background which are:

1. Peasant Movements;
2. Tribal Movements;
3. Dalit Movements;
4. Backward Casts Movement;
5. Women's Movements;
6. Industrial Working Class Movements;
7. Student's Movements;
8. Middle Class Movements;

Fundamental Duties: Rights and Duties are inter-related and these represent the sides of the same coin. The list of fundamental duties was not provided in the Constitution until 1976. In 1976, the Swaran Singh Committee was established for suggesting constitutional reforms. It is on the recommendation of this committee that a list of Fundamental Duties was inserted in the Constitution under Article 51A (Part IVA). The list of ten Fundamental Duties was incorporated by the Constitutional 42nd Amendment Act of 1976. Fundamental Duties like Directive Principles of the State Policy are non-justifiable. In 2002, by the 86th Constitutional Amendment Act, one more duty was added to the

Social movement

A social movement is a particular form of collective behavior in which the motive to act springs largely from the attitudes and aspirations of members, typically acting within a loose organizational framework. Being part of a social movement requires a level of commitment and political activism rather than formal or card-carrying membership; above all, movements move. It is different from spontaneous mass action in that it implies a level of intended and planned action in pursuit of a recognized goal. Not uncommonly, social movements embrace interest groups and may even spawn political parties, trade unions etc.

list, hence there are now eleven fundamental duties in the Indian Constitution. The Duties are:

1. To abide by the constitution and respect the National Flag and National Anthem.
2. To cherish and follow the noble ideas which inspired our national struggle for freedom.
3. To protect the Sovereignty, Unity and Integrity of India.
4. To defend the country.
5. To promote the spirit of common brotherhood among all people of India.
6. To preserve the rich heritage of our composite culture.
7. To protect and improve the natural environment.
8. To develop the scientific temper and sprit of enquiry.
9. To safeguard public property.
10. To strive towards excellence in all spheres of individual and collective activity.
11. Every parent or guardian to provide opportunities for education to his child or ward between the age of 6 and 14 years.

THE DIRECTIVE PRINCIPLES OF STATE POLICY

Directive Principles: Meaning and Nature: Part IV of the Constitution (Article 36-51) provides the Directive Principles of State Policy. These can be defined as the positive obligations of the state towards its citizens. These principles are non-justifiable which means, a court cannot enforce them. The state cannot be compelled through the courts to implement them. But they are fundamental in the governance of the country and state is expected to frame her policies to accomplish the goals enshrined in Part IV of the Constitution. Article 37 declares that the Directive Principles are 'fundamental in the governance of the country and that it shall be the duty of the state to apply these principles in making laws.' The Directive Principles constitute a manifesto for securing the socio-economic foundations of Indian democracy. Dr. B. R. Ambedkar described Part IV of the Constitution as a unique feature of the Constitution. He regarded it as an instrument of instructions which shall be respected at all costs. To him these Directive Principles of State Policy are a 'novel feature' of the constitution of India. These Directive Principles are in the nature of general directions or instructions to the state. They embody the objectives and ideals which the

Democratic Socialism

Democratic Socialism believes that both the economy and society should be run democratically to meet public demands. In general any person or organization can be labeled as a 'democratic socialist' who advocates the pursuit of socialism by democratic means. Democratic socialism is often used in contrast to the authoritarian movement in Communism (Leninism), opposing democratic centralism and the concept of the revolutionary vanguard, instead advocating for the creation of economic democracy by and for the working class.

Union and State Governments must bear in mind while formulating policy and making laws.

The aim of Directive Principles of the State Policy is to make Indian State a welfare state and to provide to its citizens justice_ social, economic and political. Article 38 reads as, "The Sate shall strive to promote the welfare of the people by securing and promoting as effectively as it may a social order in which **justice_ social**, economic and political, shall inform all the institutions of the national life." The Directive Principles of the State Policy constitute a very important part of the Constitution as it is through them the Constitution seeks to achieve the ideal of a democratic welfare state set out in the Preamble and to bring a socio-economic transformation in the society. In the words of Justice K. S. Hedge:

The purpose of the Directive Principles is to fix certain social and economic goals for immediate attainment by bringing about a non-violent social revolution. Through such a social revolution the Constitution seeks to fulfill the basic needs of the common

Social Justice.

The term 'socio-economic justice' comprehends two important elements: social justice and economic justice. Their combination into socio-economic justice is significant because social life of the community cannot be transformed according to the principle of justice unless its economic relations are suitably transformed. Social justice demands an end to the exploitation of the underprivileged sections of our society. Social justice also means that all have an equal opportunity to stand up and develop their personality. It implies absence of distinction in social status of the people because of differences in race, colour, sex, class or caste etc. However, viewed in a wider perspective the idea of social justice not only aims at the proper balance of the interest of an individual with the over-all interest of the community. In India the constitution has taken various steps to provide social justice by incorporating certain provisions in the Chapter of Fundamental Rights and Directive Principles of the State Policy.

man and to change the structure of the society. It aims at making the Indian masses free in positive sense.

The importance of these Directives can be ascertained by the fact that if the Fundamental Rights guarantee a political democracy in India, the Directive Principles ensure the eventual emergence of an economic or social democracy to sustain the former. The Directives aim at securing social justice by removing, as far as possible, inequalities especially the socio-economic inequalities.

The Preamble, the Fundamental Rights and the Directive Principles read together make it clear that the Constitution aimed at creating conditions for the building of an egalitarian society in which freedom of the individual was secured. They guide Indian policy makers to the path that will lead the people of India to achieve the noble ideals which the Preamble of the constitution proclaims: *Justice—social, economic and political; Liberty—Equality* and *Fraternity.*

There were initially sixteen Articles of the Constitution, from Article 36 to 51 that dealt with the Directive Principles. However, the 42nd Amendment added three more Articles, namely 39A, 43A and 48A. The Amendment also modified clause (f) in Article 39, and made a small change in Article 49. These Directives cover a wide range of State activity embracing economic, social, legal, educational, administrative, cultural and international issues.

(i) Article 39A has been inserted to enjoin the state to provide '*free legal aid'* to the poor and to take other suitable steps to ensure equal justice to all, which is offered by the Preamble.

(ii) Article 43A has been inserted in order to direct the state to ensure the participation of workers in the management of industry and other undertakings. This is a positive step in advancement of socialism in the sense of economic justice.

(iii) Article 48A has been inserted in order to direct the state to protect and improve the environment and to safeguard the forests and wild life of the country.

Philosophical bases of the Directive Principles

According to Sir Ivor Jennings the philosophy underlying the Directive Principles is **Fabian Socialism** without word socialism. The framers of the constitution borrowed the chapter of Directive Principles from the Constitution of Ireland. The Irish themselves were, however, in this respect most influenced by the Constitution of Republic

'Fabian Socialism'

Some thirty- five years after the *Communist Manifesto* was issued, Fabian Socialism made its appearance in England. This was the first systematic doctrine of 'evolutionary socialism', as a substitute for Marxian 'revolutionary socialism'. Fabian socialists sought to modify Marxian concepts in several ways: (a) they based their economics on the Ricardian law of rent rather than on labour theory of value; (b) they did not rely exclusively on the working class for bringing about social change but set before themselves the task of 'permeating' the middle class with the socialist message; and (c) they sought to introduce socialism, not in a single stroke, but by degrees, through state and cooperative ownership of industry, development of social consciousness – through gradual democratization of society in the political, economic and intellectual fields.

of Spain which was the first state to incorporate such principles as part of constitution.

The Directive Principles have a deep philosophical base which can be traced back to such noble declarations as French Declaration regarding Rights of Man, American Declaration of Independence and the Charter of United Nations. The makers of constitution were equally influenced by the Liberal and Socialist philosophy of the 19th century. The ideas of **Jeremy Bentham**, Karl Marx enjoy a great influence on these Directives. Further, the Directive Principles of the State Policy incorporate the major principles of Fabian Socialism and **Guild Socialism**. These Directives represent somewhat the pattern of instrument of instructions provided in the Government of India Act, 1935. At the same time it will be wrong to say that the Directive Principles are all foreign borrowings. In fact, a number of these principles are entirely Indian and Gandhian in nature like setting up of village Panchayats and cottage industries, prohibition, protection against cow slaughter etc.

Jeremy Bentham

Jeremy Bentham (1748-1832) was a UK philosopher, legal reformer and founder of utilitarianism. Bentham used the "greatest happiness to the greatest number' phrase to make radical reforms in social administration, law, government and economics in the UK in the nineteenth century. A supporter of Laissez-faire economics, in his later life he also became a firm advocate of political democracy. His utilitarian creed was developed in 'Fragments on Government and more fully in 'Principles of Morals and Legislation'.

Classification of Directive Principles

In order to understand the comprehensiveness of the Directive Principles, it is convenient to classify them into related groups. Dr. M P Sharma has suggested that they can be grouped ideologically into three categories, viz. Socialistic, Gandhian and Liberal-individualistic. We may classify them into the following groups:

1. ***Socialist Principles:*** This category includes those directives which aim at securing a **welfare state** in India. Articles 38, 39, 41, 42 and 43 are usually grouped in this category. As per Article 38, "The Sate shall strive to promote the welfare of the people by securing and promoting as effectively as it may a social order in which justice_ social, economic and political, shall inform all the institutions of the national life. According to Article 39 the state shall direct its policy towards securing: (a) adequate means of livelihood to all citizens; (*b*) a proper distribution of the material resources of the community for the common good; (c) the prevention of concentration of wealth and means of production; (d) equal pay for equal work for both men and women; (c) the protection of the strengths and health of workers and avoiding circumstances which forces citizens to enter vocations unsuited to their age or strength; (f) the protection of

Guild Socialism

A short lived but influential British socialist movement which flourished in the first quarter of the twentieth century, and which achieved is fullest exposition in the writings of G. D. H. Cole. It tried to combine good points of socialism with those of the ancient guild system. In short: (a) it upheld the Marxian emphasis on class struggle; (b) it stood for the abolition of the wage system and demanded representation of the workers in industrial control; (c) it sought to modify Syndicalism by introducing the importance of consumer side by side with the worker; (d) it sought to abolish the old state which was an instrument of exploitation. However, it insisted that a new organization must be evolved to take charge of the many civic activities necessary to the life of the community.

childhood and youth against exploitation or moral and material abandonment. Article 41 seeks within the limits of economic resources and capacity, to ensure the right to work, to education and to public assistance in cases of unemployment, old age sickness and disablement and in other cases of undeserved want. Article 42 declares that the state shall make provision for securing "just and humane conditions of work and for maternity relief." According

Welfare State Welfare State is a state that takes care of satisfying basic needs of its citizens particularly of those who cannot afford these things from their own income or other resources. A welfare state takes care of the most vulnerable sections of the society. It makes use of public resources and taxation of the relatively rich to provide for the vast network of social services and social security.

to Article 43 the state shall endeavour to secure to all workers a living wage, a decent standard of life, leisure and social and cultural opportunities for people. Article 46 lays upon the state the obligation to promote with special care the educational and economic interests of weaker sections of the society and, in particular, of the scheduled castes and the scheduled tribes and to protect them from social injustice and all forms of exploitation. Article 47 declares it as a primary duty of the state to raise the level of nutrition and the improvement of public health.

2. ***Directive Principles aiming to implement Gandhian Principles.*** There are directive principles aiming to implement Gandhian Principles. The State shall:

   a. Organize village Panchayats as units of self-government and endow them with adequate powers and authority. (Article 40)
   b. Promote with special care the educational and economic interests of the weaker sections of the society and in particular of the Schedule Castes and Schedule Tribes and to protect

them from social injustice and all forms of exploitation. (Article 45).

   c.   Try to promote cottage industries on an individual or corporate basis in rural areas. (Article 43)

   d.   Preserve and improve the breeds and prohibit the slaughter of cows, calves etc. (Article 48)

   e.   Try to secure the improvement of public health and the prohibition of intoxicating drinks and drugs. (Article 47)

3.   ***Directives relating to cultural and educational matters:*** This category of directives puts some positive obligations on the State in relation to the advancement of education and cultural rights among the citizens of India. Article 45 declares that the state endeavours to provide, within a period of ten years from the commencement of the constitution, for free and compulsory education for all children until they complete the age of fourteen years. The protection of monuments and places or objects of artistic or historic interest enumerated as an obligation of the state under Article 49 has also an obvious bearing on culture.

4.   ***Directives relating to International Peace and Security:*** These are the directive principles relating to international peace and security. Article 51 declares that the state shall endeavour to (a) promote international peace and security; (b) maintain just and honourable relations between nations; and (c) the settlement of international disputes by arbitration.

5.   ***Miscellaneous.*** Some other important directive principles are: (i) To separate the judiciary from the executive (Article 50); (ii) To secure a uniform civil code applicable to the entire country (Article 44); (iii) To organize agriculture and animal husbandry on scientific lines etc.

Implementation of the Directive Principles:

A large number of laws have been enacted by the central and state governments to implement the Directive Principles from time to time. It is generally agreed that till 1971 the courts gave greater importance to Fundamental Rights than to the Directives Principles, but that the 25th and 42nd Amendments gave precedence to the Directive Principles. In order to give effect to principles of Article 39, a series of acts was passed from time to time. Some of these were: Employees State Insurance Act, Minimum Wages Act, Wealth Tax Act, Estate Duty Act and so on. In order to reduce disparities in income, right to property incorporated in Article 31 of the Constitution was abolished. Legislatures of almost all the States and Union Territories passed Land Reform Acts which fixed ceilings on land holdings and the surplus land acquired from land owners was distributed among the landless workers. The Legislatures of almost all the States and Union Territories passed Acts for the abolition of intermediaries like *zamindars*, *jagirdars* and more than three crore farmers became the owners of land.

A large number of laws have been enacted to implement the directive in Article 40 to organize village panchayats and endow them with powers of self-government. Constitutional 73rd and 74th Amendment Acts were carried out to implement the directives relating to the establishment of Panchayati Raj System in India. To universalize education at the primary level, a scheme of free and compulsory education was initiated. This was done by amending the constitution and making Right to Free and Compulsory Education a Fundamental Right for the children below the age of 16 years.

However a lot remains to be done to achieve and truly operationalise the content of a welfare state in India. The litmus test for a civilised society is the measure and care and consideration it bestows on women, children and the handicapped. While some progress has been made for ameliorating the condition of urban women, much remains to be done for the marginalized women, children and the handicapped. Children are particularly badly neglected in the Indian Society. They are dragged into forced labour or begging and to prostitution. The constitution contemplates right to work, right to an adequate means to earn livelihood and public assistance in cases of unemployment, old age, sickness, disablement and other cases of undeserved want. These tasks remain unfulfilled.

There lies a huge difference between the opportunities enjoyed by the workers working in organized sectors and the filthy conditions the unorganized sector is in. The state is far from being able to provide humane conditions of work for the unorganized sectors or for landless agricultural labour. It is tragic to reflect that bonded labour, *beggar* and traffic in human beings continue to exist in sizeable pockets in many parts of the country.

Undeserved want in the Indian society remains unattended. India has not even been able to eradicate begging. The right to work, adequate means to earn livelihood for all and public assistance in cases of unemployment, old age, sickness and disablement appear to be distant dreams. The rural population is poorly served, if served at all, in terms of medical and health services. For most of the people in India, it has become impossible to grow old gracefully. The handicapped will also become more and more marginalized unless we think imaginatively of plans for their training, rehabilitation and productive employment.

Directive Principles of the State Policy are often criticized for their lack of legal force. Some critics consider these as 'superfluous high sounding principles' with little scope for actual realisation. K. T. Shah compares them to a cheque payable by the bank at its convenience. While there is a judicial remedy for every violation of a Fundamental Right, there is none for the enforcement of Directive Principles since they impose no legal obligations on the state. K. C. Wheare has described them as a "manifesto of aims and aspirations". Looking at the novelty of ideals these Directives aspire to accomplish, it can be stated that they are more fundamental than the Fundamental Rights, since the ideals enshrined in them are loftier in conception and seek to secure to the individual tangible benefits of greater significance than Fundamental Rights. This is why, even though made non-justifiable, the Directive Principles have thus far guided the Union and the state Legislatures in enacting social reform legislation.

Which among the two shall be given more prominence: Fundamental Rights or Directive Principles?

In favour of Fundamental Rights	In favour of Directive Principles
Fundamental Rights are in the nature of general duties which the state is oblidged to perform for the good of the individual. They are enforceable through the courts hence are to prevail over Directive Principles of the State Policy in case of the conflict between the two. Article 13(2) of the Constitution of India prescribes that the Union or the States shall not make any law that takes away or abridges any of the fundamental rights, and any law made in contravention of the aforementioned mandate shall, to the extent of the contravention, be void. This view was taken by the Supreme Court in *Golak Nath and others Vs the State of Punjab case, 1967.* The Supreme Court in its judgment clearly said that the Parliament has no power to amend any provision of Part III of the Constitution so as to take away or abridge the Fundamental Rights enshrined.	Directive Principles of State Policy are in nature of specific duties which the state undertakes to perform for social good. They are much broader in scope and more sacrocent than the Fundamental Rights. This is evident from the fact that Fundamental Rights were amended to give effect to the Directive Principles of the State Policy. The Deletion of Article 31 and the insertion of Article 21 A are clear examples. The Directive Principles of State Policy aim to make India a Welfare State. However a lot remains to be done to achieve and truly operationalise the content of a welfare state in India. Political democracy without economic democracy is a sham democracy. Despite high growth, more than three fourths of Indians are poor and vulnerable with a level of consumption not more than twice the official poverty line. Four groups of people i.e. extremely poor, poor, marginal and vulnerable constituted about 77 percent of the population in India.

Fundamental Rights represent the ethos of modernization, political democracy and are vital for the growth of individual faculties. These rights are a symbol of social transformation and hence shall be given prominence over Directives.	The SC/ST constitutes the bottom layer followed by Muslims, OBC and others. These groups experience worst human sufferings, low education level, low income, absence of work and health care and security – all have made them victims of the growing economic boom. Besides this there is also evidence to suggest that inequality is growing not only between the common man and the better-off sections of the society, but also among different regions, creating uneven regional growth and development.

CHAPTER 4

ELECTIONS AND REPRESENTATION

If Voting Changed Anything They would Abolish It
Title of book by Ken Livingstone (1987)

Elections are often thought of as the heart of the political process. Perhaps no questions in politics are so crucial as, do we elect the politicians who rule over us, and under what rules are these elections held? Elections are seen nothing less than democracy in practice. **Democracy**[4] has been derived from a Greek word *'demo'* meaning people and *'cracy'* means government or power, so democracy means rule of people. Democracy as defined by **Abraham Lincoln** is government of the people, by the people and for the people. In nutshell it can be said that any government in which people have the highest participation is democratic. Democracy links government to the

---

[4] In Bernard Crick's words, 'democracy is perhaps the most promiscuous word in the world of public affairs'. Democracy is a term used to mean anything to anyone and a term that means anything to anyone is in danger of meaning nothing at all.

people. At present democracy has become the most practicable form of the government.

Elections have today become the most visible symbol of the democratic process. It is through elections that people's participation is secured. People can participate directly as well indirectly. The direct participation of the people is called as direct democracy. But all citizens cannot take direct part in making every decision. Therefore, representatives are elected by the people. This is how elections become important. The exercise of franchise by the citizens in choice of their government is known as **'Election'**[5].

Abraham Lincoln (1809-1865) was a US politician. He expressed his democratic ideals most famously at Gettysburg, Pennsylvania, site of the battle of the Civil War where the confederation armies had been turned back from their northernmost point. Lincoln stated that, 'the world will little note, nor long remember that 'government of the people, by the people and for the people, shall not perish from the earth'.

The particular act of choice is known as 'Voting'. The people who enjoy the right to vote are termed as voters or electors and collectively they form the "Electorate'. Right to franchise is exercised by the **citizens**[6] either for the choice of their representatives or expressing approval of a particular measure put before the people. Elections are important for democracy but all elections do not make democratic systems. Even non-democratic governments hold some limited elections.

---

[5]   A device for filling an office or post through choices made by a designated body of people: the electorate.

[6]   Citizen is a full-fledged member of a political community who enjoys certain rights and performs certain duties. Citizenship is also an identity, indicating one's membership in a political community.

Methods of Election:

1. **Direct Election:** Direct election is a very simple system. Here the voters themselves go to the centre of voting and vote for or against the candidates. A candidate securing a majority of the votes cast is declared elected. This method is employed in the election of members of the **Popular House**[7] of **legislature**[8] in almost all the democratic countries of the world. In India the election of Lok Sabha, Popular House of States and the Panchayats are held by direct method of election.

    Advantages of Direct Method: There is a great number of advantages of this method out of which some are discussed as under:

    i.   *Establishes contact between voters and representatives:* Direct method establishes contact between voters and representatives and thus, gives the voters an opportunity to exercise direct influence over their elected representatives. It is thus, in accordance with the spirit of democracy.
    ii. *Voters develop interest in public affairs:* Under the system of direct election, voters take a keen interest in public affairs and always keep an eye on the activities of their representatives. It adds to the voters' sense of responsibility, political education and self respect.
    iii. *Representatives feel directly responsible to the people:* Direct elections are advantageous in as much as the representatives feel that they are directly as well as ultimately responsible to

---

[7] Popular House is that house of the Parliament in which the directly elected members of the people hold their seats. In India Lok Sabha is regarded as the Popular House of the Parliament.

[8] Legislature is a law –making assembly of elected members in a formally equal relationship to one another.

the people. This makes them more responsive to the problems of the people.

iv. ***Essential in democracy:*** Democracy is the government by the people and it cannot be real unless the people choose the government directly.

2. **Indirect Election**: Under the system of indirect election, the voters do not elect their candidates directly. They elect an **Electoral College**[9] and this Electoral College elects the representatives. The election of the President and Vice President in the USA and similarly the election of the President and the members of the Rajya Sabha in India are also elected by the Indirect Election. It is a system of double election. The final election of the representatives, thus, lies in the hands of the people.

Advantages of Indirect Election:

i. ***Favorable for countries with large population:*** Indirect Elections are favored in populous nations because direct elections in such countries will give rise to various administrative problems. For example, framers of the Indian Constitution provided for an indirect election for the President and Rajya Sabha members not only to tackle administrative problems but also entail huge expenditure.

ii. ***Eliminates Defects of Universal Suffrage:*** As we know that in an Indirect Election an 'electoral college' or an intermediately body elects members, the drawbacks of the universal suffrage are eliminated. In country where illiteracy and poverty is at high rate, the defects of universal suffrage may erupt which are removed by the body of selected persons possessing superior knowledge and intelligence.

---

[9] An Electoral College is a mechanism for the indirect election of public officials. It can be called an intermedietery body that forms the government in the Parliamentary System of Governments.

Election System in India: Elections in India provide the occasion for the widest degree of popular participation; they constitute the most important single arena for genuine competition between political groups; they are principal agency through which recruitment to a significant part of political **elite**s affected; and the skills and resources which they especially call forth figure prominently in political life in general. Elections in India can now be seen not merely as useful indicators but actually as the events through which the party system and hence, in a measure, the political system achieves their evolution.

While the constitution of India lays down the procedure for the election of the President under Article 54 and the vice-President under Article 66, the procedure for election to the Legislatures of the Union and the States is left to the Parliament, the Constitution itself providing certain principles. These principles are:

> **Elite**
>
> The term elite originally meant, and can still mean, the highest, the best, or the excellent. Used in a neutral empirical sense, however, it refers to a minority in whose hands power, wealth or privilege is concentrated justifiably or otherwise. Elite, thus, refers to a group of influential people who exercise a huge influence in the decision making of a state. The elite theory was developed by Mosca, Pareto and Michels. Elite theory of democracy believes that what is known as the rule of people, in practical is, rule of chosen few or the elites.

a. There is no provision for communal, separate or special representation. There shall be one electoral role for every territorial constituency for election to either the House of the Parliament or to State Legislature and no person shall be excluded from such roll on grounds only of religion, caste, race, gender or any of them. However, there is a provision for reservation of seats in the interest of weaker sections of the society. India is unity in diversity. Different groups based on caste, religion, class, gender, socio-economic conditions exist here. When the Constitution makers opted for a democratic system with a first past the post system, it was widely believed that these minority groups may not get adequate representation in the law making bodies. This First Past the Post System can mean that the dominant social groups and castes can win everywhere and the oppressed social groups may continue to remain unrepresented. So to ensure their proper representation, a system of reservation became necessary. Thus the constitution has a provision for the reservation of constituencies to give adequate representation for Schedule Castes and Schedule Tribes. Originally, the reservation was for ten years but it was being extended every time for the next ten years. The Seventy-ninth Constitutional Amendment has extended it to 2010.

b.   The election shall be on the basis of Adult suffrage.

Universal Adult Suffrage:

In the modern times, the traditional theories of representation have been rejected due to their limited appeal. In almost all the countries of the world, all the conditions of franchise based on property, education, race, religion or gender have been rejected. All the adults have been granted the right to vote. Now-a-days only age and nothing else is considered for the entitlement to vote. The voting age may differ from country to country e.g. in India, Britain, America, Russia the voting age is 18 years while as, it is 21 in Switzerland. It was in 1989 that the voting age in India was reduced from 21 years to 18 years by a constitutional amendment act. The biggest merit of this system is that it is based on the concept of equality which is reflected in the dictum, one person one vote, and one vote one value. All can participate in the process of making the government irrespective of their colour, gender, religion, region, caste, creed, and class or socio political background.

Article 326 of the Indian Constitution provides that the election shall be on the basis of adult franchise or suffrage, that is, every person who is not less than 18 years of age shall be entitled to vote at the election provided he is not disqualified by any provision of the constitution or any law made by the appropriate legislature on the ground of non-residence, unsoundness of mind, crime, corruption or illegal practice. Adult franchise ensures that all citizens are able to participate in the process of selecting their representatives. This is consistent with the principle of equality and non-discrimination, as the right to vote is extended to all citizens _ both men and women.

The biggest revolution since the independence of India was the adoption of universal adult franchise for elections to the legislations. In a newly independent country with enormous poverty, backwardness, illiteracy, it was an act of faith for the constitution makers to give a vote to every citizen who was an adult. Till 1989, an adult Indian meant an Indian citizen above the age of 21 years. The sixty-first Amendment Act 1989, lowered the voting age from 21 to 18 years.

Merits of universal Suffrage:

1. **Essential in Democracy:** Democracy is a government of the people, for the people and by the people. It is, therefore, important that the spirit of democracy can only be maintained if people are given right to vote without any discrimination so that they should participate in their own government.
2. **Based on Equality:** Political equality is a basic principle for democracy. It demands that the right to vote should be equally distributed among all. To exclude any class of persons from this right is to infringe their equality.
3. **Adds to Individuals' self respect and dignity:** The exercise of adult suffrage adds to self respect, dignity, sense of responsibility and political and civic education.

Demerits of universal Suffrage:

1. **The right to vote to ignorant masses may lead to disaster:** The masses do not possess the capacity to understand political affairs

and to select the right kind of candidate. Further, it is argued that extension of right to vote to ignorant masses would lead to the loss of liberty, order and civilization. As a critic said, 'Give suffrage to the ignorant, and they will fall into **anarchy**[10] today and **despotism**[11] tomorrow'. The English proverb 'masses are asses', sums up the whole story.

2. **It leads to political corruption:** Votes in the hands of backward and illiterate persons are often sold for money (notes for votes). This note for vote is rampant in India.

First Past the Post System: First Past the Post System is that kind of an electoral system under which the candidate who secures more votes than other fellow contestants in his constituency is declared elected. In India elections to the Lok Sabha and the State Assemblies are carried out using the first past the post system. The country is split up into 543 separate geographical areas, known as constituencies. Each constituency elects one representative and it is not necessary that in order to win, a candidate must get majority of votes or any minimum percentage of votes cast. One who gets more votes than others wins.

This system of representation at times is unable to satisfy minorities in obtaining an adequate representation in the legislatures. **As J.S. Mill** remarked, "Majority of the voters will have majority of the representatives but a minority of the voters will have always a minority of representations". Furthermore, the defect of this system is that under it there remains a big gap between the percentage of votes secured and the number of seats won by a candidate or a party. For example in the Lok Sabha Election of 1984 Congress won only 48% of votes but it retained 80% of

---

[10] Anarchy literally means 'without rule', or a state of lawlessness. Presently "Anarchism" has become an ideology which believes that political authority in all its forms, and especially in the form of the state, is both evil and unnecessary.

[11] Despotism means autocratic rule by one person. In its Greek sense a 'despot' was the lord or ruler of an unfree state.

the seats while as the BJP got 7.5% of the votes but could manage to win only 2 seats.

However, in India the system was chosen because of its simplicity. When the constitution was being drafted, the country was among tremendous problems. The Partition created not only the refugee problem but also intensified communal hatred. Furthermore, mass illiteracy, poverty and less political socialization became the prime factors for the adaptation of first past the post system. The other reason for the preference of this system was the fear that proportional representation may generate communal hatred as it may encourage voters from different social groups to come together to win an election in a locality. Furthermore first past the post system offers voters a choice not only between parties but specific candidates which surely is not present in the Proportional Representation.

Proportional Representation: The system of proportional representation is an electoral device designed to ensure the representation of all sections of public opinion in proportion to their voting strength. The idea of proportional representation was first advocated in the French National Convention in 1973, but it was clearly propounded by Carl Andrea, the Danish Finance Minister in 1856 and **Thomas Hare**, an English philosopher in 1858. In his book '*Election of Representatives*' Thomas Hare explained at length the proportional representation system. He believes that this system will enable even the minority class to get representation in proportion to its population. Under this system, constituencies are larger in size and they are multi-member constituencies

J.S. Mill

John Stuart Mill (1806-1873) was a UK Philosopher, economist and politician. Mill developed the philosophy of liberalism and gave it a positive dimension. His most famous works are: On Liberty (1859), Considerations on Representative Government (1861) and The Subjection of Women (1869).

where from more than one candidates are elected. The theory received support from J.S. Mill who regarded it as the greatest improvement in theory and practice of representative government. The two main schemes of proportional representation system are the Single Transferable Vote System and the List System.

Single Transferable Vote System:
According to this system, from every multi-member constituency more than one candidate is elected. The number of candidates is fixed. Every voter has one vote which he castes on the preferential basis to all candidates. Then all the ballot papers according to their first preference are collected. The candidate who gets more than the definite fixed quota is elected. The formula for determining the number of votes is as

> **Thomas Hare** *Thomas Hare (1806-1891) was a self-taught British lawyer and enthusiast for Proportional Representation. Hare's scheme was vigorously promoted by J.S. Mill as the way to ensure that all, not just the majority, were represented in a legislature*

$$\text{Definite fixed Number} = \frac{\text{Total Number of Votes} + 1}{\text{Total seats} + 1}$$

For example, if the number of seats in a constituency is three and total number of votes cast is 200, the quota will be

$$\frac{200 + 1}{3 + 1} = 51$$

Counting of votes begins with first preference votes. A candidate securing the prescribed quota of votes is declared elected and his surplus votes, if any, are transferred to the second preference indicated on the ballet papers. Now with the help of second preference votes transferred in this way, some of the candidates are declared elected. If all the candidates are not elected with second preference votes transferred in this manner, third preference votes are utilized. Moreover, if some candidates secure a very small number of votes in the first preference, and as such there being no chance for them to be elected with the transferable votes, their first preference votes are given to the second choice indicated on their ballot paper.

The main idea behind this system is that no vote is to be lost. This system is followed in Denmark, Norway, Sweden, Portugal, and Israel. In India this system is applied for the election of the members of Rajya Sabha, State Legislative Council, the President and the vice-President.

List System: Under this system political parties exhibit the list of their candidates contesting election. The names of all the candidates according to their party affiliations are given on the ballot paper. The voters make the sign of 'X' against the names of their choice. However, the counting of votes is conducted on the party basis and the candidates are declared elected on the basis of votes secured by their respective parties.

The Election Commission of India:

The makers of Indian constitution attached the highest significance to independent electoral machinery for the conduct of elections. For this it was necessary that an independent election commission should be set up in the country. Such a commission would ensure free and fair elections of the representatives of the people at all levels. It is mainly with the idea of fulfilling the long cherished desire that the election commission was established under Article 324 which reads:

"The superintendence, direction and control of the electoral rolls for, and the conduct of all elections to the Parliament and to the Legislatures of every State and of elections to the offices of President and vice-President held under this constitution, including the appointment of election tribunals for the decision of the doubts and disputes arising out of or in connection with election to the Parliament and the Legislatures of the States, shall be vested in a commission".

The election commission is the soul of democracy. To ensure free, fair and impartial elections, the constitution established the Election Commission. Under Article 324, it has been laid down that the Election Commission shall have the authority to oversee the election of the President, the Vice- President and the members of the Parliament and state assemblies.

Composition: Clause (2) of Article 324 provides that Election Commission shall consist of Chief Election Commissioner and such number of other Commissioners, if any, as President may from time to time fix. The Chief Election Commissioner acts as the chairman of the Election Commission in case any other Election Commissioner besides him is appointed. Until 1989, the Election Commission consisted of the Chief Election Commissioner only. However, on October 16, 1989 President appointed S. S. Dhanoa and V. S. Seigell as Election Commissioners, thus, for the first time the Election Commission became a multimember commission. But in less than three months the notification was revoked and Election Commission reverted with effect from 2 January 1990 to being a single member body. But, again in 1993 two Election Commissioners namely M. S. Gill and T. N. Sasha were appointed. The President also promulgated an **ordinance**[12] amending the Chief Election Commissioners (conditions of service) Act providing for 'unanimous' transaction of business but in case of difference of opinion among the three members the matter shall be decided 'according to the opinion of majority'.

Powers and Functions of the Election Commission:

The Election Commission of India has to perform multifarious duties assigned to it under the constitution. The Election Commission is responsible for superintendence, direction and control of the whole

---

[12] Article 123 of the Indian Constitution reads as, 'the President shall have the power to legislate by Ordinances at a time when it is not possible to have a Parliamentary enactment on the subject immediately'.

election process for Union as well as states. Further, preparation of electoral rolls and conduct of elections are vested in the Election Commission under Article 324 of the constitution. These words in the Constitution are very important, for they give the Election Commission a decisive role in virtually everything to do with elections. The Supreme Court has agreed with this interpretation of the Constitution. *In Bhim Singh vs. Election Commission (1996),* the Supreme Court held thus: "Having due regard to the ground realities we must emphasize that functionaries in any manner concerned with duties to conduct, supervise and control of free, fair and peaceful election to the House of People (Lok Sabha) and the Legislative Assemblies of the States need to adopt a realistic, pragmatic and flexible approach to ensure that the country shall be governed in its true secular, socialist, democratic prospective".

The Election Commission is thus duty bound to provide and to maintain a proper atmosphere conducive to a free and fair election. The Election Commission can exercise any power which is necessary to achieve this objective even if the Conduct of Elections Act and the rules made there under do not confer such powers specifically.

This principle has been forcefully established by a Constitutional Bench comprising of five judges of the Supreme Court and authored by Justice V. R. Krishna Iyer, in *Mohinder Singh Gill vs The Election Commissioner AIR 1978.* The Commission is, therefore, entitled to exercise certain powers under Article 324 itself, on its own right, in an area not covered by the Acts and the Rules.

The Election Commission is thus not only entitled to take all steps, but is under a Constitutional obligation to do so, in order to maintain communal harmony during elections, which is a necessary condition for holding free and fair elections according to the constitution. It may not only direct political parties not to field a particular candidate which vitiates the atmosphere but also direct any person making a communal speech that seeks to polarize voters not to make any speeches during the election process. And if any such person violates the code of conduct, it may even direct state governments to detain such a person in custody during the period of the elections. To uphold these objectives the Election Commission does:

1. Delimitation of constituencies is an important task performed by the EC. Under the rule of the Parliament, after every ten years of the Census, the constituencies will be delimited.
2. Preparation of the electoral rolls for the election to the Parliament and all State Legislatures, including the local bodies.
3. Superintendence, direction and control of all matters pertaining to election of the President, the Vice President, the Parliament and State Legislatures.
4. To accord recognition to political parties as national or regional parties and to allot the symbols not only to parties but to independent candidates.
5. To determine the code of conduct to be observed by the parties and the candidates at the time of election.
6. To arrange the necessary staff for the conduct of the elections.

Electoral reforms in India: Free and fair elections are essential in a healthy democracy. It is an essential condition for the success of democracy that people maintain their allegiance towards the democratic institutions based on rule of law. The more the elections are free and fair, the stronger the allegiance the people will have towards democratic institutions. To maintain this fairness in the elections various reforms were done from time to time. It was as early as 1974 that a committee called as Tarakunde Committee was formed. In 1990 the National Democratic Front Government also appointed a committee called as Dinesh Goswami Committee. Some of the important reforms undertaken are as under:

1. *Lowering of voting age:* In the Constitutional Sixty-First Amendment Act of 1989, the voting age was reduced from 21 years to 18 years.

2. *Electronic Voting Machine:* The Representation of the People's Act of 1951 was amended to facilitate the use of electronic voting machines in elections.

3. *Affidavits to be filed by Candidates on Criminal antecedents, Assets, Qualification etc.:* The Supreme Court of India ordered the Election Commission of India to call for information on affidavit from each candidate seeking election to the Parliament or State Assemblies as a necessary part of his/her nomination paper.

4. *Compulsory Identification of voters:* Since 2000, the voter identification was made compulsory. The voters were given voter cards and directed to produce them at the time of casting their votes.

Judiciary and Electoral Reforms in India: Over 65 years have passed since India got its independence. With the passage of time, one hoped, Indian democracy would become vibrant and strong. In India there are many pillars of democracy, including an independent judiciary, a free press, and free and fair elections. It may be said that India has the first two intact to a great extent, but not the third. Various political analysts argue that the present election system, which has encouraged use of black money, casteism, abusive and administrative machinery, rigging and even capturing of booths in some areas, has been fast eroding the faith of the people in free and fair elections, thus need a complete overhauling.

In India 16 general elections for Lok Sabha and a very large number of Assembly elections have been held. The conduct of these elections clearly reveals that India has achieved the status of being the "largest Democracy". But it seems a case of procedural democracy while at the substantive level India is far behind to be called a democracy. This is the reason that right from the first general election the need for electoral reforms has been the subject of wide ranging debate.

The twin issues of criminalization of politics and transparency in the funding of political parties have taken centre stage in political discourse over the past three months.

We know that candidates with criminal records are contesting elections and get elected by using strong arms. For example a record 435 candidates with criminal background stood for 11th Lok Sabha elections in 1996 and 27 of these actually made it to the Parliament. In the 14th Lok Sabha, as many as 93 MPs had criminal charges pending against them. The strength of the 15th Lok Sabha is 543, out of which 162 MPs have criminal cases numbering 522 pending against them. Out of these 162 MPs, 76 MPs face serious (murder, theft, kidnapping etc) charges.(Hindustan Times, July 11, 2013) It is a matter of great concern that between 2004 and 2009 elections, an increase about 26% in MPs with pending criminal charges and 31% increase in the number of MPs with serious pending criminal cases. In this crime politics nexus India from Kashmir to Kanyakumari is one.

The Supreme Court (SC) of India has taken a lead in trying to remove the defects in the present electoral system and to decriminalize politics. The base for this reformation was laid by the SC of India in 2002 when it delivered a judgment in Association of Democratic Reforms, requiring every candidate to disclose, at the time of filling of nomination, any charges pending against him or her for offences that may involve punishment for a period above two years or otherwise. Furthermore, the candidate has to provide information about movable and immovable assets including bank balance etc. of himself, spouse and dependents. The spirit behind this judgment was to curb the growing criminalization of politics.

The SC on September 13, 2013 ruled that returning officer could reject nomination papers of a candidate for non-disclosure and suppression of information, including that of assets and their criminal background. The court passed the judgment on a PIL filed in 2008 by NGO Resurgence India, which detected a trend among candidates of leaving blank the columns demanding information about them.

Much of the present day controversy over criminal politics generated because of a landmark judgment of the SC that could clean the Parliament and Assemblies of criminals. The SC on July 10, 2013 struck down a provision in the electoral law that protects a convicted lawmaker from disqualification till an appeal is pending in higher courts. "The only question is about the virus of section 8(4) of the Representation of the People's Act and we hold that it is ultra virus and that the disqualification takes place from the date of conviction".

The idea of two classes of people__ ordinary citizens and those elected to represent them is anathema to democracy. If an ordinary citizen is barred from contesting elections if he stands convicted on the day of polling why should an elected representative get special privilege? The verdict seeks to remove the discrimination between an ordinary individual and elected lawmaker.

To reverse the judgment, the then Cabinet approved an ordinance which aimed to shield the convicted MPs from losing their seat as per the Supreme Court's order. Some baffling and uncomfortable questions persist: why the ruling party tried to bring in an ordinance when a bill to the same effect was already pending in the Parliament? How serious was the government about ushering in an era of clean politics?

The ordinance received criticism from all corners of the society. The Left parties while opposing the decision said that the UPA government was 'repeatedly using the ordinance route which is undemocratic'. Rajiv Pratap Rudy, the general sectary of BJP at the time said, "BJP is shocked at this ordinance. We would like to know whose great idea it is__ is it Prime Minister Manmohan Singh or Rahul Gandhi or is it UPA chairperson Sonia Gandhi." Sensing the public mood and the harmful effects the ordinance can bring, Rahul Gandhi called the Ordinance a 'complete nonsense' which 'should be torn up and thrown away'. Whatever the intentions behind Rahul Gandhi's surprising move, it needs to be welcomed.

As the Lok Sabha elections start approaching, parties become busy in deciding which candidate be given the ticket. It will be a great day for India if, instead of an amendment to the Representation of the People's Act, every party ensures that no candidate against whom any criminal case is pending would be allowed the ticket.

In addition to all above mentioned judgments of the SC, the SC of India on September 27, 2013 ruled that voters have the right to reject all candidates contesting polls by casting a negative vote. If all the voters use their 'none of the above' choice, still the governments will be formed, country will be ruled.

The decisions in itself cannot bring the much needed change. The right way forward for the SC is to devise procedures that ensure quick, time bound justice. The rise of criminalized politics is not simply due to politicians becoming more crooked. It is also that endless judicial delays have created huge inducements for criminals to enter politics, and to succeed over law-abiding rivals. There is an old saying that if law-breakers are not in jail, they will be in the legislatures. That is the case today.

Shall India Replace the First Past the Post System with Proportional Representation System?

YES	NO
The First Past the Post System of representation is full of defects and drawbacks and has questioned the very basic credentials of a democratic polity. This system simply makes democracy a game of numbers, a majoritarian rule. This system of representation at times is unable to satisfy minorities in obtaining an adequate representation in the legislatures. As J.S. Mill remarked, "Majority of the voters will have majority of the representatives but a minority of the voters will have always a minority of representations". Furthermore, the defect of this system is that under it there remains a big gap between the percentage of votes secured and the number of seats won by a candidate or a party. For example in the Lok Sabha Election of 1984 Congress won only 48% of votes but it retained 80% of the seats while as the BJP got 7.5% of the votes but could manage to win only 2 seats. The system of proportional representation is an electoral device designed to ensure the representation of all sections of public opinion in proportion to their voting strength.	In India the system was chosen because of its simplicity. When the constitution was being drafted, the country was among tremendous problems. The Partition created not only the refugee problem but also intensified communal hatred. Furthermore, mass illiteracy, poverty and less political socialization became the prime factors for the adaptation of first past the post system. The other reason for the preference of this system was the fear that proportional representation may generate communal hatred as it may encourage voters from different social groups to come together to win an election in a locality. Furthermore, first past the post system offers voters a choice not only between parties but specific candidates which surely is not present in the Proportional Representation. India has yet to win freedom from all the above mentioned problems, so the first past the post system becomes inevitable to carry on with. Proportional Representation surely will lead to Bargaining Federalism, Hung Parliaments, and Coalitions in a Multiparty polity like India.

CHAPTER 5

INDIAN EXECUTIVE

'A ruler must learn to be other than good'
Niccolo Machiavelli (The Prince 1513)

The executive is the irreducible core of government. Political systems can operate without constitutions, assemblies, judiciaries, and even political parties, but they cannot survive without an executive branch to formulate government policy and ensure that it is implemented. Executive is that branch of government which is concerned with the execution of policy. It is responsible for the day-to-day management of the state. There are generally three types of executives viz, (i) Authoritarian Executive, who authoritatively rule over the people. They may vary in form according to the circumstances in which they are

> **Separation of Powers:** The doctrine of separation of powers proposes that each of the three functions of government (legislation, execution and adjudication) should be entrusted to a separate branch of government (the legislature, the executive and the judiciary respectively). Its purpose is to fragment government power in such a way as to defend liberty and keep tyranny at bay. See fig. 1.1

created and developed. (ii) The Presidential Executive which is composed of ministers and senior officials appointed by and headed by the President. The President has the ultimate say in the policies advocated by the executive branch. It is based on the doctrine of **separation of powers**. The chief executive (the President) is the real head of the state. He is elected by the people, whether directly or indirectly, for a definite period and is not responsible to the legislature though he can be removed by the process of impeachment. Thus, it is that system in which the executive is constitutionally independent of the legislature in respect to the duration of his tenure and irresponsible to it for his political policies. The United States is the best example of this system. The main features of this system are:

1. Real Authority of the President: The real executive powers are in the hands of the President who is elected by the people for a fixed period.

2. Separation of Powers: The theory of separation of powers was given by **Montesquieu**. This is the most important feature of this system of government. The separation of powers means that all the three branches of the government, i.e. Legislature, Executive and Judiciary are not responsible to one another in their matters. They are independent in their own spheres but exert a system of checks and balances.

Montesquieu *Charles-Louiis de Secondat de Montesquieu (1689-1775) was a French political philosopher, historian and novelist, often seen as one of the founders of sociology. In his best political work 'The Spirit of the Laws, 1748, Montesquieu divided political systems between despotism based on fear, republics based on virtue, and monarchies based on honour. He gave the theory of Separation of Powers which deeply influenced the framers of the US constitution*

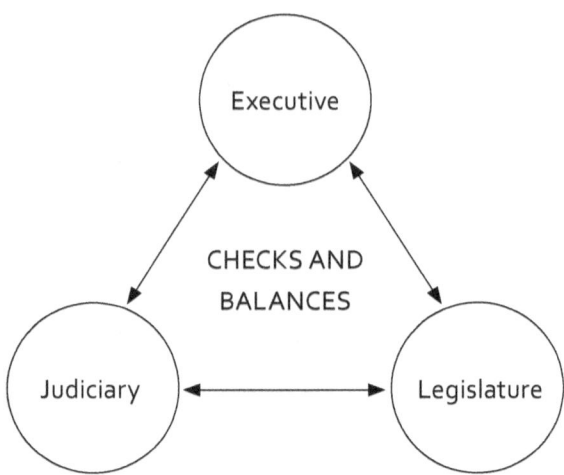

Fig 1.1. Separation of power

3. The Parliamentary Executive, (United Kingdom based model) is based upon the principle of Cabinet Government. In this system ministers are appointed and headed by a prime minister but all executive decisions are collectively made and members of cabinet are collectively responsible to the legislature from which they are drawn and whose continued support they need to stay in office.

India has adopted the Parliamentary form of executive. The constitution makers had long debates related to the form of government to be adopted for the

Government of India Act 1919: Also called as Montague-Chelmsford Reform Act. The Act made some important changes in the governance of the country. Some important changes are listed as under:

i. A provision was made for classification of central and provincial subjects. ii. The provincial subjects were divided into two groups: Reserve and Transferred. The Reserved subjects were with the Governor and Transferred subjects with the Indian Ministers. This was known as diarchy. iii. The act provided a bicameral legislature at the Centre consisting of the Council of States and the Central Legislative Assembly.

country. The practice and traditions evolved during the British rule along with the political background in India had influenced the decisions of the Constituent Assembly. The Constituent Assembly decided in favour of Parliamentary Democracy, where in the people's representatives were to get elected through a system of universal adult franchise. The country had already some experience of running the parliamentary system under the Acts of 1919 and 1935. Leaving aside a few members, all the members expressed the view that the British model was the most suitable. Jawaharlal Nehru said that 'we cannot go in the opposite direction'. Dr Ambedkar, K.M. Munshi and others also justified the adoption of the parliamentary system of government.

The makers of the Constitution had to make a choice between Presidential form of government, Gandhian concept of decentralization of power (village Swraj). Both the models were refuted. In fact K.M.Panikar suggested that the President of India should be a nominal head of the executive and should discharge all the functions which may be entrusted to him according to the constitution.

Furthermore, the makers of the Indian constitution wanted a government that would have a strong executive branch, but at the same time, enough safeguards should be there to check against the personality cult. In the parliamentary form there are many mechanisms that ensure that the executive will be answerable to and controlled by the legislature or people's representatives. So the constitution adopted the parliamentary form of government both at the national level and at the state levels.

India has, thus, adopted a parliamentary system of government similar to that of the UK and Japan. It is based on the fusion of legislative and executive powers. Under the Indian system, the Parliament is supreme as it is an elected body. There is a presence of two executives – the nominal executive and the real executive. The nominal executive is the President of India in whose name lie all the executive powers, but he exercises them only on the advice of prime minister and his Council of Ministers. Thus the prime minister and his Council of Ministers is the real executive.

The President of India: We know that in India, there is a parliamentary form of government as distinguished from the American presidential type of government. The executive, both at the Union and at the State level, is nominal (The President at the Union and the Governor in the States) and real executive is the Prime Minister at the Union and the Chief Minister in the States. The President, under the constitution has a unique position and it has been established that the Indian President is not a glorified cipher or a mere rubber stamp. It must be said that it is Prime Minister who rules the country but at the same time the President represents the country. The constitution provides him the status of statesman, guide and philosopher.

As per the constitution, the President is the head of the State and First Citizen of India, as well as the supreme commander in chief of the armed force of India. Under Article 52 part V the office of the President was established, with Dr. Rajendra Prasad as its first occupant. The President's oath of office compels him "to preserve, protect and defend the constitution and the law" and "to develop himself to the service and well being of the people of India".

Appointment of the President: The President of India is elected by an indirect election in accordance with the system of proportional representation by means of the single transferable vote.

Article 54 of the constitution says that the President shall be elected by the members of an electoral college consisting of:

a) The elected members of both the Houses of the Parliament; and
b) The elected members of Legislative Assemblies of the states.

According to Article 55, as far as practicable, there shall be uniformity of representation of different states at the election according to the population and total number of elected members of the Legislative Assembly of each state and parity shall also be maintained between the states as a whole and the Union. This second condition seeks to ensure that the votes of the state in aggregate, in the electoral college of the President shall be equal to that of the people of the whole country. In this way, the President shall be a representative of the people in different states. It also gives recognition to the status of the states in the federal system.

Qualifications: In order to be qualified for election as President, a person must:

a) Be a citizen of India;
b) Have completed the age of thirty-five years;
c) Be qualified for election as a member of the house of the people ; and
d) Must not hold any office of profit under the government of India or the government of any state or under any local or other authority subject to the control of any of the said governments (Article 58).

But a sitting President or vice – President of the Union or the Governor of any state or a Minister either of the Union or for any state is not disqualified for election as President (Art 58).

Term of the office of President: The term of the office of the President, according to Article 56, is five years with a provision for reelection (Article 57). The constitution prescribes no legal limitation on the number of terms a person may serve in the office. Dr. Rajendra Prasad was the only President of India who held the office for two consecutive terms. The President's office may terminate within the term of five years in either of the two ways:

a) By resignation in writing under his hand addressed to the vice – President of India.
b) By removal for violation of the constitution, by the process of **impeachment** (Art 56). The only ground for impeachment specified in Article 61(1) is 'Violation of the constitution'.

Impeachment: It refers to the provision of removing important public officials from their office by passing a resolution to that effect by Parliament. In India the President can be removed through impeachment motion passed by two third majority of the total membership in each House of Parliament.

Powers of the President: The role of the President in the Indian political system can be examined only after a brief review of his powers and responsibilities. His powers can be discussed under several heads.

Executive Powers:- Though he may not be the real head of the administration, all officers of the union shall be his 'Subordinates' (Article 53) and he shall have a right to be informed of the affairs of the Union {Article 78(b)}. He appoints the Prime Minister and his Council of Ministers. He also appoints the Judges of the Supreme Court and the High Courts, Governors of the State etc. The Ministers hold the office during the pleasure of the President. He also acts as the chief diplomat.

Legislative Powers: Perhaps, the most important legislative power of the President is his power to promulgate ordinances under Article 123. According to this, the President is empowered to promulgate ordinances, except when both the houses of the Parliament are in session, if he is satisfied that circumstances exist compelling him to take immediate action. Article 79 of the constitution states that, 'there shall be a Parliament for the Union which shall consist of the President and the two Houses i.e. Lok Sabha and Rajya Sabha'. As an inseparable part of the Parliament, he enjoys the following legislative powers:

1. The President has the power to summon and prorogue the sessions of the Parliament.
2. The President can address either or both the Houses of the Parliament at any time.
3. No bill can become a law without the signature of the President.
4. He nominates two persons from the Anglo-Indian community to the Lok Sabha if he feels that the community is not adequately represented.
5. He can also nominate from the fields of Arts, Science, Literature and Social Service, 12 members to the Rajya Sabha.

Judicial Powers (under Article 72): He may grant **pardon, reprieve, respite** or **remission** of punishment or may **commute** the sentence of any person convicted of any offence (a) where the punishment or sentence is by a Court Martial; (b) where the punishment or sentence is for an offence against any law relating to a matter to which the executive power of the union extends; and (c) in case where the sentence is a sentence of death. While the Governor has certain powers of pardoning the President is the only authority who can pardon a death sentence.

Military and Diplomatic powers: Article 53(2) vests the Supreme Command of the defense force in the hands of the President. The President appoints the chiefs of the Army, Navy and Air Force and enjoys the power to declare war and conclude peace.

Similarly, the diplomatic power that the President exercises in capacity of the head of the state in India, involves that the President represents the country in international forums. He sends ambassadors to foreign countries and receives their diplomats. All international treaties and agreements are concluded on behalf of

Pardon: The grant of pardon removes both the sentence and the conviction and absolves the convict from all disqualifications and punishment. It has the effect as if the convict has not committed any crime and was not convicted at all.

Reprieve: Reprieve has an effect of staying the execution of a punishment for the time being in order to allow the time for disposing the pending application for pardon, commutation etc. This is temporary concession given to the convict from immediate execution of a sentence.

Respite: Respite means awarding a lesser punishment in place of the given punishment due to some special fact. For example a physically handicapped person may be given lesser punishment in place of rigorous punishment due to his special physical condition.

Remission: Remission has the effect of reducing the amount of the punishment without changing its character. For example, the rigorous punishment of two years may be reduced to the rigorous punishment of one year. But it will always remain a rigorous punishment because its character cannot be changed by remission.

Commute: Under the commutation one form of punishment is substituted by another punishment of a lighter character. For example, the punishment of death may be substituted by the rigorous punishment or the rigorous punishment may be substituted by simple punishment. Thus the commutation changes the character of the punishment but like pardon, it does not remove conviction at all.

the President. However, these treaties and agreements are subject to rectification by the Parliament.

Financial Powers: All money bills can originate in the Parliament only on the recommendation of the President. The **contingency fund** of India has been placed at the disposal of the President. He causes the annual budget and important reports to be laid before the Parliament and recommends the introduction of money bills in the Parliament. The President appoints a finance commission every five years to recommend distribution of taxes between the centre and the state governments.

> **Contingency Fund:** Article 226 (1) of the constitution defines the consolidated fund as a fund in which all revenues received by the Government of India, all loans raised by the Government and all money received by that Government in repayment of loans shall one consolidated fund to be called 'the Consolidated Fund of India'.

Emergency powers: The part XVIII of the constitution contains emergency provisions and it gives to the President certain powers to deal with emergencies. The constitution mentions three kinds of emergencies: (a) emergency due to external aggression or internal revolt usually called as National Emergency; (b) emergency arising out of failure of constitutional machinery in the state or states, called as Constitutional Emergency; and (c) Financial Emergency arising from threat to the financial stability or credit of the country. During emergencies, the President comes to wield such extensive powers that critics of the constitution describe them as a threat to the democratic system of government.

National emergency under Article 352: National emergency is proclaimed by the President at a time when he is satisfied that the security of India or any part thereof has been threatened by war, external aggression or armed rebellion (Article 352). The term armed rebellion" was incorporated by the 44th Amendment act and it replaced the original term "Internal disturbance." Such a proclamation of emergency can be made not only when an actual violation of security of India has taken place but also when the President is satisfied that there is an imminent danger to the security of the country {Article 352 (3)}. Once issued and when duly approved by both the houses of the Parliament, an emergency proclamation can remain in force for six months. However, through subsequent approvals after every six months, the proclamation can remain operative for any length of time, e.g. during Indira Gandhi's Prime Ministeriership, an 18 months' national emergency was imposed on 25 June 1975. Imposition of Emergency earned considerable criticism because in its grab many atrocities were committed by Indira Gandhi agaist the honest officials and poor masses. All Fundamental Rights were taken away, press was censored, strikes were banned, opposition leaders were imprisoned. The imposition of emergency was a poor gamble for Indira Gandhi as well as for the Congress as it lost the elections in 1977. The grand coalition of non-congress parties under the banner of Janta Party came to power. Soon after coming to the power the Janta government in May 1977 appointed a Commission of Inquiry which was headed by J. C. Shah. The Commission was to inquire into different aspects of the emergency period, especially about the misuse of power, position etc. The Commission submitted its report in which the Commission has highlighted the cases of maladministration in the emergency period. The Commission noticed that more than 676 opposition leaders were arrested along with more than one lakh eleven thousand persons. All these detentions came under preventive detention. The Commission also declared that imposition of emergency was a grievous misuse of Article 352.

Constitutional Emergency under Article 356: Article 356 of the constitution gives to the President the power to declare emergency in a state/ states when he is satisfied that the government of the state/states cannot be carried on in accordance with the provisions of the constitution, either on the report of the Governor of the state/ states or otherwise (Article 356). This Article of the constitution is mostly misused by the political parties in power.

Financial Emergency under Article 360: The President, under Article 360 can proclaim a financial emergency in India if he is satisfied that a situation has arisen whereby the financial stability or credit of India or any part of the territory therefore stands threatened. When such a proclamation is in operation the centre can give directions to any state to observe such canons of financial property as may be essential for restoring the health of country's economy. The President can order all such fiscal measures as wage freeze, price freeze, cut in the salaries and allowances of all or any of the classes of employees. The President can order that all money bills passed by the state legislatures be reserved for his approval. But the fortunate thing is this that these provisions under Article 360 have not been operationalised.

Criticism to the Emergency Provisions: While criticizing the emergency Provisions, H.V. Kamnath observed, "There is no parallel to the chapter on emergency in any democratic constitution of the world." He dubbed them as anti-democratic, a base for a totalitarian state. Another critique K.T. Shah observed in the Constituent Assembly that, "I notice for distinct currents of thought underlying these provisions (i) to arm the centre with special powers against the units, and (ii) to arm the Government against the people. Looking at the provisions, it seems to me, the name only of liberty or democracy will remain under the constitutions."

List of Presidents of India

Sino	Name of the President	From _ To	Place of Birth	Political Party	Gender
1.	Dr. Rajendra Prasad	Jan 1950 – May 1962	Bihar	Indian Nationality	Male
2.	Dr. S. Radhakrichnan	1968 1967	Madras	Independent	Male
3.	Dr. Zakir Hussain	May 1967 – 1969	Hyderabad	Independent	Male
4.	Varahagiri Venkata Giri	May 1969 – July 1969	Madras	INC	Male
5.	Mohammad Hidayatulah	July 1969 – August1969	Lukhnow	Independent	Male
6.	V.V. Giri	Aug. 1969 – 1974	Madras		
7.	Fakhruddin Ali Ahmad	Aug. 1974 – Feb. 1977	Delhi	INC	Male
8.	Basapa Danapa Jatti	Feb. 1977 – Jully 1977.	Karnataka	INC	Male
9.	Neelam Sarjeeva Reddy	July 1977 – 1982	Andhra Pradesh	Janata Party	Male
10.	Giani Zail Singh	July 1982 – July 1987	Sandhwan (Faridkot)	INC	Male
11.	Venkataraman	July 1987 – July 1992	Madras	INC	Male
12.	Dr. Shaker Dayal Sharma	1992- 1997	Madhya Pradesh	INC	Male
13.	A.P.J. Abdul Kalam	July 2002 – 2007	Tamil Nadu	Independent	Male
14.	Smt. Pratibha Devi Singh Patil	July 2007 – July 2012	Maharastra	INC	Female
15.	Sri Pranab Mukherjee	July 2012 – Till date	West Bengal	INC	Male

THE VICE PRESIDENT

Next to the President of India, the highest position in the official hierarchy is accorded to the vice – President. Article 63 of the Indian constitution provides for the office of the vice – President. This office was created primarily for making an arrangement to fulfill a sudden temporary or permanent vacancy in the office of the President.

Election:- Article 66 of the Indian constitution reads, "The vice-President shall be elected by the members of an electoral college consisting of the members of both the houses of the Parliament, in accordance with the system of proportional representation by means of the single transferable vote and the voting at such election shall be by secret ballot." In the election of Vice – President the state legislatures do not have any role to play. All doubts and disputes regarding the election shall be enquired into and decided by the Supreme Court.

Qualifications: A candidate for the office of the vice – President must:

1. Be a citizen of India;
2. Be more than 35 years of age;
3. Possess the qualification prescribed for membership of the Rajya Sabha;
4. Not be member of either house of the Parliament or state legislature;
5. Not be a person of unsound mind or insolvent;
6. Not hold any office of profit under the union or state government or local authority.

Term: The vice – President is elected for five years. He is eligible for re- election. He may resign his office before the expiry of the normal term. His letter of resignation is to be addressed to the President.

Removal:- The vice – President can be removed from his office by a resolution of the Rajya Sabha passed by a majority of its members and agreed upon by the Lok Sabha (Article 67). However, a notice of 14 days is required to be given to the incumbent against when the proceedings of removal are to be initiated.

Powers: The vice- President is the ex- officio chairman of the Rajya Sabha and presides over its meetings. All bills, resolutions, motions or questions can be taken up by the Rajya Sabha only with his consent. He is chief spokesman of the Rajya Sabha before the President as well as the Lok Sabha.

He discharges the functions of the office of the President in case that post falls vacant on account of the death, resignation or removal of the President. The vice President can act as President for a maximum period of six months because fresh elections for the office of the President must be held within six months of the occurrence of vacancy. Similarly, if the President is unable to discharge his functions for some reason, the vice-President discharges all his functions.

PRIME MINISTER AND THE COUNCIL OF MINISTERS

The constitution of India provides for a parliamentary system and, therefore, divides the executive into two parts:

(i) The Nominal or Constitutional Executive, and (ii) The Real Executive. The President of India is a constitutional executive and the real executive authority of the Union is exercised by the Prime Minister and his Council of Ministers. The Prime Minister is the head of the Government in India. Article 74 of the constitution says, "There shall be a Council of Ministers with the Prime Minister at the head, to aid and advice the President, who shall in the exercise of his functions, act in accordance with such advice." Hence, the other ministers cannot function without the Prime Minister. Although it is considered most desirable for the Prime Minister to be a member of Lok Sabha, he can be a member of either house of the Parliament. Harold J. Laski called the Indian Prime Minister as "the pivot of the whole system of government".

> **Coalition**
> In simple words it can be defined as, when several political parties collaborate to form a government and exercise the political power on the basis of a common agreed programme. Such a system is described as coalition politics or coalition government. Such a government is usually organised when no party is in a position to get majority in the Parliament.

Appointment: The Prime Minister is appointed by the President of India. Article 75 (1) says, "The Prime Minister shall be appointed by the President .... And all other Ministers shall be appointed by the President on the advice of the Prime Minister." Usually the President invites the leader of the majority party in the Parliament to form the Council of Ministers. But, where no single party or **coalition** is in a position to form a government on its own, the role of the President in choosing the Prime Minister becomes most delicate and difficult. In such circumstances, the President may request the single largest party or alliance to form the government. In simple words it can be said that the **Hung Parliaments**[13] have affected the powers of the President in appointing the Prime Minister.

Powers of the Prime Minister: The Prime Minister performs many significant functions in the Indian political system and exercises vast powers. He is the chief executive of the nation and works as the head of the Union Government. The Prime Minister selects the members of the Council of Minister who are formally appointed by the President. He allocates portfolios among the ministers and he can drop any minister. The Prime Minister presides over the meetings of the Council of Ministers. He decides the policies of the government. He coordinates the work of different ministries and solves inter – departmental conflicts. The Prime Minister is the Chairman of the Planning Commission which is a key body in the process of planning.

The Prime Minister advises the President on all important matters like appointments of judges of the High Courts and Supreme Court, Chief Election Commissioner, Comptroller and Auditor General. He advises the President on the summoning and proroguing of the Parliament, the dissolving of the Lok Sabha and the declaration of emergencies. He acts as a link between the President and the Cabinet.

The Council of Ministers: The real executive power under the Indian constitution vests not in the President but in the Council of Ministers headed by the Prime Minister. Article 74 (1) of the constitution lays down that there shall be a Council of Ministers with the Prime Minister at the head to aid and advise the President who shall, in the exercise of his functions, act in accordance with such advice. Prior to 42nd Constitutional Amendment Act of 1976, there was no express provision in the constitution that the President was bound to act in accordance with the advice tendered by the Council of Ministers, though it was judicially established that the

---

[13]   Hung Parliament means a Parliament where no party has got the majority to form the government of its own.

President of India was not a real executive, but a constitutional head, who was bound to act according to the advice of Ministers, so long as they commanded the confidence of the majority in Lok Sabha {Article75 (3)}. The 42nd Amendment Act, amended Article 74 (1) to clarify this position. However, 44th Constitutional Amendment Act, 1978 gave President 'Right to Reconsideration'. But the power to return any bill for reconsideration can be exercised only once, on the same matter.

The process of formation of the Council of Ministers begins by the appointment of the Prime Minister by the President. After the appointment of the Prime Minister, the President appoints other ministers on the advice of the Prime Minister. The Prime Minister prepares the list of the persons whom he recommends for appointment as ministers. Article 75 of the constitution lays down the basic rules regarding the organization of the Council of Ministers. These are:

i)   The Prime Minister shall be appointed by the President and other ministers shall be appointed by the President upon the advice of the Prime Minister;

ii) The ministers shall hold office during the pleasure of the President;

iii) The Council of Ministers shall be collectively responsible to the House of the People;

iv) Before a minister enters upon his office, the President shall administer to him the oath of office and secrecy;

v)   A minister who for any six months is not a member of either House of the Parliament, shall at the expiry of that period cease to be a minister;

vi) The salaries and allowances of ministers shall be such as the Parliament may from time to time by law determine.

All the ministers, however, do not belong to the same rank. They are classified under three ranks (a) Cabinet Ministers b) Ministers of state c) Deputy Ministers.

a) **Cabinet Ministers**: Their number is usually between 15 – 20. They constitute the cabinet – the powerful policy making and decision making part of the Council of Ministers. They are the top level leaders of the party/parties in power and happen to be close to the Prime Minister.

b) **Minister of State:** They constitute the second category of ministers. They aren't the members of the cabinet. A minister of state either holds an independent charge of a small department or is attached to a cabinet minister.

c) **Deputy Minister:** They are helping ministers attached to the Cabinet Minister or the Ministers of state. No deputy Minister holds an independent charge of any department. His function is to help the minister under whom he works. They are mainly given the responsibility to prepare answers to the parliamentary questions pertaining to their respective departments and to help the process of getting the Government Bills passed by the Parliament.

Composition of the Council of Ministers: The number of members of the Council of Ministers as per original constitution up to the year 2003 was not specified. It was determined according to the exigencies of the time. For example, at the end of 1961, the strength of the Council of Ministers of the Union was 47, at the end of 1975, it was raised to 60, and in 1977 it was reduced to 24. However, the 91st Constitutional Amendment (2003) inserted provision IA in the Article 75 which provides "The total number of Council of Ministers, including the Prime Minister, shall not exceed fifteen percent of the total number of members of the House of the People." When UPA formed the government in 2009, it included 79 ministers including Prime Minister in the Council of Ministers.

UPA cabinet by Constituent Parties (2009)

Party	Cabinet Ministers	Ministers of State	Total
Indian National Congress	27	32	59
Dravida Munnetra Kazhagam (DMK)	03	04	07
Trinamool Congress	01	06	07
Nationalist Congress Party	01	02	03
National Conference	01	00	01
Muslim League	00	01	01
Total =	33	45	78

The Council of Ministers of Narendra Modi was constituted after the general election of May 2014. The results of the election were announced on 16 May 2014 and Bhartiya Janta Party came out as the majority party. Subsequently, BJP President Rajnath Singh along with other leaders of the ally parties of NDA, met President Pranab Mukherjee at President's House and handed over the support letter of 335 members of the Parliament and claimed for the government formation. Following this, Mukherjee appointed Modi as the Prime Minister of India and sought his advice for the names of the members of the Council of Ministers of his government. Narendra Modi became the Prime Minister of India and his Council assumed office on 26 May 2014. As the head of the Council of Ministers, Modi had stated that his cabinet would be compact, based on the guiding principle of "minimum government and maximum governance".[14]

Powers and Functions of the Council of Ministers:

The Council of Ministers forms the government of the Union. It is headed by the Prime Minister who is the head of the Union Government. Its powers and functions may be discussed as below.

---

[14]   For more information visit, http://en.wikipedia.org/wiki/Cabinet_of_India.

1. **Legislative Functions:** The Council of Ministers controls the legislature of the Union Government, i.e. the Parliament. It forms its policies, submits and explains them to the Parliament for approval. Since it holds majority in the Parliament, it is always sure of the acceptance of the policy. The entire legislation of importance passed by the Parliament is initiated by the Council of Ministers.

2. **Financial Functions:** The cabinet controls the financial policy of the Union. It is the Finance Minister who submits the budget to the Parliament. The Parliament approves the budget – expenditure and revenue items in its original form with the support of the subservient majority.

3. **Executive Powers:** The Council of Ministers is the executive of the Union. The ministers preside over the various departments of the government and give direction to the administration. The cabinet brings about coordination of policy among various departments and settles their conflicts. The cabinet formulates foreign and defense policies of the country and executes the five year plans.

Hung Parliament and the election of the Prime Minister:

Article 75 (1) of the Constitution of India reads: "The Prime Minister shall be appointed by the President and the other Ministers shall be appointed by the President on the advice of the Prime Minister."

Normally, the leader of the majority party is invited by the President to form the government. But the choice of Prime Minister becomes difficult when there is a 'Hung Parliament'. When elections result in hung parliaments, the President follows his own 'discretion' whom to invite to become the Prime Minister. In the exercise of such discretion, constitutional conventions play an important role in guiding the President. In the absence of clear established conventions and guidelines, the choice of Prime Minister becomes a difficult task for the President.

As we know that during 1989 to 1999 India saw many Prime Ministers coming and going without completing their five year term. As the era of coalitions was unfolding in India, so were the powers of the President to appoint the Prime Minister going through an evolving times. The elections of 1989 resulted in a hung Parliament with no party securing majority. The Congress with 194 seats was the single largest party in the House. So President R. Venkataraman first invited the Congress party leader Rajiv Gandhi, who declined to form a government. Thereafter, the President invited the leader of the National Front, V.P. Singh, to form the government. President Venkataraman applied what is called the "arithmetic test/objective test" of summoning the parties in order of their numerical strength. When, On May 15, 1996, President S.D. Sharma applied this numerical test in the appointment of A.B. Vajpayee as Prime Minister, it proved no less than a disaster. The government fell within 13 days of its appointment. The fall of Vajpayee government clearly shows that being the leader of the single largest party does not necessarily mean that he or she will command majority support in the House. It is only the leader of the party or the leader of the group or formation who is able to secure the support of the House who should be invited to form the government.

Available Options before President

Enjoying confidence of majority is what sustains the government rather than being the leader of the majority party. So in the appointment of the Prime Minister the President necessarily takes it into consideration that the Prime Minister and the Council of Ministers shall enjoy the confidence of majority. The primary factor will be his/her assessment of who as Prime Minister and which body of Council of Ministers will enjoy the confidence of the Parliament in terms of Article 75 (3) of the Constitution, which reads: "The Council of Ministers shall be collectively responsible to the House of the People."

In such circumstances, according to K. Subramanian the following appear to be the options:

(a) If there is no single party with an absolute majority, the President may look for the leader of a pre-poll alliance that has a majority.

(b) If there is no such pre-poll alliance that has a majority, the President may invite the leader of the pre-poll alliance who is supported by a sufficient number of Lok Sabha MPs to command an absolute majority.

(c) It is only when options A and B are ruled out that the President may invite the leader of a post-poll alliance. The President will make sure that the groups or parties agree to some common programme or policies. The post-poll alliance must elect its leader before the President invites it to form the government.

(d) When options A, B, and C are ruled out, the President may send a message to the House asking it to elect its leader (to seek a vote of confidence). The Constitution Review Commission, headed by a former Chief Justice of India, M.N. Venkatachelliah, recommended this option.

(e) If the House also fails to elect its leader, the President may explore the possibility of installing a 'National Government,' in which all major political parties in the Lok Sabha may be represented. Such a government would only be a caretaker government for carrying out the day-to-day administration until the mid-term elections to the Lok Sabha are conducted.

(f) If there is no possibility of installing a 'National Government,' the President may call a mid-term election. But with around 714 million voters, conducting elections in India is prohibitively expensive. Further, there is no guarantee that after such a mid-term election there will not be a hung Parliament again!

CHAPTER 6

INDIAN PARLIAMENT

We choose this system of Parliamentary democracy deliberately; we choose not only because, to some extent, we had always thought on those lines previously, but because we thought it was in keeping with our old traditions, not as they were, but adjusted with the new conditions and new surroundings, we choose it also _ let us give credit where credit is due _ because we approved of its functioning in other countries, more especially the United Kingdom.

(Jawaharlal Nehru)

The word 'Parliament' is derived from the French word *'Parlor'* which means 'to talk'. The term connotes a place where people sit and discuss national and international issues and enact legislations for their country. The modern Parliamentary system owes its origin to Western countries, particularly to United Kingdom. The term Parliamentary refers specially to a kind of democratic polity wherein the supreme power vests in the body of people's representatives called the Parliament. The parliamentary system is one in which the Parliament enjoys a place of primary and pre-eminence in the governance of the state. Under the constitution of Indian the Union Legislature is called the

Parliament. Article 79 of the constitution begins by saying that there shall be a Parliament for the Union which means that the Parliament must be always there. At the level of States their legislatures occupy the similar position. It is important to remember that in a parliamentary polity, just as government is responsible to the legislature, the legislature is also responsible to the people who are the ultimate sovereign or it can be said that this model works on the concept of **popular sovereignty**.

The Parliament consists of the President and the two Houses that is, the Lok Sabha (House of the people) and the Rajya Sabha (Council of States). The Hindi names Lok Sabha and Rajya Sabha fairly reflect the character of their composition. The Rajya Sabha is composed mainly of representatives of the State Assemblies. The Lok Sabha is composed of directly elected representatives on the basis of Adult Franchise and territorial constituencies. The President is a part of legislature, like the English Crown. Even though the President does not sit or participate in the discussions in either of the two houses, he exercises several powers and performs important functions in respect of the Parliament.

India opted for a bi-cameral legislature because of its gigantic size, diversity and federal characters. India is generally regarded as a unity in diversity. So in order to give representation to all sections in the society and

Popular Sovereignty: *When political sovereign comprises of all members of a community, i.e. the people, the idea of its supreme legal authority is expressed as 'popular sovereignty'. In other words, the idea of popular sovereignty regards people as the source of all authority in the state. In its view, the organs of state which exercise supreme power of law-making, law- enforcement and adjudication, draw their legitimacy from the will of the people. It does not rely on any superior law _ natural law, religious commandments or any other authority _ to ascertain what is right or wrong. It does not look for any source of 'superior reason' apart from the mind of people. Thus it regards people themselves, in their corporate capacity, as the embodiment of reason, the best judges of right and wrong, and hence the real source of supreme authority.*

geographical areas of the country, a bi-cameral legislature was opted. Morris Jones, while analyzing the utility of the Rajya Sabha observes, "It has three out-weighing merits. Firstly, it supplies additional political positions for which there is demand. Secondly, it provides some additional debating opportunities for which there is occasional need and thirdly, it assists in the solution of limited legislative problems.

President's Position in the Parliament: The President of India is indirectly elected by an electoral college consisting of the elected members of the Legislatives Assemblies (popular houses of the states). Though the President of India is a constituent part of the Parliament, he does not sit or participate in the discussions in either of the two houses. The President summons the two houses of the Parliament to meet from time to time. He can prorogue the two houses of the Parliament and dissolve the Lok Sabha. His assent is essential for a bill passed by both houses to become a law. Not only that, when both houses are not in session and he is satisfied that circumstances exist which render it necessary for him to take immediate action, the President can promulgate ordinances having the same force and effect as a law passed by the Parliament.

Prorogation: *The termination of a session of the House by an order made by the President under Article 85 (2)(a) of the Indian constitution. The President takes the decision in consultation with the Council of Ministers. Prorogation brings the parliamentary session to an end.*

Adjournment: *It is a short period of time for the suspension of the sittings or in other words a recess within the sittings of the Parliament. It is generally called by the presiding officer of the house. The duration of the adjournment of the house may be for a few minutes to a few days. The order to adjourn is generally passed if the normal working of the house gets disrupted due to some reason.*

Adjournment Sin die: *When the house is adjourned by the presiding officer without fixing any time/date of the next meeting. This motion does not end the session, but only suspends it or postpones the sitting for some time.*

At the commencement of the first session after each general election to Lok Sabha and at the commencement of the first session of each year, the President addresses both houses of the Parliament assembled together and inform the Parliament of the cause of its summons. Besides, he may address either house of the Parliament or both houses assembled together and for that purpose require the attendance of members.

There are certain other functions which the President is required to perform under the constitution in relation to the Parliament. He appoints the Speaker of the Lok Sabha and an acting Chairman of the Rajya Sabha. He summons the joint sitting of the both houses of the Parliament in case of disagreement between them on a bill. The President causes to be laid, before the Parliament, the budget of the government and certain other reports on constitutional functionaries like the Comptroller and Auditor_ General of India, Finance Commission, Union Public Service Commission and the like.

Composition of the Lok Sabha: The Lok Sabha (house of the people) is also known as the 'Lower House' of the Parliament and its members are elected directly by the people on the basis of adult franchise. The Lok Sabha has a unique composition because the constitution prescribes the maximum number as follows:

1. Not more than 530 members are to be chosen by direct election from territorial constituencies in the states;
2. Not more than twenty members to represent the Union Territories;
3. Not more than two members of the Anglo-Indian community may be nominated by the President if he is of the opinion that the Anglo-Indian Community is not adequately represented in the Lok Sabha.

The Lok Sabha is presided over by the Speaker who is elected by the house from its own members. The term of the house is five years from the date appointed for its first meeting. The house may be dissolved before the expiration of its full term under certain circumstances. When a proclamation of Emergency is in force, the term of the Lok Sabha can be extended by the Parliament for a period not exceeding one year at a time and not exceeding in any case a period of six months after the proclamation has ceased to operate. This has happened once, during the Emergency of 1975-177.

Powers of the Lok Sabha: The two houses of the Parliament enjoy co-equal powers and status in all spheres except in financial matters and in regard to responsibility of the Council of Ministers, which are exclusively the domain of the Lok Sabha. Although ordinary bills can be introduced in either of the two houses of the Parliament, yet almost 90 % bills are introduced in the Lok Sabha.

According to Article 75(3) of the Indian constitution, Council of Ministers shall be collectively responsible to the house of people. The Council of Ministers is responsible before the Lok Sabha for all its acts of omission and commission. The ministers remain in the office so long as they enjoy the confidence of the majority in the Lok Sabha. If the Lok Sabha rejects any policy or decision of the **cabinet,** or disapproves the budget or a bill of the government or passes a vote of no-confidence against the Prime Minister, it is taken to be a **vote of no-confidence** against the entire Council of Ministers and the whole ministry has to resign.

Cabinet

The cabinet is the senior executive organ of the government which has the responsibility of making policies on behalf of government as a whole. Cabinet System of government shares two common principles. First, they observe the principle of collective responsibility. Secondly, they observe the principle of parliamentary accountability. However, whilst the principles of cabinet government are universal, the structure membership, and operations of cabinet in practice are open to considerable variation.

No Confidence Motion: *A motion moved by a member expresses lack of confidence in the government for any reason. This motion, if allowed, may be debated upon. At conclusion of such debate, a vote of confidence is sought by the government and if fails to get the required majority of votes, it has to resign.*

The Lok Sabha has the superior position in the financial matters because all bills relating to finances can only be introduced in it. Furthermore, the house also plays a leading role in the impeachment of Judges, President, and amendment of the constitution and in approval of the declaration of emergency.

As a directly elected house, the Lok Sabha really represents the sovereignty of the people of India. The Lok Sabha, like the British House of Commons, is the real centre of power in the Union.

Composition and powers of the Rajya Sabha: The Rajya Sabha (the Council of States) is the upper house of the Parliament and is sometimes called the 'House of Elders'. The Rajya Sabha used to be seen very much as a 'talking shop' during the earlier periods of Congress dominance wherein the party dominated both Houses of Parliament. The members of the Rajya Sabha are elected by the elected members of the State Legislative Assemblies in accordance with the system of proportional representation by means of single transferable vote. The different states of the Union have not been granted equal representation in the Rajya Sabha. The number of representatives from each state in India depends largely on its population. Thus while Utter Pradesh has 31 members in Rajya Sabha, smaller states like Manipur, Mizoram, Sikkim, etc. have only one member each. Under the constitution, the Rajya Sabha consists of not more than 250 members. It includes 12 members nominated by the President and 238 members elected by the States and the Union Territories. Unlike the Lok Sabha the Rajya Sabha is a permanent body and is not subject to dissolution. The vice_ President is the ex-officio Chairman of the Rajya Sabha, while the Deputy Chairman is elected by the members of the Rajya Sabha themselves.

Powers of the Rajya Sabha: Rajya Sabha enjoys the same powers as are enjoyed by the Lok Sabha in case of ordinary bills. Rajya Sabha has equal powers with the Lok Sabha in important matters like the impeachment of the President, removal of the vice-President, constitutional amendments and removal of Judges of the Supreme Court and the High Courts. Rajya Sabha has a peculiar position as it enjoys a special power which makes it the sole authority to declare that it would be in the national interest for the Parliament to legislate in the State List. After such a declaration, it is lawful for the Parliament to make laws for the whole or any part of the territory of India with respect to that matter while that resolution remains in force. The second special power of Rajya Sabha is connected with the setting up of All India Services. Any laws connected with such a service can be initiated only if the Rajya Sabha passes such a resolution. There are certain limitations placed on the powers of the Rajya Sabha which are:

1. A Money Bill can neither be introduced in the Rajya Sabha nor can it amend or reject the Bill. The only power it has with respect to money bills is to suggest recommendations which may or may not be accepted by the Lok Sabha.
2. Rajya Sabha has no power to pass a vote of no confidence in the Council of Ministers.
3. Rajya Sabha may discuss the annual statement. It has no power to vote on the Demands for Grants.

Functions of the Parliament: the Parliament of India, like all Westminster- style parliamentary democracies, is a multifunctional institution performing a variety of roles that are inter-related and often meshing into one another. Some of the important functions of the Indian Parliament may be described as:

1. **Legislation:** The process of legislating is the basic day-to-day function of the Parliament. Despite being the chief law- making body, the Parliament often merely approves legislations. The actual task of drafting the bill is performed by the bureaucracy under the supervision of the minister concerned. Under Articles 245 and 246 the Parliament can make laws for the whole or any part of India within its area of competence as defined and delimited under the distribution of legislative powers between the Union and the States vide the Seventh Schedule. Seventh Schedule divides powers into three Lists- Union List, State List and Concurrent List. In regard to the Union List, the Parliament has

exclusive jurisdiction. Under Article 249, the Parliament enjoys the power to legislate on the State List. In addition, the Parliament can make laws in areas not mentioned in the Constitution altogether (the Residuary List).

2. **To Form the Government and to ensure its accountability:** In a parliamentary form of government the legislature and the executive organs of the government are fused together. So it becomes an important function of the Parliament to form the government. The Parliament of India, like all parliamentary democracies forms the government. Members of the Parliament, from the largest party or of the largest coalition form the government at the Centre.

Once the government is formed it is made accountable to the Parliament. Perhaps the most vital function of the Parliament is to ensure that the executive does not overstep its authority and remains responsible to the people who have elected them. If executive is not made accountable, there is danger that parliamentary democracy may slip into cabinet dictatorship. In India the real political executive is the Council of Ministers headed by the Prime Minister. On the other hand the Parliament has an unlimited power to call for information, to discuss, to scrutinize and to put the seal of popular approval on proposals made by executive. The executive remains responsible and the administration accountable to the Parliament. The function of the Parliament is to exercise political and financial control over the executive and to ensure parliamentary surveillance of administration. This control is exercised through various procedural devices like Question Hour, Motions, Resolutions, various kinds of discussions and scrutiny by Parliamentary Committees. The Parliament also controls the executive by making it responsible to itself, i.e. the executive can remain in the office so long as it enjoys the support of majority in the House. The House, however, may at any time decide to throw out the government by a majority vote, i.e. if the ruling party loses the support of majority of members of House, its government goes. Further, the Parliament has a control over public finance.

The power to levy taxes and the voting of supplies and grants- is one of the most important checks against the executive assuming arbitrary powers.

3. **Financial Function:** The Parliament is the custodian of the national purse. It is responsibility of the Parliament to control taxation and the way in which money is used by the government. The power to levy or modify taxes and the voting of supplies and grants is one of the most important checks against the executive assuming the arbitrary powers. No taxes can be levied and no expenditures incurred from the public exchequer without specific parliamentary authorization by law. The financial powers of the Parliament involve grant of resources to the government to implement its programmes. The Parliament also ensures that the government does not misspend or overspend. This is done through the budget and annual financial statements.

4. **Forum for the ventilation of Grievances:** The Parliament represents the divergent views of members from different regional, socio-economic, religious groups of different parts of the country. Good governance is the bedrock on which whole edifice of democracy is based upon. The dream of good governance cannot be materialized until and unless the Parliament acts as a forum for ventilation of

Sessions of Parliament:
A session is the period of time between the meetings of a the Parliament. There are three types of sessions as per the parliamentary practice:

a. **Budget Session:** *this is the most important and longest session of the Parliament. It occurs between February and May.*

b. **Moonsoon Session:** *This session is called during July- August of the year.*

c. **Winter Session:** *This is the shortest session of the Parliament and occurs during November - December* the grievances of the people, their difficulties and their passions, anxieties and frustrations. The Parliament is the highest forum of debate in the country. Members of the Parliament are free to speak on any matter without fear. This makes it possible for the Parliament to discuss various grievances, needs and aspirations of the people and to make necessary legislation in this regard. In recent decades, emphasis has shifted more and more towards representational and grievance ventilation role of the Parliament.

5. **Amending the Constitution of India:** Article 368 empowers the Parliament to amend the Constitution. Article 368 reads "...*the Parliament may in exercise of its constituent power amend by way of addition, variation or repeal any provision of this Constitution in accordance with the procedure laid down in this Article*". The Constitution of India provides for three categories of amendments. Firstly, some provisions of the Constitution can be amended by a simple majority. No special procedure is required in such cases and there is no difference between an amendment and an ordinary law. These parts of the Constitution are very flexible. Article 2, 3, 4, 169, Para 7(2) of Schedule V and Para 21(2) of Schedule VI fall within this category and are specifically excluded from the purview of Article 368. Secondly, those amendments that can be effected by the Parliament by a prescribed 'special majority' i.e. $2/3^{rd}$ majority of members present at the time of voting in each House of the Parliament. Thirdly, those that require, in addition to such 'special majority', ratification by at least one half of the State Legislatures. When an amendment aims to modify an Article related to distribution of powers between the states and the central government, or articles related to representation, it is necessary that states must be consulted and that they give their consent.

6. **Informational Role:** Executive is duty bound to feed the Parliament with all necessary and accurate information it requires for effective discharge of any of its functions. Information is vital to the Parliament. The Parliament enjoys almost unlimited power to call for information except that if divulging of certain

information is likely to prejudice vital national interests or the security of the state, it may not be insisted upon. So far as the activities of the government are concerned, it is the duty of the government itself to feed the Parliament with information which is full, truthful, precise and supplied in time. The most well known and effective mechanism through which members, on their own, illicit information is that of asking questions in the Houses of the Parliament. Another method for the Parliament to inform itself and receive necessary feedback is through the reports of various Parliamentary Committees. Other source of information includes the mass media, political parties, interest groups and so on. The Parliament has also its own institutionalized source of information, called the Parliament Library and its Research, Reference, Documentation and Information Service.

7. **Other Functions:** In addition to the above mentioned functions, the Parliament also performs various other functions, for example, election of President and Vice President, Impeachment of the President, removal of Supreme Court and High Court Judges, Comptroller and Auditor General, Chief Election Commissioner, Presiding Officers of the two Houses etc.

PRESIDING OFFICERS OF THE HOUSE

The Speaker: If an assembly is to function in an orderly and efficient manner, there must be someone with the authority to regulate its proceedings and working. The constitution provides for a Speaker and a Deputy Speaker for the Lok Sabha and a Chairman and a Deputy Chairman for the Rajya Sabha.

Election of Speaker: The constitution requires the Lok Sabha to elect two members of the house as Speaker and Deputy Speaker as soon as it may, after the first sitting. The Speaker and the deputy Speaker are elected in accordance with the procedure laid down under Article 93 of the Indian constitution. The President, after receiving the suggestion of the Prime Minister through the Secretary General of the Lok Sabha, approves the date for the election of the Speaker. The Secretary General, thereafter, sends a notice of this date to every member. Both the Speaker and the deputy Speaker are elected separately on motions moved and supported by the respective party leaders. A convention is, however, gradually developing whereby a candidate sponsored by ruling party is elected unopposed to the office of the Speaker and the candidate for the post of deputy Speaker is generally from the opposition party and is supported by the ruling party to ensure his unanimous election.

Tenure of the Office: The Speaker and the deputy Speaker will normally hold office during the life of the house, but their offices may terminate earlier in any of the following ways:

i)   If a member holding an office of the speaker or deputy speaker ceases to be a member of the Lok Sabha;

ii) By resignation in writing, addressed to the deputy Speaker, and vice versa;

iii) By removal from the office by a resolution, passed by a majority of all the then members of the house. Such a resolution cannot be moved unless at least 14 days notice has been given of the intention to move the resolution. When a resolution for his removal is under consideration, he cannot preside over the meetings even though present in the house, till the fate of the motion has been decided.

Position and Powers of the office of the Speaker: Generally speaking, the position of the Speaker in India, more or less corresponds to that of the Speaker of the House of Commons. His office is one of prestige, splendor and authority. He is the Head of the Lok Sabha. The smooth and orderly conduct of the business in the house is primarily his responsibility. Within the house and in all matters connected with the House, his word is final. Independence and impartiality are the two important attributes of the office of the Speaker. This is sought to be ensured in many ways. In the warrant of precedence, the Speaker has been given a very high position. He comes next only to the President, the vice – President and the Prime Minister. He ranks higher than all Cabinet Ministers other than the Prime Minister himself.

The Speaker enjoys vast powers to ensure the smooth and orderly conduct of the business of the house. No member can speak unless he "catches the speaker's eye". It is for the Speaker to determine in what order members would speak and how long a member should be allowed to speak. All the parliamentary committees of the Lok Sabha are constituted by him or by the House. They function under his control and direction. He appoints the chairman of all committees and issues directions in matter relating in their working and the procedure to be followed by them. Besides presiding over his own house, the Speaker possesses certain powers not belonging to the Chairman of the council of states e.g. Article 118 (4) empowers the Speaker to preside over the joint sitting of the two houses of the Parliament. The constitution also gives the Speaker a special power in so far as the relations between the two houses in certain financial matters which fall within the exclusive jurisdiction of the Lok Sabha. If he certifies a Bill to be a 'Money Bill' his decision is final.

In view of the vital and vast responsibilities that a Speaker has to fulfill, Jawaharlal Nehru said,

The speaker represents the house. He represents the dignity of the house, the freedom of the house and because the house represents the nation, in a particular way, the Speaker becomes the symbol of nation's freedom and liberty. Therefore, it is right that should be an honoured position, a free position and should be occupied always by men of outstanding ability and impartiality.

The deputy Speaker : Indian constitution mentions under Articles 93 to 95 that whenever the office of the Speaker is vacant or the Speaker is absent from a sitting of the house, the deputy Speaker presides over the deliberations of the house and so presiding, exercises all the powers of the Speaker in the house under the rules of procedure. The deputy Speaker is the chairman of the Budget Committee which approves the Budget proposals of the secretariat before these are sent to the Ministry of Finance for incorporation in the general Budget.

Unlike the Speaker, the deputy Speaker has a right to speak in the house, to take part in its deliberations and to vote on any proposition before the house as a member, but this he can do only when the speaker is presiding. When himself in the chair, the deputy Speaker cannot vote except in the event of equality of votes.

The Chairman of Rajya Sabha: While the house of the people has a Speaker, the council of states has a Chairman (who presides over that house) and performs the function of an ex – Officio. The vice – President of India is the ex – officio Chairman of the Rajya Sabha. He presides over the Rajya Sabha by virtue of the office of the vice- President that he holds. The vice President is not a member of either house of the Parliament or of a house of legislature of any state. He holds office for five years from the date on which he enters office or until he resigns his office or is removed from his office.

The functions and duties of the Chairman of the Rajya Sabha are more or less the same as the Speaker in the Lok Sabha.

HOW LAWS ARE MADE?

The Legislative procedure in the Parliament: Law making is still deemed to be the pre-dominant function of the Parliament, even though today it is not the only function it performs not is the Parliament the only actor in the drama of law-making. Carefully studied, it is the government which, in actual practice, makes legislative proposals and the Parliament, after discussion and debate, puts its seal of approval. A definite procedure is followed in the process of law making. All legislative proposals are initiated in the Parliament in the form of Bills. The procedure of passing different kinds of bills by the Union Parliament has been discussed under Articles 107-111 of the constitution of India. Before discussing how bills are passed, let us examine various types of bills which come before the Parliament.

1. **Government Bills:** A bill introduced by any member of the Council of Ministers is called a Governmental Bill. Most laws that find their way to the Statute Book are through the governmental bills.

2. **Private Member Bill:** A bill introduced by any member of the Parliament other than a Minister is called a Private Member Bill. Although the Private Member Bills that become laws are few but they serve a good purpose in as much as they bring to the attention of the government and the public the need to amend an existing law in the light of the changing conditions or to enact a needed piece of legislation.

3. **Ordinary Bills**: All bills which are not Constitutional Amendment Bills and Money Bills are called as Ordinary Bills or draft proposals for ordinary legislation.

4. **Money Bills:** The definition of a Money Bill is given in Article 110 of the constitution of India and no bill is a Money Bill unless it satisfies the requirements of this Article. The Article lays down that a bill is

a Money Bill if it contains only provisions dealing with all or any of the six matters specified in this Article which are as under:

a. The imposition, abolition, remission, alteration or regulation of any tax;
b. The regulation or borrowing of money by government;
c. the payment of money into or withdrawal of money from the Consolidated or the Contingency Funds of India;
d. the appropriation of money out of the Consolidated Fund of India;
e. Declaring of any expenditure to the expenditure charged on the Consolidated Fund of India, or the increasing amount of any such expenditure.
f. Any matter incidental to any of the matters specified in sub-clauses (a) to (f) of Article 110 (1).

5. **Financial Bills:** Generally speaking, a Financial Bill may be any bill which relates to revenue or expenditure. These, besides providing for any of the matters specified in the constitution for a Money Bill, also provide for other matters. These bills can be divided into two categories:

i. Those bills which make provisions for matters specified in Article 110 for Money Bills but do not contain solely those matters, e.g. a bill which contains a taxation clause but does not deal solely with taxation.
ii. Bills containing provisions involving expenditure from the Consolidated Fund.

Although Financial Bills of the first category cannot be introduced in the Rajya Sabha but the Council of States has the same power to reject or amend such a Financial Bill as it has in the case of non-Financial Bills.

HOW DOES THE PARLIAMENT MAKE LAWS?

The main function of every modern the Parliament has been usually recognized as law-making. A definite procedure is followed in the process of law-making. The measures introduced in the Parliament for law-making are called 'Bills' or Draft Acts. Even before a Bill is introduced there may be a lot of debate on the need for introducing such a bill. In order to become a law, the bill has to pass through various stages. The procedure of passing different kinds of bills by the Union Parliament has been discussed under Article 107 to 111 of the constitution of India. All bills which are not Constitutional Amendment Bills and Money Bills are Ordinary Bills. An Ordinary Bill has to undergo following stages to become a law.

i. **Draft of Bill:** As soon as a legislative proposal is conceived, the ministry concerned works out its political, administrative, financial and other implications. The Ministry of Law and the Attorney General of India are consulted in respect of legal and constitutional aspects. Professional and various **interest groups** are sometimes also consulted. After the proposal has been thoroughly examined from all points of view, it is submitted to the Cabinet for approval, when the Cabinet has approved

Interest groups

An interest group or pressure group is an organized association that aims to influence the policies or actions of government. Interest groups differ from political parties in that they seek to exert influence from outside, rather than to win or exercise government power. Further, interest groups typically have a narrow issue focus, in that they are usually concerned with a specific cause or the interests of a particular group, and seldom have the broader programmic or ideological features that are generally associated with political parties.

the proposal, the government's draftsman gives it the shape of a Bill. The Bill is, then, examined in detail by the administrative machinery in consultation of all other authorities concerned and given a final shape.

ii. **Introduction or First Reading:** When the draft of the bill is completed, the bill is introduced in the Parliament. A bill other than Money Bill or Finance Bill may be introduced in either house of the Parliament {Article 107 (1)} and requires passing in both houses before it can be presented for the President's assent. A bill may be introduced either by a Minister or by a Private Member. The difference in the two cases is that any member other than a minister desiring to introduce a bill has to give notice of his intention and to ask to leave of the house to introduce which is, however, rarely opposed. If a bill has been published in the official gazette before its introduction, no motion for leave to introduce the bill is necessary.

Usually, the introduction which is the first reading of a bill is only a formality and by convention there is no discussion at this stage. But, if introduction of a bill is opposed on the ground that the proposed legislation is outside the legislative competence of the Parliament, the chair may permit a full discussion in which the Attorney- General also participates. After a bill has been introduced in the house, it is published in the Gazette of India.

iii. **Motions after Introduction or Second Reading:** Second Reading forms the most elaborate and vital stage in the life of a bill because it is at this stage that it receives detailed and minute examination. After a bill has been introduced, the member in charge of bill may make one of the following motions in regard to the bill, viz_

a. That it be taken to consideration;
b. That it be referred to a Selected Committee;
c. That it be referred to a Joint Committee of the house with the concurrence of the other house;

d. That it be circulated for the purpose of eliciting public opinion there.

If a bill is referred to a Selected Committee or a Joint Committee the Committee considers the bill clause by clause just as the house does. Amendments can be moved to various clauses by members of the Committee. The Committee can also take evidence of experts, associations or public bodies who are interested in the measure.

If a motion for circulation of the bill for the purpose of eliciting opinion there on is adopted, the secretariat of the house circulates letters to the state governments and Union territories asking them to publish the bill in their Gazettes for inviting opinions of local bodies, associations, individuals or institutions concerned with the bill. The period for eliciting opinion is generally specified in the motion for circulation of the bill, where no debate has been specified, the state governments are asked to send opinions within three months of the adoption of the motion.

In case the Minister prefers to move the motion that the bill, as reported, be taken into consideration, a debate is allowed. The scope of the debate is confined to the bill as reported by the Committee and the principle of the bill is not open to discuss again.

Deadlock
When the Parliament cannot make any progress on any issue or matte, the situation is termed as *deadlock*. It may be caused if the two houses fail to agree either as to the provisions of the bill as introduced or as to the amendments that may have been proposed by either. For resolving the deadlock, a joint sitting of the two houses of the Parliament is called by the President.

iv. **Third Reading or Passing of the Bill in the House where it was introduced:** When all the clauses and schedules, if any, of the bill have been considered and voted upon in the house, the minister can move that the bill be passed. At this stage discussion is confined to arguments either in support of the bill or for its rejection without referring the details thereto further than is absolutely necessary. After the motion that the bill may be passed is carried, the bill is taken as passed as far as that house is concerned.

In passing an ordinary bill, a simple majority of members present at voting is required.

v. **Passing of the Bill in the other House:** When the bill is passed in one house, it is transmitted to the other house. There, again, it goes through the three stages. The house which receives the bill can take either of the following courses;

a. It may reject the bill all together giving rise to a **deadlock** between the two houses.

b. It may pass the bill with amendments. In this case, the bill will be returned to the originating house. If the originating house accepts the amendments of the other House, the bill will be presented to the President for the assent (Article 111). If however, the originating house does not agree to the amendments proposed by the other house, and the disagreement between the two houses continues, resulting in a deadlock. The President may summon a joint sitting to resolve the deadlock {Article 108 (1) (b)}.

c. It may take no action on the bill, i.e. keep it lying on its table. In such a case if more than six months elapse from the date of the reception of the bill, a deadlock is deemed to have taken place. To resolve this deadlock the President may summon a joint sitting {(Article 108(1)(c)}

vi. **President's Assent:** when the bill has been passed by both the houses either singly or at a joint sitting, the bill is presented to the President for his assent. The President can use his legislative power in the following ways:

a. The President can withhold his assent and if he withholds his assent, there is an end to the bill;

b. The President can give his assent; the bill becomes an act from the date of his assent;

c. Instead of either refusing assent or giving assent, the President may return the bill for reconsideration of the houses with a message requesting them to reconsider it. If, however, the houses pass the ill again with or without amendments and the ill is presented to the President for his assent after such reconsideration, the President shall have no power to withhold his assent from the bill.

THE PARLIAMENTARY CONTROL OVER THE EXECUTIVE

The Parliament and the executive: We know that the real political executive in India is the Council of Ministers headed by the Prime Minister. There is, however, a clear distinction between the functions of the executive and the functions of the Parliament (Article 75). The Parliament is to deliberate, discuss, legislate, advise, criticize and ventilate public grievances. Also, it has a legitimatizational role. The executive is to govern, albeit on behalf of the Parliament and the people.

While the executive has almost unlimited right to initiate and formulate legislative and financial proposals before the Parliament and to give effect to approval policies unfettered and unhindered by the Parliament. On the other hand the Parliament has an unlimited power to call for information, to discuss, to scrutinize and to put the seal of popular approval or proposals made by the executive. The executive remains responsible

Zero Hour: *This period follows by the Question Hour. Generally begins at noon 12: 00 O' Clock, hence the name Zero Hour. The members normally use Zero Hour for discussions on various issues of national importance.*

Quorum: *It is minimum number of members whose presence is essential to transact the business of the house.*

Vote on Account: *The vote on account generally enables the government to draw some amount from the Consolidated Fund of India, as there usually remains a time gap between the presentation of the annual budget and its approval.*

Guillotine: *The act of putting all the demands for grant to vote, without discussion on the last day earmarked for the discussing of the budget is called as guillotine.*

Lame-duck Session: *This session is held when the new the Parliament has been elected or elections are due in near future but the old the Parliament meets for the last time before it is dissolved. This session of the Parliament is called as the Lame-duck session.*

and the administration accountable to the Parliament. The function of the Parliament is to exercise political and financial control over the executive and to ensure parliamentary surveillance of administration. This control is exercised through various procedural devices like Question Hour, Motions, Resolutions, various kinds of discussions and scrutiny by the Parliament committees.

Question Hour: The first hour of every sitting in both houses is devoted to asking and answering of questions. It is known as the "Questions Hour". During this hour, matter concerning the government of India is raised and problems are brought to the notice of the government to seek their intervention to meet any situation, to redress public grievances or to expose some administrative abuse or excess. Most of the questions aim at eliciting information from the government on issues of public interest such as, price rise, availability of food grains, atrocities on weaker sections of the society, riots, black marketing etc. The government is thus put on trial during this hour.

Question Hour forms the most interesting part of parliamentary proceedings because it is the most effective method of keeping vigil on executive and the administrative agencies of the government. No other business evokes as much interest among the public, the press and the members themselves as the question hour. The questions asked during the questions hour can be classified as under:

i) **Starred Questions:** Starred questions derive their name from the fact that they are always distinguished by an asterisk. A starred questions is one to which a member desires an oral answer in the House. Answers to such questions may be followed by supplementary questions by members.

ii) **Unstarred Questions:** An unstarred question is so named because it does not carry an asterisk mark. In the case of unstarred question a written answer is laid on the table by the concerned Minister. Consequently, no supplementary question can be asked thereon.

iii) **Short Notice Questions:** A short notice question is one which relates to a matter of urgent public importance and can be asked with notice shorter than the normal period prescribed for a question.

The Parliament also controls the executive by making it responsible to itself, i.e. the executive can remain in the office so long as it enjoys the support of majority in the Parliament. When the Parliament is sitting, the continuance of the government in office depends from moments to moments on its not losing the confidence of the house of the people. The house may at any time decide to throw out the government by a majority vote i.e. if the ruling party loses the confidence of the majority of the members of the house, its government goes. Want of parliamentary confidence in the government may be expressed by the house of the people by:

a) Passing substantive motion no-confidence in the Council of Ministers;
b) Defeating the government on a major issue of policy;
c) Passing an adjournment motion;
d) Refusing the vote supplies or defeating the government on a financial measure.

The Parliament has a control over public finance. The power of levy or modify taxes and the voting of supplies and grants is one of the most important checks against the executive assuming arbitrary powers. The Articles from 114 – 116 along with Article 265, clearly mentions that no tax can be legally levied and no expenditure incurred from the public exchequer without specific parliamentary authorization by law.

Is Indian Parliament Losing its Credibility?

The working of the Parliamentary democracy with a competitive party system, it is argued, has bred instability in the country. The Parliament, the supreme representative institution of the people, is said to have become largely dysfunctional as a result of frequent adjournments following pandemonia and long jams in the two Houses. From One Party Dominance to Rainbow Coalitions, Indian Parliamentary system has always become a hot debate. Criminalization of politics and politicization of crimes has worsened the situation. Political corruption, nepotism, hooliganism have become unwanted realities. Communalization of politics and politicization of religion has polarized the whole society. Criminals are making it to the Parliament. As we know that candidates with criminal records are contesting elections and get elected by using strong arms. For example in the 14th Lok Sabha, as many as 93 MPs had criminal charges pending against them. The strength of the 15th Lok Sabha was 543, out of which 162 MPs had criminal cases numbering 522 pending against them. Out of these 162 MPs, 76 MPs face serious (murder, theft, kidnapping etc) charges.(Hindustan Times, July 11, 2013) It is a matter of great concern that between 2004 and 2009 elections, an increase about 26% in MPs with pending criminal charges and 31% increase in the number of MPs with serious pending criminal cases. In this crime politics nexus India from Kashmir to Kanyakumari is one.

Rude acts of misbehavior the MPs of the Parliament indulge in, has put a huge question mark on the sacredness of the institution. Recently cameras showed MPs punching each other, throwing chaples, shoes, water bottles, papers, mikes, Chairs etc. at each other, thus paralyzing the Parliament. Discussions in the Parliament degenerate into party squabbles, there being no decorum and violent and undignified acts taking place. The compromise with morality and Rule of Law is defended by those in power on the ground of "Coalition Drama". Often the Speaker has difficultly in keeping order. *Aya Ram Gaya Ram* is still the nature of politics and defections are iron laws in India.

Under such scenario the public has come to believe that politics has become the most lucarative profession and and those who go there are only interested in making maximum money in the shortest possible time and national interest or spirit of public service are the last priority for them, if any.

Looking on the plight of Parliamentary systemn K. M. Munshi was among the first to announce the failure of the Parliamentary democracy and British Cabinet system. He said, 'if I had to make a choice again. I would vote for the Presidential form of government so that, whenever the politians fail the country, there is at least one strong organ of the sate capable tiding over the crisis.' During the proclamation of National Emergency (1975-77) A.R. Antulay the then Chief Minister of Maharastra initiated the move for a switch-over to the Presidential system in India. N. A. Palkhiwala also expressed his support for Presidential system provided a fair balance of powers is maintained.

CHAPTER 7

THE SUPREME COURT OF INDIA

Judges judge but who will judge the judge

The constitution may provide fundamental rights to the individuals but it has to provide a sound and sophisticated mechanism which will ensure that the citizens' rights and liberties are secured or protected. This mechanism will provide an answer to the questions like: Who will solve the disputes emerging out of our living a group life? Who has to interpret or expound the statutes and the Constitution? How to ensure the rule of law reigns supreme? If there be no remedy to a citizen when his rights are violated, then, the instruments which confer rights would be worthless. That is the reason why Alexander Hamilton has said: "Laws are a dead letter without Courts to expound and define their true meaning and operation". Thus, an independent impartial judiciary becomes indispensable in a democratic polity. This is why "Judicial Review" and "Independent Judiciary" are among the "Fundamental Features of the Indian Constitution".

ORGANIZATION AND COMPOSITION OF THE SUPREME COURT:

In the law, the judiciary or judicial system is the system of courts which administer justice in the name of the sovereign or state, a mechanism for the resolution of disputes. Unlike other federal constitutions, the constitution of India provides for a single integrated judicial system with the Supreme Court at the apex, High Courts at the state level and District Courts at the local level.

Judiciary of India as of today is the continuation of the British legal system established by the English in the mid 19th century. It was for the first time in India that under The Government of India Act 1935 an All India Court, called as 'Federal Court' was set up. On January 28, 1950, two days after India became a sovereign, democratic, republic, the Supreme Court came into being. The inauguration took place in the Chamber of Princes in the Parliament building which had earlier been the seat of the Federal Court for 12 years.

Under the federal constitution a Supreme Court is an essential part of the constitutional scheme. The Supreme Court of India, however, is more than a federal court. Under Article 32, it is made the protector of all the fundamental rights embodied in the constitution and it has to guard these rights against every infringement at the hands of either the Union Government or the State Governments. Article 13 declares that any law which contravenes any of the provisions of the Part on Fundamental Rights shall be void. Supreme Court is the highest court of appeal in both civil and criminal cases. It gets not only the opportunity to interpret the constitution and the laws enacted by the Parliament but also the laws passed by the various State Legislatures. It stands at the apex of India's judicial hierarchy, with effective power to supervise and control the working of the entire system and to ensure the realization of the high judicial standards that it might set as an integral part of the democratic system of government to be established by the Constitution.

Composition of the Supreme Court: The Supreme Court stands at the apex of the judicial system of India. The original constitution of India (1950) provisioned for a Supreme Court with a Chief Justice and seven lower-ranking judges. The Parliament was given the power to make laws regarding the constitution, organization, jurisdiction and powers of the Supreme Court. The Parliament increased the number of judges from 8 in 1950 to 11 in 1956, 14 in 1960, 18 in 1978 and 26 in 1986. The Supreme Court at present consists of the Chief Justice and 30 other judges. The Chief Justice is appointed by the President in consultation with such judges of the Supreme Court and High Courts as he deems necessary. The other judges of the Supreme Court are appointed by the President in consultation with the Chief Justice. However, he may also consult other judges of the Supreme Court and High Courts while appointing a judge of the Supreme Court.

The position of the President in this regard underwent a drastic change following Supreme Court judgment of 1993 in *S.C. Advocates on Record Association Vs Union of India* case. The Court held that in the matter of appointment of judges of Supreme Court and the High Courts, the President is bound to act in accordance with the opinion of Chief Justice of India, who would tender his opinion on the matter after consulting his colleagues. Thus, the discretion of Prime Minister and the President regarding the appointment of judges has been reduced. In the selection of candidates for the appointment of judges of the Supreme Court and the High Courts, the judiciary plays a major role and the executive merely acts as a check on the exercise of power by the Chief Justice.

The Chief Justice and other judges of the Supreme Court hold office till they attain the age of 65 years. They can resign from their office by addressing their resignation to the President. They can be removed from their office through the process of Impeachment. The judges can be removed only on the grounds of proved misbehavior or incapacity. So far no Supreme Court judge has been removed from office through impeachment.

Independence of Judiciary: Simply stated independence of judiciary means that

1. The other organs of the government like the executive and legislature must not restrain the functioning of the Judiciary in such a way that it is unable to do justice;
2. The other organs of the government should not interfere with the decisions of the judiciary;
3. Judges must be able to perform their functions without fear and favour.

The constitution has made elaborate provisions to ensure the independence of judiciary.

1. The salaries and allowances of judges have been charged on the Consolidated Fund of India and are not subject to vote of the Parliament.
2. The salaries and other service conditions of judges cannot be changed to their disadvantage during their tenure.
3. The removal of judges has been made quite difficult. They can be removed from their office through the process of Impeachment. The judges can be removed only on the grounds of proved misbehavior or incapacity.
4. Judges are barred from carrying any practice before any court in India after their retirement.
5. The decisions and actions of judges cannot be criticized and a person can be punished for contempt of the court.
6. The conduct of judges cannot be discussed in the Parliament or state legislature.
7. The appointment of judges of Supreme Court does not depend on the discretion of the President. The President has to consult the judges of the Supreme Court and such other courts as he may deem fit, while appointing the judges.

8. The court enjoys complete freedom with regard to appointment of officers and servants of the court.

Supreme Court: Jurisdiction and Powers:

The Jurisdiction of the Supreme Court under the constitution is quite wide. It is the final Court of Appeal in respect of civil and criminal matters. What follows would give us an idea about the extensive jurisdiction the Apex Court enjoys as well as the powers conferred upon the Court under the constitution.

Supreme Court's Original and Exclusive Jurisdiction in Respect of Certain Disputes under Article 131: Original jurisdiction means cases that can be directly considered by the Supreme Court without going to the lower courts before that. The Supreme Court has Original and Exclusive Jurisdiction in any dispute:

i) between the Government of India and one or more States; or

ii) between the Government of India and any State on one side and one or more States on the other side; or

iii) Between two or more States, if the dispute involves a question of law or fact on which the existence or extent of a legal right depends.

A Court is said to have Original Jurisdiction when it has authority to hear and determine a case in the first instance. The Court's Jurisdiction is exclusive when no other court has the authority to hear and decide the case. The functions of the Supreme Court under Article 131 are purely of a federal character and are confined to disputes between the Government of India and any of the States of the Union, the Government of India and any State or States on one side and any other State or States on the other side, or between two or more States *inter se*. What is necessary under Article 131 is that the existence or extent of a legal right must be in issue in the dispute between the parties, that is, between the Government of India and one or more States, etc. The rationale underlying Article 131 is if there be a dispute between two or more states, it is not proper that the dispute be agitated before the court of one of the disputants that is, disputing parties. Further, under Article 131, the Plaintiff State need not assert a legal or a constitutional right. It is enough if it can challenge the right claimed by the Respondent State.

One class of disputes, though of federal nature, is excluded from this original jurisdiction of the Supreme Court, namely, a dispute arising out of any treaty, agreement, covenant, engagement, sanad, or other similar instrument which having been entered into or executed before the commencement of this constitution continues in operation after such commencement or which provides that the said jurisdiction shall not extend to such a dispute.

Appellate Jurisdiction of the Supreme Court under Article 132:

The Supreme Court is the highest court of appeal and its writs and decrees run throughout the country. Broadly speaking, four types of cases fall within the appellate jurisdiction of the Supreme Court, i.e. Constitutional, Civil, Criminal, and such cases where it may grant special leave to appeal. The Supreme Court shall have the final say on questions involving the interpretation of the Constitution. Different opinions by different High Courts on Constitutional Questions would create confusion among the lawyers and citizens. Article 132, therefore provides that an Appeal shall lie to the Supreme Court from any Judgment, Decree or Final Order of a High Court, whether in Civil or Criminal or other proceeding, if the High Court certifies that these involve a substantial question of law as to the interpretation of the Constitution.

Supreme Court's Appellate Jurisdiction in Civil Matters (Article 133):

The Supreme Court is empowered to entertain Appeals from the Judgment, Decree or Final Order of a High Court in Civil Proceedings that is proceedings of civil nature. The Proceedings are civil in nature if a person seeks relief in a Civil Court when his civil rights are infringed by another person or by the State. After the conclusion of the proceedings, the Civil Court may declare that the plaintiff's claim is justified and he is entitled to relief. To invoke the Supreme Court's appellate Jurisdiction, the following conditions have to be fulfilled:

i)   What is being appealed against must be a Judgment, Decree or Final Order of a High Court in a Civil Proceeding.

ii) The High Court must certify that the case involves a substantial question of law of general importance and that it (the High Court) is of the opinion that the substantial question of law... needs to be decided by the Apex Court. It can be said that the Judgment, Decree or Final Order —all seem to convey the same meaning, that is, the Civil Court's pronouncement that finally or conclusively determines the rights of the parties in a controversy or suit.

It should be noted that under Article 133, no appeal can be made against the Judgment, Decree or Final Order of a single Judge of a High Court unless the Parliament enacts a law to remove this restriction.

Appeals to Supreme Court in Criminal Matters (Article 134):

The Criminal Appellate Jurisdiction of the Supreme Court can be invoked against the Judgment, Final Order or Sentence of a High Court in a criminal proceeding when the High Court has certified that the case is a fit one for appeal to the Supreme Court. The grant of certificate by the High Court would be justifiable when difficult questions of law or principles are involved in the case. Ordinarily, the High Court's Certificate would demonstrate that the case involves a substantial question of law or principle. No doubt, in granting or not granting the certificate under Article 134(1) (c), the High Court enjoys discretion but the discretion is judicial one which has to be judicially exercised in the light of well-established principles. The Supreme Court's Criminal Appellate Jurisdiction can be invoked in the following circumstances:

a) When the High Court has reversed the decision of acquittal of the accused by the Sessions Court and sentenced him to death; or

b) When the High Court has withdrawn for trial before itself any case from any court subordinate to it and has convicted the accused person and sentenced him to death.

The Parliament may by law enlarge the appellate criminal Jurisdiction of the Supreme Court. In 1970, the Parliament enacted a law which enables an accused to appeal to the Supreme Court when the High Court "has not sentenced him to death under Article 134(2) (6)(1) but has sentenced him to imprisonment for life or for a period of not less than ten years. The Supreme Court (Enlargement of Criminal Appellate Jurisdiction) Act, 1970 has substituted the words underlined above for the words "to death".

Appeal to Supreme Court by Special Leave (Article 136):

Under Article 136, the Supreme Court may, in its discretion, grant special leave to appeal from any judgment, decree, determination sentence or order in any case or matter passed or made by any court or tribunal in the territory of India. Under Articles 132 to 135, the Supreme Court's appellate Jurisdiction can be ignited by fulfilling the conditions mentioned there-under. But, under Article 136, Supreme Court's permission or leave is required. Such permission or leave can be granted by the Court in its discretion. Further, appeal may be allowed against determination, sentence or order (need not be a 'final order') of a court (need not be a High Court) or tribunal (Industrial Tribunal, Income Tax Tribunal).

Supreme Court may be inclined to grant special leave in situations where a party has suffered gross injustice on account of violation of natural justice or where the tribunal's order or determination is so palpably wrong or absurd as to shock the court's conscience.

Since Article 136 speaks of judgments, decrees, sentence, orders, determinations of Courts or Tribunals, purely administrative or executive order or direction cannot be the subject-matter of appeal and the court would be disinclined to accord leave. The Court has to be convinced that there are special circumstances which warrant its intervention. For example, when the Tribunal has been improperly constituted; where the procedure followed is unjust, unfair, and unreasonable; when the Tribunal has assumed a jurisdiction which in law it does not enjoy.

The Supreme Court has no power or Jurisdiction to grant special leave against the Judgment, Decree, Sentence, Determination, Order passed or made by any Court or Tribunal functioning under any law relating to the armed forces Article 136(2).

Supreme Court's Power to Review its own Judgments, Orders (Article 137):

The Supreme Court has the power to review its own decisions. Article 137 of the Constitution lays down that *"the Supreme Court has the power to review any judgment pronounced or orders made by it."* In Judicial decision-making, the general proposition is that there should be finality attached to Court's Judgments and that there should be an end to law suits. A rigid adherence to this proposition may, in some cases; result in gross and manifest injustice, a court cannot be allowed to be a court of injustice. Thus Supreme Court itself ruled that there is nothing in the Constitution which prevents the Supreme Court from departing from its previous decisions if it is convinced of its error and its beneficial effect on the general interest of the public. In Golak Nath case (1967) the Supreme Court reversed its earlier decisions given in the Shankri Prasad and Sajjan Singh cases, and in the Keshvananda Bharti case; the judgement in the Golaknath case was reversed. If, in a case, the court finds that a particular provision of the Act was not brought to its notice or evidence which would have tilted the scales of Justice was not available at the time of its pronouncement, then, it may be inclined or probably pleased to review its earlier judgment at the instance of the aggrieved. Article 137 expressly empowers the Supreme Court to review its Judgments. Review is permissible on the following grounds;

   i)   Discovery of new and important matters of evidence;
   ii)   Mistake or error of law apparent on the face of the record;

Advisory Jurisdiction under Article 143:

Normally, the Court's function is to decide the controversy presented to it and render its judgment. Again, Courts do not take sue motto notice of a prevalent controversy and offer their opinions. The Court's Jurisdiction has to be invoked by the aggrieved party through appropriate means, But, Article 143 enables the Supreme Court to render Advisory Opinion in certain contingencies. Such Advisory Opinion of the Supreme Court rendered at the instance of the President of India may enable the Parliament to pass appropriate Legislation or to introspect and effect suitable amendments to the existing law.

Article 143 enables the President to refer to the Supreme Court a question of law or act which in the opinion of the President is of such nature and such public importance that it is expedient to obtain the Court's Opinion on it. It has to be noted that a question of law which the Supreme Court has already decided in a dispute presented to it cannot be the subject-matter of a reference by the President for Advisory Opinion, because, the implication would be that the President would be inviting the Apex Court to act as an Appellate or Reviewing Authority over its earlier decision while seeking its Advisory Opinion under Article 143. On a Presidential Reference for Advisory Opinion, the Attorney- General would be given notice and all concerned may also be served notices to appear as parties or as interveners. The Court, after hearing, reports to the President. The Advisory Opinion tendered need not, rather, should not bind the President. Conversely, the Supreme Court for germane reasons may decline to express its opinion, especially, when the reference is vague.

Power to Enforce Fundamental Rights or
Writ Jurisdiction under Article 32:

As we know that part III of the Indian Constitution deals with the Fundamental Rights. These Fundamental Rights guaranteed to the citizens would remain as pious constitutional declarations if the repositories of the rights are not assured that in case of any violation of those rights they can look up to some authority for their enforcement. It is, at this juncture, Article 32 comes into play and acquires significance. Dr. Ambedkar had remarked that Article 32 "is the soul of the Constitution and the very heart of it" and without this Article our constitution would be a nullity." Article 32 is in the company of other Fundamental Rights in Part III. But, unlike other rights, "it is remedial and not substantive in nature".

Article 32(1) declares: "The right to move the Supreme Court by appropriate proceedings for the enforcement of the rights conferred by this part is guaranteed". To be noted is the right to move the Supreme Court for the enforcement of the fundamental Rights is itself a Fundamental Right. Thus, the Supreme Court is the ultimate protector and guarantor of the fundamental rights and a solemn duty has been cast upon this Court to protect the citizens' fundamental rights "zealously and vigilantly". Clause (2) of Article 32 empowers the Supreme Court to issue writs including the writs of habeas corpus, mandamus, quo warranto, certiorari and prohibition for the enforcement of the fundamental rights. The Court's power is not confined to the issuance of the above writs, it can issue directions or orders which appear to the Court to be appropriate for the enforcement of the fundamental rights. The Court's power is not only preventive, in the sense, preventing violations of fundamental rights, but also remedial, in the sense, the Court can award compensation and exemplary costs when the state has violated the fundamental right to life and personal liberty guaranteed under Article 21.

The Writ jurisdiction of the Supreme Court is sometimes treated as an 'Original' jurisdiction of the Court in the sense that the party aggrieved has the right to directly move to the Supreme Court by presenting a petition, instead of coming through a High Court by way of appeal.

Supreme Court's Power to Commit a Person for Contempt (Article 129): The Supreme Court is a court of record. Article 129 reads, "*The Supreme Court shall be a court of record and shall have all powers of such a court, including the power to punish for the contempt of itself.*"

A Court of Record is a Court whose records are of evidentiary value and cannot be questioned when produced before any court. Records of the Supreme Court are admitted as final evidences and cannot be questioned when these are produced and referred to in any other court. Article 141 declares: "*the law declared by the Supreme Court shall be binding on all courts within the territory of India.*" Power to punish for contempt is conferred to uphold the majesty and dignity of the court, to prevent scandalisation of the judiciary, to ensure that the stream of justice remains unsullied, to bar interference in the administration of justice. However it should be noted that reasonable criticism of a judicial act in the interest of public good does not constitute contempt. The power of the Supreme Court to punish for contempt extends to all Courts and Tribunals subordinate to it. For the exercise of the power to punish for contempt, no one has to appraise the court. The court can act suo motto.

JUDICIAL ACTIVISM

Traditionally recognized as one of the essential organs of the state, the judiciary's role has been that of rule interpretation, and upholding the law of the land. In modern states which have adopted the idea of constitutionalism and limited government an independent judiciary has become one of the requisites of a democratic government. Any constitutional arrangement based on written constitution, which clearly puts limits on governmental powers and defines the rights of citizens or between the individuals and the state, requires neutral agency to decide disputes among citizens or between the individual and the state. Therefore, applying laws to particular cases and upholding the constitution, the judiciary is also responsible for safeguarding the rights of the individuals, institutions of the state itself.

The Supreme Court enjoys wide powers as an apex court in the judicial system of India and its decisions are binding on all the courts within the territory of India as stated in Article 141. It is a guardian of Fundamental Rights, Article 32, and is the ultimate court of appeal having, Constitutional (Article 132), Civil (Article 133) and Criminal jurisdiction (Article 134). It is the final interpreter of the constitution enjoying the power of Judicial Review.

The goal of the constitution enunciated, by the founding fathers, in its the Preamble, is to secure to the people of India Justice _social, economic and political; liberty of thought, expression, belief, faith and worship and equality of status and opportunity. For achieving this goal, the constitution has created three state organs, the legislature, the executive and the judiciary with their separate fields of jurisdiction, but the ill health of both legislature and executive has tilted and disturbed the so called balance of distribution of powers and functions between the three wings of the state. The weak functioning of the executive because of criminalization of politics and politicization of crimes, lumpanization, exploitation, casteism etc., has made the Indian state what Gunar Myrdal famously called as

"**Soft State**", precisely it does not have the will and the requisite discipline to implement the laws made by it. To quote M.K. Phalkiwala, "we have too much government too little administration, too many public servants too little public services, too many controls too little welfare, too many laws too little justice; I do not know who runs the country."

Judicial activism is only an extension of judicial review power. Broadly speaking judicial activism falls into two categories. One is largely acceptable while the other is not permissible at all. The first consisting of evolving of new principles, new maxims, new concepts going beyond the traditional rule of '*lacus standi*' which was based on the fact that judicial remedy can be sought only by those who have suffered an injury due to a violation of a legal right by some public authority. **The Public Interest Litigation (PIL)** choose to liberalize this rule by holding that for any person to espouse a public cause, he or she did not have to be directly affected. This introduction of PIL, is cited by the Supreme Court as a measure to achieve the constitutional imperatives of a welfare state. The PIL has been used for providing various types of reliefs to the under trail prisoners, to prohibit traffic in women, to check custodial violence, for the release of bounded labour, for the enforcement of labour laws, for environment protection and so on. The Supreme Court of India has conveyed a clear message to all the instrumentalities of governance that it cannot stand idly by, particularly when there is abuse of power and misgovernence. According to Upendra Baxi, the duty of the court

Soft State: *The term 'Soft State' was first noted by the famous economist Gunar Myrdal in his classical book, 'The Asian Drama' in the context of South Asia for the inability of the states to implement their economic plans and programmes efficiently and effectively. Now the term has acquired additional dimensions of meaning that subsumes a comprehensive collapse of even the most basic functions of the state. A contemporary political commentator Atul Kohli has aptly drawn attention to the paradox of the enormous expansion of the state power in India at the same time when its powerlessness to act effectively is equally obvious.*

is not only to protect the constitution by nullifying unconstitutional acts but further to advance and achieve constitutional intent.

The second extends to laying priorities, policies and programmes and giving directions to execute them when they are not obligatory, and are entirely in the direction of the executive and the legislature of other authorities and thereby usurping their functions, power and wisdom. There have been occasions where the judiciary has overstepped its limits by issuing directions in matters which are purely administrative and about which the courts do not possess the requisite expertise and proficiency. Such decisions land the administrative agencies in practical difficulties. Would not such approach strike at the very basis of the Indian democratic polity which postulates that the government of the country should be carried on by the elected representatives of the people, accountable to them? Would it not result in judicial oligarchy dethroning democratic supremacy? Would not such an approach disturb the delicate balance of distribution of powers and functions between the three wings of the state_ the Legislature, the Executive and the Judiciary? Would it not result in judicial oligarchy dethroning democratic supremacy? Critics argue.

The Public Interest Litigation (PIL): *In Indian law, Public Interest Litigation means litigation for the protection of the public interest. It is litigation introduced in a court of law, not by the aggrieved party but by the court itself or by any other private party. PIL is the power given to the public by courts through judicial activism. Now any public spirited citizen can move /approach the court for the public cause by filling a petition: 1. In Supreme Court under Article 32 of the constitution; 2. In High Court under Article 226 of the constitution; and 3. In the Court of Magistrate under Section 133 of Indian Panel Code.*

Judges Judge, create history in the name of PIL or judicial activism, but judiciary like the legislature, is also manned by human beings who come from the same social milieu and are subject to same human frailties and social constraints. No institution has a monopoly right to weaknesses or to making mistakes. Courts may also go wrong, overstep the limits of judicial discretion and restraint and make mistakes. Even Supreme Court recognized its fallibility. Besides this the Transparency International Report of 2007, while projecting the judiciary as third most corrupt institution in the country, concluded that 77% of corruption in judicial system has been lawyer-driven. These with their absolute powers, are a source of threat to the independence of the judiciary.

JUDICIAL REVIEW IN INDIAN CONSTITUTION

The power of judicial review is the power of the judiciary to 'review' and possibly invalidate laws, decrees and actions of other branches of government, notably the legislature and the executive. In its classical sense, the principle of judicial review stems from the existence of a codified constitution and allows the courts to strike down as 'unconstitutional' actions that are deemed to be incompatible with the constitution.

In post-independence India, the inclusion of explicit provisions for 'judicial review' were necessary in order to give effect to the individual and group rights guaranteed in the text of the Constitution. Dr. B.R. Ambedkar, who chaired the drafting committee of our Constituent Assembly, had described the provision related to the same as the 'heart of the Constitution'. Article 13(2) of the Constitution of India prescribes that the Union or the States shall not make any law that takes away or abridges any of the fundamental rights, and any law made in contravention of the aforementioned mandate shall, to the extent of the contravention, be void.

While judicial review over administrative action has evolved on the lines of common law doctrines such as 'proportionality', 'legitimate expectation', 'reasonableness' and principles of natural justice, the Supreme Court of India and the various High Courts were given the power to rule on the constitutionality of legislative as well as administrative actions. In most cases, the power of judicial review is exercised to protect and enforce the fundamental rights guaranteed in Part III of the Constitution. The higher courts are also approached to rule on questions of legislative competence, mostly in the context of Centre-State relations since Article 246 of the Constitution read with the 7th schedule, contemplates a clear demarcation as well as a zone of intersection between the law-making powers of the Union Parliament and the various State Legislatures. Hence the scope of judicial review before Indian courts has evolved in three dimensions – firstly, to ensure fairness in administrative action, secondly to protect the constitutionally guaranteed fundamental rights of citizens and thirdly to rule on questions of legislative competence between the centre and the states.

CHAPTER 8

INDIAN FEDERALISM

'All politics is local'

Thomas O' Neill

Meaning of federalism: Federalism is a dynamic theory of nation and state building. The word federalism is derived from a Latin word *'foedus'* that literally means 'a treaty' or 'an agreement'. Obviously the essential feature of modern federal state is that the two or more independent states agree to form a new state. According to Daniel J. Elazara, "a federal system provides a mechanism which unites separate politics with an overarching political system so as to allow each to maintain its fundamental political integrity". This he calls as 'self rule plus shared rule'. Its hallmark is, to quote Rasheeduddin Khan, 'unity of polity and plurality of society'. As a theory of nation building, federalism seeks to define state _ society relationships in such a manner as to allow autonomy of identity of social groups to flourish in the constitutionally secured and mandated institutional space. The federal constitution recognizes the special cultural rights of people, especially the minorities. In this sense it is very close to the theory of **multiculturalism,** yet different because the niceties of federalism lie in its fundamental stress on institutionalization of diversities and facilitating socio-political cooperation between two sets of identities through various structural mechanisms of 'shared rule'. M.J.C Vile observes, 'federalism is a system of government in which neither level of government is wholly dependent on the other nor wholly independent of the other". Instead, he lays stress on the 'mutually interdependent political relationship' between the centre and regional authorities.

Essential Features of a federal polity: Scholars may differ in defining 'federalism' but the consensus of opinion is that a federal system involves the fallowing essential features:

i.   **Dual Government:** while in a unitary state, there is only one government, namely national government, in a federal state, there are two governments, the national or federal government and the government of each component state.

ii. **Distribution of powers**: The central principle upon which the federal government is formed is division of powers as authority between the federal government and the

Multiculturalism: *Multiculturalism is used as both a descriptive and a normative term. As a descriptive term it refers to cultural diversity arising from the existence within a society of two or more groups whose beliefs and practices generate a distinctive sense of collective identity. Multiculturalism is invariably reserved for communal diversity that arises from racial, ethnic or language differences. As a normative term, multiculturalism implies a positive endorsement of communal diversity, based either on the right of different cultural groups to respect and recognition, or on the alleged benefits to the larger society of moral and cultural diversity. Multiculturalism, in this sense, acknowledge the importance of beliefs, values and ways of life in establishing self-understanding and a sense of self-worth for individuals and groups alike. Critics of multiculturalism argue that multicultural societies are inherently conflict-ridden and unstable, and view normative multiculturalism as an example of political correctness.*

states, though the method of distribution may not be alike in the federal constitutions.

iii. **Supremacy of the Constitution**: A federal state derives its existence from the constitution. Every power_ executive, legislative or judicial_ whether it belongs to the federation or to the component states, is subordinate to and controlled by the constitution.

iv. **Authority of courts**: It is essential to maintain the division of powers not only between the coordinate branches of the government, but also between the federal government and the states themselves. This is secured by vesting in the courts of a final power to interpret the constitution and nullify any action on the part of the federal governments or state governments and their different organs which violate the provisions of the constitution. In other words it can be stated that to prevent conflicts between centre and states, there is an independent judiciary to settle disputes.

Federalism in India: The constitution of India provides a federal system of government in the country even though it described India as a 'union of states' (Article 1). The term 'Union' of States, implies that firstly, the Indian federation is not the result of an agreement between independent units, and secondly, the units of the Indian federation cannot leave the federation.

India is the land of continental proportions and immense diversities. There are hundreds of languages spoken in India. It is the home of several major religions. There are several million indigenous people living in different parts of the country. In spite of all these diversities people share a common landmass, history and many other important features. This has led Indian national leaders to visualize India as a country where there is unity in diversity. Sometime it is described as unity with diversity. Thus federalism was adopted by the Constituent Assembly, in recognition of the regional heterogeneity of India. Its adherence to the concept of **Cooperative Federalism** can be explained in the form of the then prevailing situation in post-partition India. There was an urgent need felt among the members of the Constituent Assembly to check communalism, deal effectively with acute food crisis, integrate the **princely states**[15] in India and undertake the task of initiating and implementing the policies of industrial and agriculture development.

The roots of Indian federalism can be traced back to British colonial regime. Before the independence, the British government had initiated the federation in India under the Government of Indian Act, 1935. The most remarkable feature of the Act was that it envisaged a 'federation of all – India,' consisting of the British provinces and Indian states willing to join it.

Traditionally legal scholarship has characterized Indian federalism as 'quasi federal'_ a unitary state with subsidiary federal principles rather than a federal state with subsidiary unitary principles (K.C. Wheare). This interpretation is because of the unionist bend of the constitution and the manner by which the word 'Union' was inserted instead of 'federal'.[16] Livingstone and D. D. Basu are of the opinion that it is functional aspect and not institutional which determine the

Cooperative Federalism
Granville Austin prefers to call Indian Federalism as Cooperative Federalism which means that the Union and State governments work in harmony in carrying out community Developmental Programs etc. Inter-governmental-level-co-operation in different fields has been the most significant aspect of Cooperative Federalism. Planning at both levels is done in a cooperative manner, in which the basic norms of development are set by the Central Government in discussion with the States.

---

[15]   Princely states are those states which were ruled by the Princes at the time of Partition. There were 565 Princely who were given option to join either India or Pakistan.

[16]   Article 1 of the Indian Constitution states that 'Indian that is Bharat, shall be a Union of States'.

kind of federation. That is why D. D. Basu calls Indian federation as '*sui generis*'. [17]

Indian federalism is complex enough to defy singular generalization and characterization. At best one can characterize it as 'Union type Federal Polity'. Such a polity usually combines the features of duel federation; Cooperative-collaborative federalism and the inter-dependent federalism.

The federal features of the Indian constitution include:

1. A written constitution which defines the structure, organization and power of the central as well as state governments.
2. Supremacy of the constitution, which implies that both the centre and the states are sub-ordinate to the constitution and are expect to act according to its provisions.
3. A rigid constitution, which can be amended only through a special procedure, which is quite different from the ordinary lawmaking procedure. Some provisions of the constitution can be amended only with the consent of legislatures of majority of states.
4. An independent judiciary which acts as the guardian of the constitution and ensures that the centre and the states operate within their respective spheres. It also acts as the guardian of fundamental rights of citizens.
5. The creation of an Upper House – Rajya Sabha in which the states have been given representation.
6. A clear division of power between the centre and the states. Like every other federal constitution, the constitution of India divides powers between the Union Government and the State Governments. It divides all the subjects in three parts.

---

[17] *Sui generis* means a system of government neither purely federal nor purely unitary but a combination of both.

i. Union List contains 97 subjects over which the Union Government legislates and administers them in whole of India.

ii. State List contains 66 subjects over which each State Government legislates and administrators them in its own territory.

iii. Concurrent List contains 47 subjects over which both Union and State governments can legislate.

Union list includes subjects like	State list includes subjects like	Concurrent list includes subjects like
Defense	Agriculture	Education
Atomic energy	Police	Transfer of
Foreign affairs	Prison	property other than
War and peace	Local Government	Agricultural land.
Banking	Public Health	Forests
Railways	Land	Trade Unions
Post and telegraph	Liquor	Adulteration
Airways	Trade and commerce	Adaptation and
Currency and coinage	Live stock and animal	succession,
Foreign trade	husbandry	Criminal law,
	State public services	Electricity.

The Unionist Bend of Indian Federalism: Article 1 of the Indian Constitution describes India as a 'Union of States'. The emphasis of India being a Union was to convey the fact that it was not a result of a compact or agreement between the constituent units but a declaration by the Constituent Assembly deriving its authority from the people of India. Further, the conceptualization was clearly intended to convey the federal nature of the polity but with a subordinate position to the states and structural – functional balance in favor of the supremacy of the Union.

D. D. Basu analyzed that "even though there is a distribution of powers between the Union and the States as under a federal system, the distribution has a strong central bias and the powers of the states are hedged in with various restrictions which impede their sovereignty even within the sphere limited to them by the distribution of powers basically provided by the constitution". Looking on this scheme of distribution of powers between the centre and the states, K.C. Wheare called Indian federalism as quasi-federal, a unitary state with subsidiary federal principles rather than a federal state with subsidiary unitary principles. Some of the important provisions that create a strong central government are as under:

1. The very existence of a State Including its territorial integrity is in the hands of the Parliament. The Parliament is empowered to 'form a new State by separation of territory from any State or by uniting two or more States.... It can also alter the boundary of any State or even its name. The Constitution provides for some safeguards by way of securing the view of the concerned State legislature.

2. The Constitution has certain very powerful emergency provisions, which can turn Indian federal polity into a highly centralized system once emergency is declared. During an emergency, power becomes lawfully centralized. The Parliament also assumes the power to make laws on subjects within the jurisdiction of the States.

3. Even during normal circumstances, the central government has very effective financial powers and responsibilities. In the first place, items generating revenue are under the control of the central government. Thus, the central government has many revenue sources and the States are mostly dependent on the grants and financial assistance from the centre. Secondly, India adopted planning as the instrument of rapid economic progress and development after independence. Planning led to considerable centralization of economic decision making. Planning Commission appointed by the union government is the coordinating machinery that controls and supervises

the resources management of the States. Besides, the Union government uses its discretion to give grants and loans to States. This distribution of economic resources is considered lopsided and has led to charges of discrimination against States ruled by an opposition party.

4. The Governor has certain powers to recommend dismissal of the State government and the dissolution of the Assembly. Besides, even in normal circumstances, the Governor has the power to reserve a bill passed by the State legislature, for the assent of the President. This gives the central government an opportunity to delay the State legislation and also to examine such bills and veto them completely.

5. There may be occasions when the situation may demand that the central government needs to legislate on matters from the State list. This is possible if the move is ratified by the Rajya Sabha. The Constitution clearly states that executive powers of the centre are superior to the executive powers of the States. Furthermore, the central government may choose to give instructions to the State government. The following extract from an Article of the Constitution makes this clear.

Article 257 (1): The executive power of every State shall be so exercised as not to impede or prejudice the exercise of the executive power of the Union, and the executive power of the Union shall extend to the giving of such directions to a State as may appear to the Government of India to be necessary for that purpose.

6. The all-India services are common to the entire territory of India and officers chosen for these services serve in the administration of the States. Thus, an IAS officer who becomes the collector or an IPS officer who serves as the Commissioner of Police, are under the control of the central government. States cannot take disciplinary action nor can they remove these officers from service.

7. Articles 33 and 34 authorize the Parliament to protect persons in the service of the Union or a State in respect of any action taken by them during martial law to maintain or restore order. This provision further strengthens the powers of the Union Government. The Armed Forces Special Powers Act has been made on the basis of these provisions. This Act has created tensions between the people and the armed forces on some occasions.

Reasons for Making Centre Strong: India's constitution, observes Paul R. Brass 'was born more in fear and trepidation than in hope and inspiration'. Brass is realistic and balanced in his observation when he remarks that the India's constitution- makers thought they had good reasons to be fearful of disorder, even chaos, in the subcontinent as a consequence of the actions of a multiplicity of dangerous forces arising out of political movements associated with communalism, secessionism and revolutionary communism. Moreover, some of these forces were associated with acts of violence, revolutionary insurrection, extensive communal killings and war. The response of India's constitution makers to these threats and dangers was to use them as a basis for framing a constitution with numerous provisions designed to deal effectively with the threat of disorder through the creation of a strong centralized state.

When the Constituent Assembly first met in 1946 and early 1947, the idea was to have a federation with a centre having limited powers, to which Muslim League agreed but Nehru was not in favour of a weak centre. Before the Union Constitution Committee could transact any worthwhile business, the Mountbatten Plan of 1947 was announced. All hopes of preserving the unity of India vanished and the partition of the country on communal lines became a firm decision. As was expected, a decisive swing followed in favour of a strong centre. Once partition had become a reality, there was no need to appease the Muslim League and restrict the powers of the Union Government. Therefore, the Union Powers Committee was unanimous in its view that it would be injurious to the interests of the country to provide for a weak central authority which would be incapable of ensuring peace, of coordinating vital matters of common concern, and of speaking effectively for the whole country in the international sphere.

Besides the concerns for unity, the makers of the constitution also believed that the socio-economic problems of the country needed to be handled by a strong central government in cooperation with the states. Poverty, illiteracy and inequalities of wealth were some of the problems that required planning and coordination. Thus the concerns for unity and development prompted the makers of the constitution to create a strong central government.

The growing power of the central governments in the matters originally allotted to the state or regional governments has changed the structure of "federation" to a Unitarian Federation. India acts more as a Unitarian Federation than a 'Federation'. The main forces that have contributed to the growing strength of national governments seem to have been six fold _ war politics, depression politics, welfare politics, techno politics, grants in aid politics and party politics.

What made Partition of India inevitable?

The contradictory nature of the reality of 15 August 1947 continues to intrigue historians and torment people of both sides of the boarder to this day. A hard earned prize freedom was won after long, glorious years of struggle but a bloody, tragic partition rent as under the fabric of the emerging free nation. The question, who partitioned British India still holds the interest of historians, political scientists, economists, academicians and what not. Some blame Muslim League and its popular leadership, most importantly Jinnah, some blame British for their policy of Divide and Rule and some other blame the Rightists ideology of RSS, Bajrangdal, Hindu Mahasabha and the like and others blame Indian National Congress (INC) and its leadership especially Nehru and Patel. This plurality in theories clearly indicates that there were different forces working altogether for the same cause.

Broadly speaking a triangular set of forces were emphasizing the growth of communalism, hence preparing the communal clouds to rain and flourish the partition. The political triangle was consisting of British which used the weapon of Divide and Rule, Muslim League which demanded for Pakistan and Congress demanding for transfer of power. British chose communalism to counter and weaken the growth of national movement in India and to safeguard their interests. The Muslim Leaders such as Sir Syed Ahmad and Jinnah, who in the initial years of their lives stood for Hindu Muslim unity were also swept by the tides of communalism. In the latter part of their lives they became the champions of Two Nation Theory. On the other hand the split of 1907 in Indian National Congress gave extremists a solid command on their faction of INC and they openly went on Hindu orthodoxy and tried to provide Hindu ideology or at least a Hindu idiom to its day to day political agitation. Tilak used the Ganesh Puja, the Shivaji festival etc. to propagate nationalism and the anti-partition Bengal agitation was initiated with dips in Ganges. What was more worse, Bakim Chander and many other poets and writers in various languages described Muslims as foreigners in their poems, plays and dramas and identified nationalism with Hindus.

There is no denying of the fact that Jinnah, Iqbal, Sir Syed started their careers as nationalists and utilized their energies for Hindu Muslim unity but the million dollar question is what made them to change their mind? Let us take the case of Jinnah....

Jinnah was born on Christmas day 1876 in a tenement house in Karachi. He started out as an Indian nationalist in 1906 when he first attended the Congress (NC) Session. He was opposed to separate electorates and did not join the Muslim League (ML) until 1913. He was an indefatigable champion of Hindu –Muslim unity and a composite India. During his power, ML and NC would hold their sessions together. He was the centre figure of the famous Lucknow Pact of 1916. But the Congress members, especially Nehru and Patel killed this Pact and made Jinnah to admit that 'no new pact was possible'.

Reinterpreting Jinnah, Ayseha Jalal in her work: '*Jinnah - The Sole Spokesman*' argues that until 1947 Pakistan was only a bargaining counter and that what Jinnah really wanted was power at the centre in a union of Pakistan and Hindustan. The argument portrays Jinnah in as a man with an inward mission of his own, one which he could not communicate even to this own followers. She portrays the Lahore Resolution of 1940 as a serious setback for Jinnah, envisaging as it did the creation of two Muslim Federations, abolishing the centre and leaving minority province Muslim high and dry.

Jinnah's acceptance of the Cabinet Mission Plan is seen as a part of the same strategy. It offered him what Asyesha Jalal argues he had wanted from the beginning, a chance to find a solution within the unity of India by giving maximum autonomy to the regional units and allowing for a federal government at the centre with limited powers. This plan explicitly rejected Pakistan; but ML along with Jinnah accepted it.

Anita Inder Singh has shown in her work on partition that Jinnah entered into negotiations willing to consider the preservation of some sort of centre but most reluctant to see the establishment of either a central legislature or a constitutional assembly for India as a whole. H.V. Hudson in his book; '*The Great Divide*' argues that Jinnah should have argued that Hindu and Muslims constitute two nations and still accepted Pakistan to include undivided Punjab and Bengal with substantial Hindu and Sikh minorities.

Saleem M. M. Qureshi in his book: '*Politics of Jinnah*' says that Jinnah was disappointed with the partition because it divided Punjab and Bengal. Jinnah says, "My Pakistan contains heart, that is, Punjab and Soul; that is, Bengal, without which Pakistan would mean truncated and moth-eaten Pakistan."

Now the question arises who then made Jinnah to demand a separate homeland for the Muslims? Shri Shanker Sharan in his Article "Advani is Right' published in Mainstream of June 18, 2005 blames Nehru and other Congressmen for the partition. He says 'His (Jinnah's) alienation from the NC came because the Congress would not concede him the kind of national role a man of his vast ability deserved.

He was never made the President of the NC to which exalted post even a young Jawaharlal was appointed in 1929, 1936, 1937, 1946 and 1951. On December 1928 an All Party Conference accepted Nehru's Report and rejected the Jinnah's proposals, what are known as Jinnah's Fourteen Points. This created a disappointment in Jinnah's mind and he began to think of parting of ways'.

Furthermore it was not Jinnah who killed the last option for a united India under the Cabinet Mission Plan, but Jawaharlal Nehru who out rightly rejected the Plan. Nehru's claim of autonomous rights for the Constituent Assembly killed the trust and the consensus of which the Cabinet Mission had succeeded. Jinnah, therefore, withdrew the ML's support from the plan and announced Direct Action which led to the riots in Calcutta, Nokhaila and Bihar and thus sealed the fact of a united India.

Gandhi tried to save a United India by the last and supremely courageous offer of Prime Ministership to Jinnah, but Nehru and Patel killed it with the view that Indian people will not accept it.

The new epoch in the history of the subcontinent was unfolded by Advani's trip to Pakistan in June 2005, which proved to be a great turnover in the contemporary political history. L.K. Advani, who redefined Indian politics, polarized society with the Ayodhya movement, had suddenly discovered the virtues of Hindu- Muslim brotherhood. As he set foot on the Pakistani soil, almost a magic realism, the Hindu hawk transformed into a Muslim- loving dove. He with a guilty conscience said that the demolition of Babri Masjid was the saddest day of his life. He further said, 'partition is irreversible' but further stated that there is a Pakistani in every Indian.

In praise of the Quid-e-Azam, he declared him a 'great man, an apostle of Hindu –Muslim unity and above all a secular.' Referring to his presidential speech of Constituent Assembly of Pakistan in August 11, 1947, he reminded his words – *you are free to go to your temples, you are free to go to your mosques or other places of worship in the state of Pakistan. You may belong to any religion, caste or creed – that has nothing to do with the business of the state.*

This declaration created a mismatch between the party and its leaders. The BJP was plunged into what they might call as *"dharma sankat"* of epic proportions. VHP leaders called Advani a traitor. The RSS was stunned and angry upon Advani's ideological transformation. The more crucial battle was being waged within the BJP where even Advani's loyalists were unwillingly to endorse his statement. It was same Jinnah who according to some partitioned the Nation and now he has partitioned the BJP. The battle changed its colour when Advani refused to backtrack and offered his resignation from the post of party presidentship.

History repeated itself four years later with his party colleague Jaswant Singh being expelled from the party in the same situation, by the same democratic stalwarts, for the same reasons and on the same remarks as were done by his predecessor L. K. Advani. In his book; *'Jinnah – India, Partition, Independence'* Jaswant Singh ridiculed both Nehru and Patel and held them responsible for the partition of the nation and maintained that Jinnah was 'demonized' for no reason.

The gulf within the party is widening and the members seem to oscillate between the secular ideology of the state and the conservative ideology of the party. In the *'Chitan Baithak'* (brain storming session) held in Simla, the BJP has completely dissociated itself from the contents of the book. The book generated a huge uproar in the BJP camp and the bombardment of comments became a usual fashion.

Leaders from Sushma Suraj to Monohar Joshi, Bal Thackray to Rajnath Singh all raised their protest against the remarks of Jaswant Singh. Rajnath Singh took objection to ridiculing of Sardar Vallabhai Patel by Jaswant Singh, saying the first Home Minister played a historic role in unification and consolidation of India amidst serious threats to its security and integrity. Shive Sena chief, Bal Thackray flayed Jaswant Singh and said that calling the founder of Pakistan secular was an insult to all those who shed their blood for India's independence. Ruling Congress party also joined the race and bravely announced that the nation will teach lessons to those raising fingers at the freedom fighters, referring to Singh's attacks on first PM of India Jawaharlal Nehru and Sardar Vallabbhai Patel.

It is because of the pressure from the patron organization RSS that the main opposition party expelled one of its senior most leaders, Jaswant Singh, who was the chairman of Public Accounts Committee (PAC), for praising Pakistani founder Mohammad Ali Jinnah in his book. Reacting to this, Sigh said that it was a dark day for India where debating, discussion or even disagreement on a written material was a taboo. It is sad for India and a very dark day, if intellectual freedom is kept hostage of political whims.

Nation cannot be build on tricks! This is for what the rightists dare to speak the truth publically.

Centre–State Relations: Areas of Tension: From one side the constitution recognizes the separate identity of the regions or the states and yet gives more powers to the centre. Once the principle of identity of states is accepted, it is quite natural that states would expect a greater role and powers in the governance of the states and the nation as a whole. This leads to various demands from the states which ultimately generates tensions and conflicts in centre-state relations. Till the Fourth General Election of 1967, the centre-state relations were cordial and cooperative, reflecting an example of what Granville Austin called as "Cooperative Federalism". It is not that during this period, there were no tensions and conflicts, but these conflicts were treated as an inter-party affair (as the Congress was in power at both centre as well as in states) which took the shape of a family quarrel and as such, it was comparatively easy to resolve it, particularly on account of the presence of Nehru and the prestige that he commanded at the national and the state levels. During this period it appeared that the federal system was operating in a unitary party framework.

However, the year of 1967 was a watershed in Indian elections in a true sense because for the first time a challenge was posed to the ruling party and seemingly its support base was on the decline. Congress got only 283 seats out of 520, i.e. only 54% majority in the Parliament, unlike early three elections when it had got 70-75% seats. Fourth general election is regarded as 'Political earthquake' in Indian politics. Congress lost power in eight states to coalition of associated national and regional parties. It also lost

2.5% to 18% seats in the states where it retained power. The Congress thus faced the danger of being reduced to a minority party. Thus, the 1967 elections represented a major step in the direction of an increasingly competitive polity. Congress lost power in eight different states to non-congress parties and its support base was on decline. The formation of the non-congress governments had a considerable impact on the nature of federal polity. It resulted in demands for greater powers and greater autonomy to the states. In fact, these demands were direct fallout of the fact that different parties were ruling at the centre and in many states. The post-Fourth General Election tensions in centre-state relations are characteristic of the transition from the stage of one party dominant politics to the multiparty competitive politics. After the rise of coalition politics since 1990s Indian federalism achieved a character of 'bargaining federalism'.

Bargaining Federalism
Bargaining Federalism is mostly found in the states having multiparty system with diverse national interests. Indian federalism since 1990 provides a good example of what Professor Moores Jones called as 'Bargaining Federalism'. Bargaining federalism is traceable first, in the rise of regional parties; second, coalition politics; and third, in the existence of (formal as well as tacit) and operation of various institutional agencies such as Planning Commission, Finance Commission, Inter- State Council, NDC etc. In bargaining federalism regional parties get the maximum benefit by bargaining with the national parties.

Tamil Nadu was the first state to revolt against the Centre and threatened of secession. Subsequently the ruling party DMK of Tamil Nadu lobbied for setting up of **Rajamannar Commission (see table 1)** to examine the working of the constitution. The Rajamannar Commission recommended revoking of the federal relations by transferring some Union Subjects to the State List. Further, it recommended the abolition of Articles 249, 356 and 357 of the Indian Constitution. Centre State relations came under close scrutiny once again in 1977 in the form of a memorandum (**West Bengal Memorandum, see table 2**) on Centre-state relations submitted by the Left Government in West Bengal. To investigate the centre-state relations the government formed the **Sarkaria Commission** in June 1983, **(see table 3)**. The atmosphere became chaotic as the Shorimani Akali Dal also adopted the famous **Anand Pur Sahab Resolution**.

Anand Pur Sahab Resolution: For voicing its concern for the need to provide autonomy to the states, Shiromini Akali Dal (SAD) prepared and passed a resolution in 1973 at Anandpur Sahab. Besides other things SAD demanded that various areas like Dalhousie, Pinjore, Ambala and other Punjabi speaking areas be immediately merged with the Punjab under one administrative unit. Further, it demanded greater autonomy for the state in internal matters and held that the Central intervention should be restricted to Defence, Foreign Affairs, Post and Telegraphs, Currency and Railways. The rest of the departments should be under direct countrol of the Punjab.

Table 1
Rajamannar Committee Report 1971

The government of DMK in Tamil Nadu appointed a commission headed by P.V Rajamannar, a retired chief Justice of Madras High Court. The Commission submitted its report in 1971. Some recommendations are as:

1. Transfer of certain subjects from Union and Concurrent Lists to State List along with Residuary powers of legislation and taxation to be vested in the state legislatives.
2. Stress on formation of Inter-state Council, comprising of CM's with the Prime Minister as its chairman which will channelize the Parliament's decisions and state interests and will act as a watch dog for states.

3. Abolition of Planning Commission and its place must be taken by a statutory body, consisting of scientific, technical, agricultural and economic experts, to advise the States which should have their own Planning Boards.

4. It recommended the deletion of Articles 356, 357 and 360, along with the directives imposed by the Centre to States.

5. Equal representation of states in Rajya Sabha.

6. State Cabinet's consultation will be mandatory for the appointment of the Governors.

7. Amendment to the Article 312.

8. High Courts should be the highest courts for matters falling in the state jurisdiction.

9. Non-interference to the territorial integrity of the State.

Table 2

West Bengal Memorandum: Document for State Autonomy.

The CPIM government of West Bengal produced its own document on centre-state relations and suggested:

1. Jurisdiction of the centre should be restricted to only: Defense, Foreign Affairs, Foreign Trade, Currency and Communication and Economic Cooperation.

2. The Central Forces (BSF, CRPF, and Industrial Forces) shall have no right to operate in the states.

3. The Centre and States should have separate administrative services with exclusive jurisdiction on them.

4. Equal representation to all states in Rajya Sabha and special status for JAMMU AND KASHMIR under Article 370 should be maintained.

5. Residuary Powers should be transferred to states.

6. Abolition of Article 249, which gives to the Parliament power to legislate on the State List under the plank of National Interest.

7. Deletion of Articles 356, 357, 360, 200, 201. Articles 356, 357, 360 deal with Emergency while as Articles 200 and 201 deal with Governor's power to reserve Bills passed by the assembly for the President's assent.

8. The Parliament's right to amend the boundaries of the states should be amended.

Table 3.
Sarkaria Commission

The growing demands of decentralization lead to the formation of Sarkaria Commission in June 1983. Justice R.S. Sarkaria was made the chairman and Mr. B. Sivaraman, the Cabinet Secretary, Mr. S. R. Sen, a former Executive Director of IBRD and Rama Subramaniam (Member Secretary), were nominated as the members. The Commission submitted its report in 1988. The important recommendations of the Commission are as:

1. Formation of an inter-governmental council consisting of Prime Minister and Chief Ministers of states to decide collectively on various aspects of governance that causes friction between Centre and States.

2. Sparing use of Article 356 of the Constitution should be made and all possible alternative governments must be explored before imposing presidential rule in the states. The state assembly should not be dissolved unless the proclamation is approved by the Parliament.

3. It rejected the demand for the abolition of the office of governor as well as his selection, from a panel of names given by the state governments. However, it suggested that active politicians should not be appointed governors when the State and Centre are ruled by different political parties, the governor should not belong to the ruling party at the Centre. Further, the retiring governors should be debarred from accepting any office of profit.

4. The judges of High Courts should not be transferred without their consent.

5. The three language formula should be implemented in its true spirit in all the states in the interest of unity and integrity of the country.

6. The work of Union and State governments, which directly affects the local people, must be carried out in the local language.

7. Central control over radio and TV should be relaxed and the individual *kendras* should be free to decide about the timing for the relay of national look-up programs.

8. It favoured amendments for sharing certain taxes between the Centre and the States, even though it generally opposed the curtailment of the Centre's powers.

9. In the financial sphere it did not favour any drastic changes in the basic scheme of division of taxes but favoured sharing of corporate tax and levy of consignment tax.

10. It did not favour disbanding of All-India Services in the interest of the country's integrity. Instead, it favoured new All-India Services.

11. It made a strong case for inter-state councils but insisted that these should be used only for the purpose mentioned in Article 263 of the constitution.

12. It favoured retention of the National Development Council and suggested activation of the Zonal Councils.

13. It found the present division of functions between the finance commission and the planning commission as reasonable and favoured continuance of this arrangement.

14. It favoured determination of terms of reference of the finance commission in consultation with the state governments. It also suggested setting up of similar expert bodies at the state level.

CHAPTER 9

DYNAMISM IN INDIAN PARTY SYSTEM

Politics is all about who Gets What, When and How.

Harold Lasswell

A party system is indispensable to democracy. It is impossible to visualize a healthy polity without a vigorous party system. The institutionalization of Indian National Congress in the first ever meeting on 28th December 1885 in Bombay, which subsequently became a national event, and graduating in course of time to an all embracing political party, is rightly considered as the moment of founding of political party and the beginning of party politics in the Indian context. Of course, a whole range of factors came into play before the untiring efforts of A. O. Hume and some prominent Indian personalities which led to the formation of Indian National Congress.

As the Congress consolidated organizationally and gained a legitimacy both with the government and with the people, a political process conducive for the crystallization of political parties and political groups was set up in motion. The founding of Indian National Congress deserves to be regarded as the birth of a party system in India because it set in motion a process that, on the one hand, was a signal to a number of ideas to bloom, on the other hand, in the process of its evolution and growth, rules of political mobilization and competition were written.

There is an agreement among students of political parties in India about their evolution route through the social reform movements, social literacy, religious and other associations, to the founding of Indian National Congress, the Muslim League and sprouting of other political groups within and outside the two main streams of parties. Ajay K. Mehra has identified the process and interrelationships at four levels, which created the base for a party system in India.

First, as various associations were sprouting and taking firm roots during the 19th century, both before and after the revolt, there were interactions amongst them. The Brahmo Samaj under the leadership of **Raja Ram Mohan Roy,** had various discords within it. Second, as the Congress graduated from being an elite debating club and transcended the political mendicancy during the first decade of 20th century, the conflicts within organization, and organizational efforts to manage such conflicts aided evolution of a party system. The formation of Muslim League and the Surat Split paved the way for maturation of party system. Third, with elections becoming more and more competitive, political groups began to take shape of parties, and parties together as a party system. Finally, the interference of conflicting interests at the intra-party and inter-party levels and party's capacity to resolve conflicts helped in the emergence of the party system.

> **Raja Ram Mohan Roy (1772-1833)** *was born in an orthodox Brahman family at Radhanagar in Bengal. He is regarded as the Father of Modern India for his valid contribution in reforming the Indian society and polity. He was called as the 'religious Benthamite' for his utilitarian views on religion. His most famous book is "Tuhfat-ul-Muwahhidin (A Gift to Deists). For carrying out religious reforms he founded the Atmiya Sabha in 1815, Unitarian Association in 1821 and the Brahmo Sabha in 1828, which later became the Brahmo Samaj. He is best known for his efforts to abolish the practice of Sati.*

By 1951, a year after the new constitution was put into effect and the time when preparations for first general election were on, four major groups of parties had emerged in the Indian political arena. One group, more or less accepted the basic democratic, secular state provided in the Constitution. The Congress, the parties that came out of it, were part of this group. The Communist Party of India and various Marxist parties formed another group. A third group consisted of Hindu sectarian parties like **Bhartia JanSang**, Hindu Mahasabha etc. A fourth group of parties was indifferent to the constitutional framework and concentrated on parochial or regional demands e.g., Akali Dal of Punjab, National Conference of Jammu and Kashmir etc.

One Party Dominant System: Congress swept the poles in first three general elections and came out as a single largest party. In the first three general elections, Congress secured 364 seats, 371 seats and 361 seats respectively. This back to back victory of Indian National Congress resulted in the formation of particular party system generally described as the one-party dominant system. Although various parties contested elections but could not challenge the Congress dominance. Commenting upon the nature of the Congress dominance, Rajni Kothari called it a one party dominant system. But this Congress system remained only up to 1967 when the Congress lost power in eight different states to regional parties and other non-congress parties. The fourth general elations were held at a time when the nation was facing tremendous pressures from within as well as from outside. The defeat in Indo-China war of 1962, followed by the death of Nehru eroded the credibility of Congress. Furthermore,

Bhartia JanSang: Bhartia Jansang was formed in 1951 by Shyama Prasad Mukherjee. Its lineage however can be traced back to RSS and the Hindu Mahasaba before independence. It emphasized the idea of one country, one culture and one nation and believed that the country could become modern, progressive and strong on the basis of Hinduta. At present these three organizations work under one organization called as BJP, which was formed in 1980.

the rising food crises, devaluation of the Indian rupee, famine in Bihar stunted growth, growing discontentment among large sections of people, all want against the Congress. The unification of non-congress parties further added to vulnerability of the Congress.

Once the Congress system started collapsing as a result a 'market polity' emerged on the forefront. Moris Jones summed up this situation as 'dominance coexisting with competition but without a trace of alternation'.

1967 was a watershed in Indian elections in a true sense because for the first time a challenge was posed to the ruling party and seemingly its support base was on the decline. Congress got only 283 seats out of 520, i.e. only 54% majority in the Parliament, unlike early three elections when it had got 70-75% seats. The fourth general election is regarded as 'Political Earthquake' in Indian politics. Congress lost power in eight states to coalition of associated national and regional parties. It also lost 2.5% to 18% seats in the states where it retained power. The Congress thus faced the danger of being reduced to a minority party. Thus, the 1967 elections represented a major step in the direction of an increasingly competitive polity.

The defeat led to a vertical split in the party in 1969. The syndicates, who played a crucial role in the instillation of Indira Gandhi as Prime Minister, went against her. This powerful group blamed Indira Gandhi for the defeat of 1967. The factional rivalry between the syndicate and Indira Gandhi came in the open in 1969 following President Zakir Hussain's death. Indira backed V.V. Giri as against the official candidate Sanjeeva Reddy. The defeat of Sanjeeva Reedy formalized the split in Congress. In 1969 the Congress got divided into Indira faction and the Syndicate faction. As the two factions of the Congress battled for the partie's political legacy and popular support base, it was the Indira's Congress which claimed a definite edge. Mrs. Gandhi's leadership, her new policies, new political process with a pyramidal decision making structure helped the Congress to regain its last ground.

After the split of 1969, Indira Gandhi made some sweeping reforms. From agrarian reforms to the nationalization of banks, she put the Congress on a socialistic path. Sensing public support for her policies she decided to go directly to the people and receive a fresh mandate by holding mid-term polls in 1971. To gain more and more vote share she gave a famous slogan of *gareebi hatao* (remove poverty). This helped Congress to regain its image and made Indira Gandhi popular as the savior of the poor. The Congress won 352 seats with about 44% of the popular votes on its own. The Indira Gandhi led Congress achieved the status of being the real Congress. The war of 1971 further strengthened the Congress. India's victory and the division of Pakistan were credited around Indira's head. She came to be called as godess Durga. In sum, it can be said that the 1971 elections restored the Congress position after the set back of 1967. Furthermore, Congress also swept majority of the seats in 1972 Assembly Elections. Thus Congress acquired dominant position both in centre as well as at the state level.

Two Party System: Indira Gandhi began to lose her popularity and credibility due to a nationwide drought in 1971, 1972 and 1973. These droughts brought a position of starvation in the places like Bengal and Bihar. This was followed by the strike of the railway workers and the mass movement against the authoritarian rule of Indira Gandhi. The first major agitation against the authoritarian rule of Congress was launched by the students of Gujrat. The students were soon joined by the opposition parties which raised the issues of high price on the basic commodities, corruption in the higher ranks. In Bihar Jaya Praksah Narayan gave a call of Total Revolution. The decision of the Allahabad High Court in June 1975 against Indira Gandhi acted as a fuel to the fire. The verdict put a huge question mark on her Prime minister-ship. Ultimately she found herself placed in a situation where the imposition of Emergency was the only way to keep things under control. Thus the Emergency was imposed on 25 June 1975 for 18 months.

Imposition of Emergency earned considerable criticism because in its grab many atrocities were committed by Indira Gandhi agaist the honest officials and poor masses. All Fundamental Rights were taken away, Press was censored, Strikes were banned, Opposition leaders were imprisoned. The imposition of Emergency was a poor gamble for Indira Gandhi as well as for the Congress as it lost the elections in 1977. The grand coalition of non-congress parties under the banner of Janta Party came to power. The exchange of power between Janta Party and Lok Dal clearly explained the voter consciousness and power of the ballot.

The Janta Party was formed when Jan Sang, Bhartiya Lok Dal, Socialist Party, Congress (O) and Congress rebels joined hands to keep Congress out of power. The Janta Party was a quick-fix coalition of several non-left parties with leaders like Morarji Desia, Jaya Prakash Narayanan etc. Janta Party succeeded in overthrowing the Congress regime in the elections of 1977. After 18 months of National Emergency the government decided to hold elections. All opposition leaders and political activists were released from the jails. As the elections were held in March 1977, the opposition got a very little time to prepare. When the emergency was lifted after 18 months the non-congress parties fought the elections by forming a coalition called as Janta Party. The party's election manifesto declared that the party would strive for the establishment of socialistic society based on democratic and Ghandian values. The party showed its commitment in secularism. In the 1977 elections the Janta Party's victory reflected not simply the consolidation of the opposition vote but a substantial shift away from the Congress.

The Janta Party's victory marked the end of one party dominance at the centre. During 1977-1979 it looked for the first time in India a two party system appeared when two parties the Janta Party and the Congress together accounted for more than 50% of votes and seats. The political system dominated by one person prior to 1977 was replaced by collective leadership of the new party where bargaining once again became a prominant feature of politics. This verdict of 1977 also brought to the forefront a North- South divide in India as in North India Janta Party swept all the seats and in the South Congress came as victorious. The experience of 1977-79 gave new mantra to democratic politics that governments that are seen to be unstable and quarrelsome are severely punished by the voters.

Janta Party was a coalition of various parties with deep ideological differences. The party fought the 1977 election on the slogen of Restoring Democracy and became victorious. But the internal conflicts, ideological differences, and the absence of spirit of compromise led to the break down of Janta Party in 1979. Morarji Desai lost his majority in less than 18 months and a new government headed by Charan Singh was established but that too could not survive for long. Hence the mid term elections were held in 1980 which was won by Congress. Indira Gandhi returned to power with a bang winning 353 seats. The victory of Indira Gandhi is attributed to the solid support extended by the minorities all over the country.

Regionalization of National Politics: The phase from 1980-89 was a developmental phase in various senses. Bhartiya Janta Party was formed and with that roots for a sound opposition. The Bhartiya Janta Party was formally launched as an independent political organization in February 1980. The party adopted four fundamentals i.e. one country, one nation, one culture and a rule of law that would determine its future course of action. The BJP support base is essentially the same as that of the erstwhile Jana Sang. It is a party of the urban educated Hindu middle classes, professionals, small businessmen and white collar workers. In UP, Maharastra, Delhi, Rajasthan BJP remained a dominant political party. BJP won only two seats in 1984 elections but emerged as a powerful party in 1989 elections by winning 88 seats. Naturally the BJP worked hard before as well as after the elections and succeeded in putting together a 24 – party coalition, known since then as national democratic alliance (NDA).

The rise of regional parties has changed the nature of political system in India. They have put an end to the one party dominance and have brought a new system of coalition politics. If we analyze the elections of 1996, 1998, 1999, we observe that no single party was in a position to form the government on its own. This phenomenon led to the increasing role of regional parties and the formation of coalition. For example in 1996 UF Government was formed by 13 parties and NDA Government of 1998 was formed by 24 parties. These trends have nationalized the regional parties and regionalized the national parties. The growing influence of regional parties is ascribed to, what Yogender Sharma has remarked as 'Second Democratic Upsurge'. The increased political consciousness of underprivileged sections and the V. P. Singh's Mandel Card brought a bottom top approach in Indian party system. The Constitutional 73rd and

74th Amendment Acts and the process of Sanaskritisation made a virtual end to the one party dominant system in Indian politics.

There are two categories of regional parties in Indian politics today. First there are old regional parties like the National Conference of Jammu and Kashmir, Shiromani Akali Dal in Punjab, DMK and AIADMK in Tamil Nadu and some tribal regional parties mainly in the North East. The origins of these parties go back to the period between the two world wars. They mostly arose in areas with strong regional identities. Secondly there are a number of new regional parties that came to be formed in the 1980's – e.g, Telego Desam in Andra, Asom Gana Parishad in Asam, Meso National Front in Mizoram and a number of tribal parties mainly in the North East.

Era of Coalitions: The decade of 90s witnessed the rise and fall of many coalitions. The elections of 1989 again put the supremacy of the Congress under an acid test. Congress was short of majority so were the other parties. Under these circumstances a grand coalition was formed by the name of United Front. United Front was led by Janta Dal and supported by the Left parties in West Bengal and Kerala, DMK in Tamil Nadu, National Conference of Jammu and Kashmir, Akalidal in Punjab. The National Front Minority Government was supported up by both Left and the BJP -a strange combination. Yet this unlikely combination materialized due to the common objective to keep the Congress out of power. V.P. Singh decided to implement Mandal Commission which created a lot of disturbance at the national level. But it could keep the power only for 11 months, when it finally broke down due to intense factionalism.

We know that the elections of 1996, 1998, 1999, resulted in hung parliaments and no single party was in a position to form the government on its own. The two main parties Congress and the BJP realized this political reality and formed two grand coalitions under the banner of UPA and NDA. NDA ruled the centre from 1999 to 2004 was defeated by the UPA government led by the Congress. Congress prepared itself for the election by forming alliance. It formed its own alliance with RJD of Lalu Prasad, DMK, JMM etc called as the UPA (United Progressive Alliance). The Congress led UPA won the elections by getting 219 seats and formed the government. The National Common Minimum Programme acts as a roadmap for the Government. This surprising verdict of election 2004 signifies a fundamental change in Indian democracy. In fact, this is the first general election since 1977 that has upset every electoral poll calculation and poll prediction. The Congress won 145 seats which is its highest since 1991 while the BJP won only 138 which is its worst since 1991. It is since 2004 that a bi – nodal system emerged in India i.e. UPA and NDA and among them the national power oscillates.

These umbrella type alliances are playing a seesaw type of power game; when one rules the other remains in opposition. Stating otherwise, when one is up, the other is let down. The BJP was waiting for its turn to get up as it dipped down in 2004 when the situation drifted in favor of Congress. The elections of 2009 put a huge question mark on the speculations made by political analysts and political pundits about the BJP's big show. BJP failed to make any ditch and the blame game within the party started. The saffron brigade started losing its colour, charm, health and even the leadership.

Beginning of a New Era: In the 16th Lok Sabha elections BJP secured a landslide victory by winning 282 seats alone and a total of 335 with its allies. This has happened for the first time in Indian politics that a non-congress party has managed to secure 31 per cent of the vote share. The BJP's massive victory will have a profound impact on the functioning of party politics in India for a long period to come. The era of hung parliaments, instable governments and coalition dramas has virtually ended. Opposition is demoralized as the Congress could manage only 44 seats, an all time low. The BJP's win signifies many things in one go:

i.   The end of Congress system, as Amit Shah, the BJP's National President, stated, "Our historic victory marks the beginning of the end of the Congress era".
ii. The triumph of democracy over dynasty.
iii. Revivalism of Hinduism as a massive political force which may disturb the communal balance in the Indian society.

iv. Indian Federalism will become Cooperative Federalism rather than a Bargaining Federalism.

v. India has reached very close to a Totalitarian system with one man acting as a vanguard of whole nation. The Modianization of India may threaten democracy and establish a dictatorship, a one man's rule.

CHAPTER 10

LOCAL SELF GOVERNMENT IN INDIA

India resides in villages, to develop India we have to develop the villages.

Gandhi

Democracy is about meaningful participation. It is also about accountability. Strong and vibrant local governments ensure both active participation and purposeful accountability. The ethos of democracy can find real nourishment only when power reaches the grass-roots level. This is possible with the establishment of Panchayati raj or local self government institutions. Indian democratic system has three levels of governance- national, state and grass-root level or local level. Local Self Government means government at local level; termed as, first tier of democratic setup, where decisions are to be made at the local level. A local Government is a "Statutory authority" in a specified local area (village or town or city) having the power to raise revenue through taxes for the performance of local services like Civic Amenities i.e. sanitation, education, water supply etc. It is constituted by the elected representatives of the local people and enjoys autonomy from state or central control sufficient to enable it to function and perform its services adequately. Local government operates at the lowest level of society i.e. at the grass-root level close to the people, touching their everyday life. Local self governing institutions, as such, are considered as the cradle of democracy. In India, local self governing bodies comprise the Panchayati Raj and Nagar Palikas system. The panchayats are meant for villages while as Nagar Palikas or Municipalities are meant for towns and cities.

Characteristics of Local Government:

a) **Local Area:** A local government like any other government has to operate in a geographical area – a small or local i.e. Village, town or a city, in contrast to the whole country or state. The population of the area may vary from one area to another. In a village, the population may be just in thousands but in metropolitan cities like Delhi, Kolkata, and Mumbai it may run to several millions.

b) **Statutory Status:** The local government enjoys statutory status i.e. it is created by a specific law or statue. Local governments are created by the law of the legislature and it is from that law it derives all its status and powers.

c) **Autonomous status:** Autonomy of the local government is the natural consequence of their statutory status. The local governments are free and autonomous in exercising their powers and performing their duties. As they are created by the act of legislatures, so their powers and functions are clearly mentioned in the act.

d) **Local Participation:** Participation of the local people in decision – making and administration of the local authority is important that is what gives it the character of self- government. It is called democracy at the grass-root level. In democratic countries, participation of people is ensured by making the local bodies.

e) **Local Accountability:** Since local government provides services like civic amenities to the people of the area, it is appropriate to the local people that it is accountable to them. The control of local people will compel it to serve them better.

f) **Local Finances:** Local governments have two important Sources of finances:

   i) Grants in aid given by central or state government; and
   ii) Taxes and Levies imposed by the local governments themselves.

g) **General purpose body/ multipurpose body:** Local government is a general purpose body. It is multipurpose and performs functions like health care, primary education, sanitation, water supply, regulation of local fairs and markets, maintenance of parks, libraries local transport and so on and so forth.

Importance and Advantage of Local government: Local self governments are essential for vibrant and sound democracy. As we know that democracy demands greater participation of people and local governments encourage people to participate, thus empowering democracy. Jawaharlal Nehru emphasized the importance of local government when he said that, "local self government must be the basis of any true system of democracy. Democracy at the top may not be a success unless you build it on a sound foundation from below". Historically too, the local government preceded national government because governance began with the organization of people into small communities in a limited area cooperating with each other and making self–governing communities. It is vital for national progress. The existence and functioning of local governments at grass-root level has many advantages. That advantage primarily lies in the convenience that citizen has for getting matters settled quickly and at a least cost.

Some important advantages are given as:

1) **Grass-Root democracy:** Local government provides scope for democracy at the grass-root level. If direct democracy can still be practicable, it is only at this level.

2) **Serves as a Training School:** Local government is an excellent ground for creating and training future leaders. The participation

of people at the local level in the management of their own affairs, gives them necessary experience to handle bigger affairs later at the state or national level. Lord Bryce regarded local government as the best school of democracy.

3) Encourages participation of people in public affairs.

4) It is more competent to solve local problems because local problems can be best solved locally. It is necessary in a democracy, tasks which can be performed locally, should be left in the hands of the local people and their representatives. Common people are more familiar with their local government than with the government at the State or central level.

5) Local government is economical.

6) It reduces the burden of the central government.

7) Local government serves as a 2 – way channel of communication between itself and the central government.

Evolution of Local government in India: Local governments have deep roots in Indian soil. It is believed that India possessed local self governments from ancient times. The earliest period in Indian history belongs to Indus Valley Civilization which was essentially urban in character. The people of this civilization had the proud distinction of giving to the world its earliest cities, its first urban civilization, its first town planning, and first drainage system. Vedic Literature has provided some references to an organized system of rural self governmental institutions. Aryans were village people and Vedic state was essentially a country state with "village" as the basic unit of administration. The village government was usually carried on under the supervision of village headman called "Gramani". There are also references of Samiti (Assembly) and Sabha. The Jain and Buddhist literatures give the proof of local self government during 600 B.C to 600 A.D. **Kautilyas** Arthashastra (400 B.C) also provides an exhaustive account of the system of village administration at that time. Village headman was known as Adhyaksha and also villages were self – sufficient. In fact, the institution of village panchayats in one form or the other has had an unbroken continuity almost all over India and throughout her long history.

British Period: With the beginning of the British rule in India came centralization of administration and gradual erosion of surviving local self governing institutions. In course of time, they were replaced by formally constituted institutions of village administration. It is a historical fact that the present structure of the local government is a legacy from British rule in India. But, British did take certain steps to stabilize the local self government in India. It was as early as 1687 that a municipal corporation came to be formed in Madras. It was the first local governing body, although it did not survive for a long time. The Charter Act of 1793 was the first statutory enactment regulating Municipal administration. In 1793, Municipal administration was set-up in three presidencies, Madras, Bombay and Calcutta, and the British Government authorized the Governor General of India to appoint 'Justices of Peace' in these presidencies. These officers were empowered to levy taxes. In 1870 the viceroy, Lord Mayo, passed a resolution for decentralization of power to bring about administrative efficiency in meeting the demands of the people. It was in the wake of this resolution that the first significant step to revive the traditional village Panchayat system in Bengal was taken in 1870 through the Bengal Chokidari Act.

> **Kautilya (370-283 BCE)**
>
> *The real name of Kautilya was Chanakya who managed the first emperor Chandragupta's rise to power at a young age. Originally a scholar of economics and politics, Chanakya played an important role in the establishment of the Maurya Empire. He authored an ancient political treatise 'Arthasastra' meaning economics and as such he is considered as a pioneer of the fields of economics and politics in India.*

However, the real landmark in the emergence of the concept of local self government was "**Lord Ripon's** historical resolution of 1882" in which he enunciated a comprehensive political philosophy involving the transfer of power from the imperial level to the local representatives. He is regarded as the father of local self governments in India and his resolution is considered to be the Magna Carta of local democracy in India. The resolution called upon the provincial governments to establish a network of local boards charged with definite duties and entrusted with definite funds throughout the country.

In 1906, the Congress under the presidentship of **Dadabhai Naoroji,** accepted 'self-government' as the political goal for the country. Then came the Royal Commission on Decentralization in 1907. It suggested a 'three – tier' instead of 'two – tier' pyramid arrangement for rural local governments. The British government's declaration of August 1917 promising 'Responsible Government' through gradual development of self – governing institutions was another landmark in the evolution of local governments in India. After this many important Acts _____ Act of 1919 (Diarchy System of government); Act of 1929 and Act of 1935 (Diarchy replaced by Provincial autonomy) were passed for the creation and strengthening of local self government.

However, it is important to note that there was little success as for as the functioning of these institutions is concerned.

> **Lord Ripon (1827-1909)** was a staunch Liberal Democrat who remained Viceroy of Indian from 1880 to 1884. He is generally regarded as the father of modern local self institutions in India, because it was he who established the Panchayati Raj institutions in a modern sense. Like Lord William Bentinck, Lord Ripon was a champion of education of the Indians. In order to reform Indian Education System he appointed a Commission in 1882, popularly called as Hunter Commission. He resigned from his post on Ilbert Bill controversy, hence helped the cause of Indian nationalism. The Indians by and large hailed him as "Ripon the Good".

Post Independence development in Local Self-Government: The independence of India gave a new impetus to the local government. The popular national and State governments gave a different atmosphere for the functioning of local government. The whole system of local self government was restructured. The development of local self – government in the post – independence period has been neither continuous nor appreciable although as compared with the pre-independence period the development is more rapid, widespread and determined, but it is not uniform. The municipal administration has received much less attention than given to rural local self government. The local government found no mention in the constitution except at two places: one in the chapter on Directive Principles of state policy (DPSP) under Article 40 and two, in the entry 5 in the list II (State List) of seventh schedule of the constitution. The constitution placed local government in the state list of functioning. Article 40 of DPSP says that; State shall take steps to organize village panchayats and endow them to function as units of self government.

Factors which were Responsible for the Growth of PRI's in India:

1) **Influence of Mahatma Gandhi:** Mahatma Gandhi gave a new philosophy of ruralism. He was very much in favour of panchayats so that villages become self – sufficient both economically and politically. He believed that strengthening village panchayats was a means of effective decentralization.

> **Dadabhai Naoroji (1825-1917),** *known as the Grand Old Man of India, was a Parsi intellectual, educator, cotton trader, and an early Indian political and social leader. He is credited with the founding of the Indian National Congress, along with A. O. Hume in 1985. He was a Member of Parliament (MP) in the United Kingdom House of Commons between 1892 and 1895, and the first Asian to be a British MP. He gave his famous theory of Drain of Wealth in his book "Poverty and Un-British Rule in India".*

2) The Article 40 of the DPSP reflects the Indian influence and gives importance to Panchayats.
3) The five year plans emphasized the important role which the local governments could play in securing the participation of people in this process.

4) Community Development Movement which was inaugurated in 1952 laid special emphasis on the development of local community as distinguished from the development of country as a whole.

Planning Commission in 1950 appointed a Team for the study of community Projects and National Extension Service (NES). Thereafter, Central Government appointed a number of commissions and committees from time to time, on the subject of rural and urban local governments. Important are:

Balwant Rai Mehta Committee (1957)

Ashok Mehta Committee on PRI'S (1978).

G.V.K. Rao Committee to review the existing administrative arrangements for rural development and Poverty Alleviation Programmes (1985).

The P.K. Thungun Committee in 1989 recommended constitutional status for the local government bodies. A constitutional amendment to provide for periodic elections to local government institutions, and enlistment of appropriate functions to them, along with funds, was recommended.

Balwant Rai Mehta Committee: In January, 1957, the government of India appointed a Committee to examine the working of Community Developmental Programme (1952) and National Extension Service (1953) and to suggest measures for their better working. The chairman of the committee was Balwant Rai Mehta and it submitted its report in November 1957 and recommended the establishment of the scheme of "Democratic Decentralization" which ultimately, came to be known as 'Panchayat Raj'. The Committee was appointed to enquire into, among other things, the lack of initiative, apathy and indifference on the part of the rural population in developmental and administrative tasks. Balwant Rai Mehta Committee is very important as for as the establishment of local self government in Indian is concerned. In fact, Panchayat Raj Institutions have been setup in India as a result of the recommendations of this committee.

Main Recommendations of Balwant Rai Mehta Committee

1) It recommended for the establishment of three tier system of decentralization or Panchayat Raj System namely, 'Gram Panchayat/ Gram Sabha' at the village level (village Panchayat); The Panchayat Samiti at block level and the Zilla Parishad at the district level.

2) The village Panchayat was to be constituted by direct election on the basis of adult franchise with a special provision to co- opt two women members and one member each from Schedule Caste (SC) and Schedule Tribes (ST). The Panchayat was to have specific items of revenue like a share in land revenue and certain obligatory duties like acting as the agent of the Panchayat Samiti for executing schemes.

3) Indirect election for Zilla Parishad and Panchayat Samiti members. The Panchayat Samiti was to be indirectly elected by the village Panchayats, some representation being given also to municipalities and cooperative organizations in the Block area. The Zilla Parishad consisting of the Presidents of the Panchayat Samities, members of state legislatures and the Parliament and all district level officers of the developmental departments as members and with the District Collector as the Chairman.

4) All planning and developmental activities should be given to these bodies.

5) Adequate resources (financial) should be given to these local bodies.

These recommendations were accepted by National Developmental Council on 12th January 1958, and by the Union government, and State governments as well. The important recommendation was the genuine transfer of powers to the people. Rajasthan was the first state to introduce Panchayat Raj system in 1959, followed by Andhra Pradesh in the same year. The Punjab in 1961 and then other states also followed. In some areas these bodies were strong while as at other places they couldn't function due to various reasons. In 1962 the country's attention was diverted towards 'Chinese war' and the defense budgets increased with the result the community development programme suffered for want of funds. Later during Indira Gandhi's time, a considerable decline occurred in the powers of Panchayati Raj institutions because she believed in centralization of power rather than in decentralization. However, it would be of interest to note that throughout the period 1950 – 1964, the government headed by Nehru was all along keenly interested in the decentralization of governmental authority and in the establishment of village panchayats.

Ashok Mehta Committee: In 1977, Janata Party came into power which revived the local self government in December 1977. Janata Party appointed a high level committee on Panchayat Raj Institutions under the chairmanship of Ashok Mehta. It submitted its report in August 1978 and made 132 recommendations to serve and strengthen the declining Panchayat Raj system in the country. Following were the main recommendations of the Committee:

1. Establishment of a two- tier Panchayat Raj system instead of three-tier system which Zilla Parishad at the district level and below it, the Mandal Panchayat at local level consisting of a group of villages (with population of 15,000 to 20,000). It stressed for direct election for both these tiers, which should be conducted by Chief Election Officer of the state under directions of Chief Election Commissioner.
2. There should be an official participation of political parties at all levels of Panchayat system.
3. A district should be the first point for decentralization under popular supervision below the state level.
4. The PRI's should have compulsory powers of taxation to generate their own financial resources.
5. Zilla Parishad should be the executive body and made responsible for planning at district level.
6. Developmental functions should be transferred to Zilla Parishad.
7. Seats for SC and ST should be reserved on the basis of their population.

8. State governments shouldn't supersede the Panchayat Raj Institutions. In case of supersession, elections should be held within 6 months from the date of supersession.
9. Voluntary organizations must play important role in mobilizing people in favour of Panchayat Raj.

But due to the collapse of the Janata Government before the completion of its term, no action was taken on the recommendations of Ashok Mehta Committee as the Indira's Congress was not interested. The decline of Panchayat Raj Institutions had started from mid sixties. In many states a tendency to postpone the Panchayati elections indefinitely was noticeable. In some states, parallel bodies came to be set – up at the district level, thus reducing the role of Panchayat Raj in development planning and implementation. Some major problems and short comings in the working of Panchayat Raj Institutions can be identified as:

1. Elections not being held on a regular basis.
2. Lack of adequate transfer of powers and resources to Panchayati Institutions.
3. Lack of Panchayati Raj bodies to generate their own resources such as tax on sale of land.
4. Non–representation of women and weaker sections in the elected bodies.

During 1980's in the 6th and 7th five year plans, it was proposed to strengthen democratic decentralization. In 1985 the Planning Commission appointed a 12 member committee under the Chairmanship of G.V.K. Rao, to review the existing administrative arrangements for rural development and poverty alleviation programmes (CAARD). It strongly recommended the revival of Panchayat Raj Institutions all over the country and highlighted the need to transfer power of state to democratic bodies at the local level. It also stressed for regular elections for Panchayats and their strengthening by increased people's participation.

In June, 1986 **Rajiv Gandhi** appointed another committee on Revitalization of Panchayat Raj institutions for democracy and development under an eminent jurist L. M. Singhavi. It suggested that Panchayat Raj institutions should be constitutionally recognized, protected and preserved. It also suggested a constitutional provision to ensure regular, free and fair elections for Panchayati raj institutions.

It may be recalled here that the Asoka Mehta committee made the first official recommendation for including Panchayati raj in the Constitution in keeping with its approach that panchayats should be regarded as a political rather than mere developmental institutions. This committee also favoured participation of political parties in Panchayat elections with their symbols.

Rajiv Gandhi

Rajiv Ratna Gandhi(1944-1991) was the seventh Prime Minister of India, serving from 1984 to 1989. He took office after the assassination of his mother Indira Gandhi in 1984. He became the youngest Prime Minister of India. In 1968 he married Maino, an Italian lady, who changed her name to Sonia Gandhi. In 1991 he was assassinated by a suicide bomber from the LTTE. Rajiv Gandhi was posthumously awarded the highest civilian award by the government of India, Bharat Ratna in 1991.

Accepting these recommendations of the committees the central government headed by Rajiv Gandhi brought in the constitutional 64th amendment bill which was passed by the Lok Sabha in 16th August 1989. Unfortunately, this bill could not be enacted as it was not approved by the Rajya Sabha. Then, the National Front Government soon after assuming office in November 1989, under the Prime Ministership of V.P. Singh, announced that it would take steps to strengthen Panchayat Raj Institutions. Thus, in September 1990, a bill was introduced but lapsed because of fall of the government. The Congress under the Narashima Rao once again took up the matter of Panchayat Raj Institutions. It introduced the two constitutional amendment bills, 73rd and 74th, for Panchayat Raj Institutions for local as well as for Municipalities (urban bodies) respectively. These were introduced in Lok Sabha in September 1991 and passed in December 1992.

73rd Amendment Act of 1992

The constitutional base for Panchayat Raj was required because state governments were not enthusiastic about the creation of Panchayat Raj bodies and to share power with them in their states. Under the Indian constitution, local self-government and Panchayat Raj is a state subject and the central government can't pass any legislation unless the constitution is amended. Hence 73rd Constitutional Amendment Act, 1993 became a necessity. Once passed the 73rd Amendment was approved by 17 State Assemblies and received the Presidential assent on 20th April 1993. Thus it emerged as the 73rd Constitutional Amendment Act 1992, and it came to force on 24th April 1993 which is a red – letter day in the history of Panchayati raj in India. This Act has added **Part IX** to the constitution of India entitled as 'The Panchayats' and consists of provisions from the Article 243 to 243(A-O). In

Part IX The Panchayats

Act 243 ___ Definition

243 A _____ Gram Sabha Powers & functions

243 B ___ Constitution of Panchayats

243 C___ Composition

243 D___ Reservation of seats

243 E ___Duration of Panchayats etc.

243 F__ Disqualification of membership

243 G ___ Poor, Authority & responsibility of Panchayats 243 H ___ Poor to improve taxes by a Funds of the Panchayats.

243 I ___ Constitution of Finance Commission.

243 J ___ Audit of Accounts of Ps.

243 K ___ Elections to Panchayats.

243 L _____ Application to UTS.

243 M ___ Part not to apply to certain areas.

243 N _____ Continuance of existing laws and policies.

243 O _____ Bar to interference by courts in election.

(11th Schedule)

11th Schedule (29 subject)

Agriculture, Land Reforms, Animal Husbandry, Irrigation, Fisheries, Social Forestry, Social Welfare

Health, Sanitation, Drinking water, fuel and fodder, roads, culverts, bridges, ferries, waterways and means of communication, rural electrification, education including primary and secondary education, libraries, cultural activities, maintenance of community assets etc.

addition the Act has added **11th schedule** to the constitution. It contains 29 functional items of the panchayats.

Salient Features of 73rd Amendment Act, 1992:

1. It provided for the establishment of 3 – tier system of Panchayati raj for all states having population of over 20 lakh. The structure was to be; panchayats at the village level, intermediate level and district level. 'Gram Sabha' was to be the foundation of the Panchayat Raj. It consists of all the voters in the Panchayat area (village).

2. The members of all these panchayats will be directly elected by the people.

3. The term of each Panchayat would be 5 years and elections will be held regularly after every 5 years under the supervision, direction and control of state.

4. The act also provides for the reservation of seats for schedule castes, and Schedule Tribes in proportion to their population, at all three levels and also reservation of seats (1/3rd) for women at all levels (not less than 33%).

5. To appoint State Finance Commission to make recommendations as regards the financial powers of the panchayats (by the Governor of the state after every 5 years).

6. To constitute District Planning Committee to prepare draft development plan for the district as a whole.

Panchayats were given the following powers and authority to function as institutions of self – government:

i. Preparation of plans for economic development and social justice.

ii. Implementation of Schemes for economic development and social justice in relation to 29 subjects given in the 11th schedule of the constitution under Article 243G. To levy, collect and appropriate taxes, duties, tolls and fees. Thus, this Act has given a new shape to PRIs. It has also protected the autonomy of the states as for as elections to them have been left to state Election Commission and Funds are allocated by states but at the same time it has given wide range and real powers to panchayats.

Panchayati Raj Structure and Functions:

Part IX of the Indian constitution envisages a three- tier system of panchayats, namely:

a. Panchayats at the village level;
b. The intermediate Panchayat placed between the village and district panchayats in states where the population was above 20 lakh; and
c. The district Panchayat at the district level.

Village Level: There are two institutions at the village level which are considered as the basic units of the Panchayati raj system. They are Gram Sabha and Gram Panchayat.

Gram Sabha: The Gram Sabha is the lowest ladder of the Panchayat Raj. It consists of all the eligible voters in the village or a group of villages in which the gram Panchayat has jurisdiction. It usually meets thrice a year. It performs the following functions:

a. To approve the administrative report of the Gram Panchayat;
b. To approve the annual budget and the accounts and audit report of the preceding year;
c. To approve the development programmes, like community service, projects to be undertaken during the year.
d. To elect members of the Gram Panchayat.

Gram Panchayat: Gram Panchayat is the first executive tier of the Panchayati raj system. The members of Gram Panchayat are elected for a period of five years by the Gram Sabha on secret ballot basis. They are called Panches while the President is called Sarpanch. A Gram Panchayat has jurisdiction over a village or group of villages. The functions of the Gram Panchayat are broadly divided into civic, administrative, law and order, commercial, welfare and development.

Civic functions are the obligatory functions of the Panchayat which include sanitation, maintenance of roads, bridges, drainage, wells and tanks providing water for domestic use and supervision of street lights.

Administrative functions include maintenance of budget and accounts, collection and maintenance of records and statistics, registration of both death and, marriages, maintenance of records of village cattle and land management. Law and order functions include watch-and- ward service.

Commercial activities include supervision of community orchards, fisheries, and Panchayat enterprises. Welfare functions include providing aid to handicapped, relief to flood and famine victims, welfare programmes for women, youth, children and backward classes, maintenance of Panchayat schools, libraries and reading rooms and holding of village fairs.

Development functions include promotion of cottage industries, small scale industries and cooperatives, preparation and execution of the village agricultural and irrigational plans.

The sources of income for Gram Panchayats are:

1. Income from taxation on property, profession, animals, vehicles, electricity, water etc.
2. Grants-in- aid from state government; and
3. Public contribution and voluntary donation.

Intermediate Level: The intermediate level of Panchayati system consists of Panchayati Samiti which functions at the Block level. It consists of the Sarpanches of the panchayats within its jurisdiction or of members elected indirectly by the Panches, or of directly elected members. Schedule Casts, Schedule Tribes, Other Backward Classes and women are given representation through reservations. The general body of Panchayat Samiti meets once in three months.

The functions of the Samiti can be divided into:

a. delegated; b. community development; c. supervisory.

The delegated functions include the implementation and coordination of the policy directives of the state government in respect to development programmes.

Community development functions relate to social welfare programmes regarding agriculture, fishers, small scale industries and health.

Supervisory functions inciude supervising the Gram Panchayats, Block Development Officers and Vikas Adhikaris. The main sources of income include: grants-in-aid given by the state government; and part of taxation from land revenue.

The Panchayat Samitis function mainly through standing committees. These committees look after finances, welfare and development work. The Block Development Officer (BDO) acts as the chief executive officer of the Block Samiti.

District Level: At the district level is the Zilla Perished which is the highest tier in the system. The Zilla Perished has: a. presidents of Panchayat Samities as ex-offiico members; b. MLA's, MLC's and MP's of the area as associated members; c. representatives of women, SC's, ST's and OBC's as co-opted members; and d. representatives of cooperative societies in the area as ex-officio members.

The chairman and vice-chairman of the Zilla Perished are elected by the presidents of Panchayat Samities in the district. The members have a three to five year term of office. The Perished meets every three months.

The functions of the Zilla Perished are of advisory, financial, supervisory, co-coordinative, developmental, and civic and welfare nature.

The Zilla Perished advises the government in matters relating to developmental activities in the district and in the matters of implementation assigned to Zilla Perished by the government. It approves the budget of Panchayati Samities and distributes the funds allotted among the Panchayat Samities.

It supervises the functions of Panchayat Samities and Gram Panchayats;

It coordinates the developmental plans and projects in the Blocks and looks after the development work in the district;

It looks after the construction of roads, bridges, parks, water supply etc.

74th Constitutional Amendment Act (Urban Local Self Government):

Prime Minister Rajiv Gandhi showed his sincerity in providing constitutional status to the urban local bodies, and his government introduced 65th constitutional amendment bill in the Parliament in 1989, but it was rejected by Rajya Sabha. Then, 74th constitutional amendment bill was introduced by **P.V. Narasimah Rao** in September 1991, which was passed by both the houses of the Parliament in December 1992 as the Constitutional 74th Amendment Bill. It received approval of more than half of the states in 1993 and came into force on 1 June 1993. This amendment introduces a new **part IX – A** in the constitution relating to "Municipalities". It contains provisions from Article 243-P to Article 243 –ZG. In addition, the act has also added **12th schedule** to the constitution which contains 18 functional items of municipalities and deals with Article 243 W. The new laws under the constitution

P.V. Narasimah Rao (1921-2004). *Pamulaparti Venkata Narasimha Rao was an Indian lawyer and politician who served as the tenth Prime Minister of India. He was the first Prime Minister from non-Hindi speaking south India. Under his Primeministership India adopted a new model of economy called as Liberalization, Privatization and Globalization (LPG) model. Rao's term also saw the destruction of Babri Masjid in Ayodhya in Uttar Pradesh which triggered one of the worst Hindu-Muslim riots in India since 1947.*

have made municipal elections mandatory every five years. Some main features of the Act are as follows:

i) The Act provides for the constitution of three types of municipalities in every state.

    a. A Nagar Panchayat for a transitional area (an area in transition from rural to Urban);

    b. A Municipal Council for a smaller urban area;

    c. A Municipal Corporation for a larger urban area;

ii) Devolution of more and more functions and taxation powers;

iii) Revenue sharing with state government funds;

iv) Regular conduct of elections and direct elections of members;

v) Reservation of seats for SCs', STs', and for women;

vi) Restriction on the formation of townships only to industrial areas where the entire municipal services are provided or proposed to be provided by the industry;

vii) Formation of District Planning and metropolitan Planning Committee. Etc.

viii) It also provides for constitution of ward Committees, consisting of one or more wards, within the territorial area of a Municipality having a population of 3 Lakh or more. The essence of this provision is to bring about proximity between the people and local governments so that these committees could play an effective role at the Mohalla level in the delivery of municipal services.

12th Schedule (Article 243W)

i. Urban Planning including town planning,
ii. Regulation of land use and construction of buildings;
iii. Planning for economic and social development;
iv. Roads and bridges;
v. Water supply for domestic, industrial and commercial purposes;
vi. Public health, sanitation conservancy and solid waste management;
vii. Fire services;
viii. Urban forestry, protection of environment and promotion of ecological aspects;
ix. Safeguarding the interests of weaker sections of society, including the handicapped and mentally retarded;
x. Slum improvement and up gradation;
xi. Urban poverty alleviation;
xii. Provision for urban amenities and facilities such as parks, gardens and playgrounds;
xiii. Promotion of cultural, educational and aesthetic aspects;
xiv. Burials and burial grounds, cremations, cremation grounds and electric crematoriums;
xv. Cattle pounds, prevention of cruelty to animals;
xvi. Vital statistics including registration of births and deaths;
xvii. Public amenities like street lighting, parking lots, bus stops and public conveniences;
xviii. Regulation of slaughter houses and tanneries

Nagar Palikas System: The local representative bodies in towns and cities are called Municipalities. Part IX A of the constitution gives three types of institutions of local self government for the urban areas. They are:

1. Nagar Panchayat, for a transitional area, i.e. an area which is being transformed from a rural area to an urban area;
2. Municipal Council for a smaller urban area;
3. Municipal Corporation for a larger urban area.

Nagar Panchayat: A Nagar Panchayat consists of three categories of members: (1) Elected members- they are elected from single- member wards by the registered voters who are above the age of 18 years. The panchayats are divided into as many wards as is the number of members to be elected. (2) Nominated members- the State government may nominate one or two members to the Nagar Panchayat from amongst the persons who have special knowledge or experience in municipal administration. (3) Ex-officio members like MPs, MLAs or MLCs who represent the constituency comprising the Nagar Panchayat.

The Nagar Panchayats perform various functions like water supply, drainage, street lighting, sanitation, primary education, management of fairs etc.

Municipal Council: It is established for a smaller urban area. But what is a smaller urban area has to be decided by the State Government, thus the size of Municipal Councils varies from state to state. It may be noted that in an industrial area Municipal Councils may not be established. The membership of the Municipal Council is almost same as that of the Municipal Panchayat.

The Council functions through its committees. The number of such committees varies from State to State. The most important committee is Wards Committee. Wards Committee is mandatory for one or more wards comprised within the territorial area of municipality having a population of three lakh or more. The Council performs the functions mentioned in the 12th Schedule of the Constitution.

Municipal Corporation: These are the top most urban local government bodies set up in big cities which are described as 'larger urban areas' in 74th Constitutional Amendment. Its members are called Councilors, and they are elected by the people on the basis of adult franchise, usually for a period of five years. Seats are reserved for SCs, STs, OBCs and women.

The Corporation is headed by a Mayor who is elected by the members of Corporation. However, the chief executive officer of the Corporation is the Municipal Commissioner, who is appointed by the State Government.

The Corporations performs the same functions as are mentioned in the 12th Schedule of the Constitution.

RURAL LOCAL GOVERNMENT IN JAMMU AND KASHMIR

As we have seen that Panchayati Raj system has a long history in India, but in the State of Jammu and Kashmir it was only in 1935 when the first Village Panchayat Regulation Act No. 1 was promulgated by the then Maharaja Hari Singh. This Act was limited in its objectives and elitist in nature. The Preamble of the regulation had stated that, "it was expedient to establish in Jammu and Kashmir Village Panchayats to assist in the administration of civil and criminal justice and also to manage sanitation and other common concerns of village". Under this resolution, 5 – 7 panches constituted a Panchayat; one among them was "Panchayat Officer or Wazir-e-Wazarat". A cluster of villages constituted Panchayat and Panchayats were assigned the usual civic functions and some judicial responsibilities.

The 1935 regulation was amended in 1941 to widen the list of functions. In 1947, the State Government launched an ambitious programme of rural reconstruction. The State leadership's political commitment to democratic decentralization and social justice had been outlined in the National Conference's policy document "Naya Kashmir" released in earlier 1944. National Conference had called for the constitution of all institutions of democracy, from panchayats to the National Assembly, through election. The reforms, 'Land to the Tiller' were carried soon after independence. They created a sound basis for development of panchayats at the grass-roots.

In 1951, by an Act, the Panchayat Raj Institutions were adopted to be re-established and various features of their activities and allied objectives defined. This Act further provided for "Adult Franchise" for the election of Panchayat members. Based on the directional thrust of the Balwant Roy Mehta Committee, the Jammu and Kashmir Government enacted "Village Panchayat Act in 1958" replacing 1951 Act. The Act of 1958 laid stress on revenue resources through taxes without any commitment on the part of the Government in this behalf.

The Panchayats in the state continued to remain dormant even after the Indira Gandhi – Sheikh Abdullah Accord of 1975. The popular government in 1976 introduced the 'Single Line Administration' with the objective of securing a mechanism for development at district level. In spite of these measures, the Panchayats could not work efficiently. In order to review the democratic process at the grass-roots level, the 1958 Act was replaced by the Jammu and Kashmir Panchayat Raj Act 1989. The Act was described as a radical step as it aimed at promoting and developing the Panchayati Raj system in the State as an instrument of vigorous local self government.

The act provides for a 3 – tier Panchayat Raj System. These tiers were the 'Halqa Panchayat', the 'Block Development Council', and the 'District Planning and Development Board'. It also provided for the establishment of the 'Panchayat Adalats' and to secure the full involvement of people, through direct elections of panches and sarpanches and chair persons of the bodies at the block level.

Halqa Panchayat: It is the village level unit in 3 – tier structure of Panchayat Raj system. The Act gives a wide range of powers to the Halqa Panchayat, which is the soul of the system. It is the centre around which the planning, developmental and political activities of people at the grass-root level would revolve. Every Halqa Panchayat would have 7 to 11 panches and a Sarpanch. (An amendment to the 1989 Act regarding reservation for women was made by the state legislature in April 1997).

Functions of Halqa Panchayat ranged from development of agriculture, social forestry, and marketing of agricultural produce to regulation of fairs and festivals and sanitation, preparation and implementation of poverty alleviation and employment generation schemes, and implementation of the scheme of universalisation of elementary education etc.

Every halqa Panchayat was to have a fund called 'Halqa Panchayat Fund', which will be raised from the grants of the government loans granted by financial institutions or other such agencies, taxes and levies etc.

Block Developmental Council (BDC):

It consists of all the Sarpanches in the Block and all the chairpersons of the marketing societies within its jurisdiction. The chairperson of the BDC would be elected by all the Sarpanches and Panches of that Block. The Block Development Officer (BDO) would act as Secretary to BDC, whose term was five years.

Functions of BDC:

i)   Construction, maintenance and supervision of inter – Halqa Panchayat Communication system.

ii) Administrative and the technical guidance to Halqa Panchayats and review of their work.

iii) Supervision and monitoring of various developmental programmes undertaken by Halqa panchayats.

The remarkable feature of the council is the direct election of the Chairman, and exclusion of members of legislature and the Parliament from holding any office in it.

District Planning and Development Board (DPDB): All the Block Chairpersons would together constitute the DPDB which would also have MPs, MLAs, and MLCs and Chairpersons of Municipalities/ notified area committee as members. Its Chairperson is nominated by the State Government from amongst members. The Deputy Commissioner (DC) of the district would be the Chief executive officer (CEO) of DPDB. The DPDB would be the highest authority in the power structure of the Panchayat Raj system. It was to consider and guide the formulation of developmental programmes for the district and indicate priorities for various schemes and consider issues relating to the speedy development and economic upliftment of the district. The Board shall formulate and finalize the plan and non plan budget, lay down the policy guidelines for the BDC and Halqa Panchayats, Supervise and coordinate poverty alleviation and employment generation programmes etc.

Urban Local Self Government in Jammu and Kashmir:

The state of Jammu and Kashmir witnessed government at the local level in urban areas when in the year 1886 two municipalities were established, one for Jammu and one for Kashmir, under 'Jammu and Kashmir Municipal Act No. 16 of 1886.' The number of such local self governing bodies has now gone to 71 which include 6 Municipal Councils and 63 Municipal Committees in the state.

Local self government has a vital importance in the matters of development, upliftment of weaker sections like slum improvement, providing better health, hygienic and civic amenities in local areas. As per the statistics of 2011, the urban population of Jammu And Kashmir state constitutes 33% of total population. Therefore, local self governance has a vast coverage area. Almost all the important cities, towns and tourist attraction places come under the control of local self governance.

The department of urban local bodies has a great role and significance and importance in comparison to other departments of the state, in view of having responsibility to deal with the urban areas. The 74th Amendment Act to the constitution of India opened new vistas to the widening domain as functions of the local self government institutions. The Jammu and Kashmir legislature passed a legislation known as Jammu and Kashmir Municipal Corporation Act 2000 incorporating all the functions and duties enshrined in the 74th Amendment Act.

The Municipal sector envisages classification of the following three:

a) A Municipal Committee for a small town.
b) A Municipal Council for a medium town and
c) A Municipal Corporation for the capital cities.

Any Municipality is eligible to be declared as a corporation provided the population thereof exceeds 4 lakh. In the case of Municipal Councils and Committees no population criteria has been fixed. At present there are 3 Municipal councils in the Kashmir division___ Anantnag, Baramullah and Sopore and 31 Municipal committees of Kashmir (34 including Leh and Kargil) and 415 wards.

Functioning: As per the Act 2000, Municipal Councils/ Committees perform following functions:

i.   Preparation of plans for economic development and social justice.
ii. Performance of functions and implementation of the schemes, which may be entrusted to them.
iii. Urban planning including town planning.
iv. Regulation of land, use and construction of buildings.
v.   Public health; Sanitation, Environmental protection, Slum improvement and upgrade, promotion of Education, culture etc.
vi. Provision of urban amenities and facilities like parks, playgrounds and genders.
vii. Safeguarding the interests of weaker section of society.
viii. Urban poverty alleviation.
ix. Registration of birth and deaths, Burials and burial grounds, Cremation and Cremation grounds.
x.   Regulation of Slaughter houses, Street lightening and Bus Stops etc.

Urban committees ensure better municipal administration in cities. The procedure for the constitution of the municipalities in the state of Jammu and Kashmir has been given in Jammu and Kashmir Municipal Act Samvat 2008.

Four types of local urban bodies constituted in the state of Jammu and Kashmir:

1) Municipalities (3) ____ Jammu, Srinagar and Poonch.
2) Town Area Committees (5) ____ Kautha and Udampur in Jammu and Anantnag, Baramullah and Sopore in Kashmir.
3) Notified Area Committees (46).
4) Cantonment Boards (2) ____ Satwari (Jammu) and Badami Bagh (Srinagar) respectively.

The Panchayat elections in the state of Jammu and Kashmir were held once from 1978 to 2011- by Farooq Abdullah's government in 2001-02. With poor voter turnout and less than 30 per cent of members getting elected in the Valley- in contrast to Jammu and Ladakh- the Mufti Syeed government scrapped it summarily by way of legislation next year. It was in 2011 the Panchayat elections were again held in the state after a gap of 32 years. A total number of 33,540 panchs and sarpanchs were elected with a record number of 80 per cent voter turnout. Omar Abdullah, the Chief Minister of Jammu and Kashmir, signaled a massive expenditure through the newly elected Panchayat Raj institutions. In June 2012, the Chief Minister announced to spend 1000 crore through the Panchayat institutions that year. Ali Mohammad Sagar, the Rural Development Minister told that the government spend Rs 775 crore on Mahatma Gandhi National Rural Employment Guarantee Act (MNREGA) alone in 2011 and for 2012 the government has a set target of Rs 1500 crore which will be spent through Panchayat Raj institutions. The panchayats have really changed the face of development_ from bottom to top rather than from top to bottom.

The municipal election in the state in general and in Kashmir Valley in particular was a sort of challenge before the authorities. The gap of 25 years for municipal election and the political environment of the Valley had driven the grass-root democracy to such a situation where real spirit of civic government was forgotten. In the year 2004 – 2005, when these elections were ordered, nobody hoped for such an enthusiasm of people for participation in municipal elections.

The employees of local body institutions accepted the challenge for completion of the democratic process and the process was completed in March 2005 and Committees were constituted. By participation of general public in election process, it is being observed that the democratic setup has helped a lot in taking care of local problems and other developmental activities.

Pledging to empower local self-government institutions, Omar Abdullah said in May 2011 that his government will hold elections to municipal bodies after Panchayat polls are over. Omar Abdullah said, "I want to transform that power from the Secretariat to the people at lower levels and my endeavour is to achieve this goal during the current financial year."However, these elections were not conducted and remained an unfulfilled dream.

Decentralization of powers is a pre – requisite of a democratic country. Local self government implies the decentralization of powers so that the elected bodies may function independently with authority and resources to bring about economic development and social justice. The real test of the decentralization lies in its contribution towards people's empowerment by way of providing them a significant role in decision making and in the entire process of governance. Experience shows that in India, the institutions of local self government are operating among a number of pulls and challenges. Even though the 73rd and 74th Constitutional Acts brought historical power to the grass-root bodies recognizing them as the third-tier of government and creating a channel for effective decentralization, still there is a huge gap among the Indian states in realizing the real essence of governance and decentralization.

Among the various problems faced, the important one is the excessive state control over the bodies and reluctance of the states (in varying degrees) to grant functional, and more particularly financial powers to the directly elected representatives in the Panchayat Institutions.

The local MPs and MLAs consider the new emerging leadership in the Panchayats and Nagar Palikas as their rivals in the power structure who threaten to take away their share of the cake.

Decentralization of power has also brought decentralization of corruption. Some elected representatives- sarpanchs or panchs- are unfortunately acting like dictators in their own villages promoting nepotism by favouring their own kiths and kins. Lack of awareness in implanting the system, the bureaucratic delay, political interference, social pressures have made the Panchayati Raj to look like a Sarpanch Raj rather than Panchayat Raj.

The state government often delays Panchayat elections on purely political considerations because the states retain some power relating to the conduct of elections under the state acts. The State Election Commissions have to depend upon the state governments for logistic support that includes staff and other machinery. It must be agreed that 73rd and 74th amendments have the potential of bringing about revolutionary changes in the political power, structure and the system of governance.

CHAPTER 11

CHALLENGES TO INDIAN DEMOCRACY

India is a multi-national nation, a diversified one; having deep chasms (both political, Social and cultural) and wide fault lines. It is a nation with thousands of years of history but yet unable to cultivate a single national identity. We can simply say we are an ancient people learning to live in a recent nation. It is in the name of this so called national identity that people are persuaded to vote for it, to go for kill and to be killed. National identity for India would be a formidable challenge for the wise and the visionary. The venerable words of the Preamble attracted every curious eye and noble soul. It is this venerability of the Preamble that has made it front page of Earnest Barker's '*Principles of Social and Political Theory 1967*'. But it is unfortunate to look about the things turning upside down. The unity of India, the integrity of its democratic, secular institutions, and the commitment and the capability of its Central and State governments to do well by the country's billion-plus, have come under intense pressure from various phenomena.

Religious Extremism:

Communalism is a powerful force in India. The challenges of casteism, communalism and religious fundamentalism involving separatism in India are the major threats to Indian state. They weaken the working and stability of the democratic state of India and militate against the basic principles governing national life and providing means to its new identity. 'Casteism' and 'Communalism' are tearing apart the rich and closely-knit fabric of Indian cultural pluralism. In India eight major religious communities co-exist, namely the Hindus (82%), Muslims (12.12%), Christians (2.6%), Sikhs (2%), Buddhists (0.7%), Janis (0.4%), Parses (0.3%) and Jews (0.1%). Quite often communalism is wrongly used as a synonym for religion or simply for a sense of belonging to a community. A communalist is basically interested in using and exploiting religion and that too for political, electoral and economic gains. Communalism is exploitation of religion, sometimes open and sometimes subtle.

Communalism, especially the majority communalism in India is on rise and it has challenged not only the democratic credentials of Indian polity but is a great threat to the unity and integrity of the nation. Communalism is not a phenomenon confined to any one community; the followers of all religious denominations have been susceptible to its influence. Yet, the organizational advance, social reach, political clout and ideological influence that Hindu Communalism achieved during this period were so extensive that it could succeed in bringing the government under its control. The communal violence of the twenty- first century is qualitatively different from the communal incidents of the 20th century. If the 20th century conflicts were mostly spontaneous, the recent events are meticulously and systematically organized. What happened in Gujarat in 2002 and in Orissa in 2007 are glaring examples. In both cases they were not riots or conflicts between the members of two communities but were practically genocides.

In the name of Ram the foundations of India's secularism heritage shook on December 6, 1992, when the Hindutva hordes tore down the domes of the Babri Masjid. The barbaric event, officially acknowledged now as a conspirational venture by the Sang Parivar and its party with a difference, ensured that L. K. Advani's epical rath run with modern technology reached its logical end- the corridors of power in New Delhi. The facts reveal that BJP reached its zenith of popularity from 1989 (11.5

% votes) to 25-59 % in 1998, thanks to Gujarat carnage, Babri Masjid demolition, Rath Yatra and Mumbai Riots etc. To this and other such episodes, the then worthy PM made a frontal attack, a brave one by a weak PM – That when I look at the record of Advani, all I can discover is the prominent role he played in the destruction of Babri Masjid, what else has he done as a politician for national welfare? He further said, we know for example that when he was the Home Minister the attack on the Parliament took place, he was the Home Minister who took over the massacre that took place in Gujarat".

The recent episode in the national politics has put huge question marks on the secularization of Indian democracy. Democracy was shaken when the whole India watched and listened Varun Gandhi saying, 'this is not the hand (of the Congress), this is the hand of Lotus. It will cut the throats of Muslims after the elections". Varun Gandhi is a novice but even a consummate politician like Atal Bihari Vajpayee could occasionally trip up. In a venomous speech at a BJP meeting in Goa in April 2002, shortly after the anti-Muslim violence, which shook Gujarat that year started, Mr. Vajpayee who was Prime Minister at that time, declared, "Where ever Muslims live, they do not like to live in co-existence with others, they do not like to mingle with others; and instead of propagating their ideas in a peaceful manner, they want to spread their faith by resorting to terror and threats."

The story does not end here, from Mumbai to Gujarat, Orisa to Karnataka, Jammu and Kashmir to Punjab we have a long list of state sponsored massacres and communal riots. The majority terrorism is on rise. On a National Integration Council meeting, the CPIM's intervention stated: "Police investigations in the past few years have noted the involvement of Bajrang Dal or other RSS organizations in various bomb blasts across the country- in 2003, in Parbani, Jalna and Jalgaon districts of Maharashtra; in 2005, in Mau district of Utter Pradash; in 2006, in Nanded; 2007, blast in Samjhauta Express, in September 29, 2008, blasts in Malegaon etc. are the incidents of militant communalism. The Sacher Committee Report has shaped the community consciousness among Muslims and they feel alienated from the mainstream. Their demands for development are looked suspiciously by the right wing political parties. This can have a profound effect on the political situation in India. At the BJP's National Executive Meeting in Lukhnow on January 2007, Rajnath Singh (then BJP President) asked the people to give the BJP 10 years in power and they will, by 2016 do away with the policy of appeasement of Muslims forever.

What is alarming is the show case put forward by the Raj Thakra's MNS (Maharastra Navnirman Sena) in the 2009 assembly polls in Maharastra. MNS captured 13 seats while in 2004 it was virtually absent. This strong preference to MNS by the voters shows that Indian Minds are looking for more communal leadership than RSS and BJP. BJP leaders agreed that the MNS not only hurt the BJP- Shive Sena alliance in Mumbai – Thane, as expected, but also made a surprisingly strong showing in other regions as well. BJP leadership blamed the top brass leadership of the coalition for failing to deliver on its promise of a Ram Temple at Ayodhya; and on whose campaign the coalition secured a victory in 1992-93 poles.

MNS is strongly stickled to its political vandalism. From *gundagardi* to beating of women in pubs, from changing of signboards to Marathi to the slogan 'Maharastra for Marathis', the party has reaped a good harvest. The *gundaraj* of the party made a recent show in the Mumbai Assembly when a Samajwadi Party MLA, Abu Azmi was attacked and beaten for taking the oath in Hindi. The act came after MNS President Raj Tachkeray's open letter to party legislators asking them to take oath in Marathi, and his veiled warning in press statement against using any other language.

Raj Thackeray even did not bother to let even master blaster Sachin Tendulkar who said, "I am an Indian first and Maharastrian second and Mumbai belongs to all Indians". The reply Sachin got from Raj Thackeray was that Sachin's remarks had shaken Maharastrians. To quote Raj Thakray, "you left your usual ground and entered the political arena and you said everyone in India has an equal right over Mumbai. Sachin, hearing these words, the Maharathi heart is torn........you have been run out from the pitch of the Marathi heart".

Raj Thakray is not only popularizing and legalizing violence, but he is also earning respect for it. The recent case of dismissed crew of Jet

Airways, who knocked on his door seeking his intervention in the labor dispute, demonstrates this fact. Not surprisingly, K. L. Prasad the joint commissioner (law and order), Mumbai had to accept that Thakray was running a parallel government. India's dream for deepening democracy seems to remain bleak and unfulfilled under the current situation as regionalism has taken the lead from democracy and is deepening under the leaders like Raj Thakray. The danger is that many a fanatic group espousing a similar agenda in other states may get emboldened which will lead us towards a more violent community conflicts.

Modi will lead the BJP in 2014 Lok Sabha elections, as the party named him as its Election Campaign Committee Chairman. In the party's executive meet in Goa, it was decided to give Modi what he wanted. The move was widely seen as just a step away from making Modi the Party's prime ministerial candidate. A day before the crucial BJP executive meeting in Goa, party stalwart, L.K. Advani showed his reluctance on the appointment of Modi and stayed away from the meet. His statement that Madhya Pradesh Chief Minister Shivraj Singh Chuhan was a better prime ministerial candidate, has once again put him on a different track which the party does not like to play on. The supporters of Modi protested against Advani, shouted slogans against him. Advani responded by quitting all major party posts after accusing most of its leaders of pursuing 'personal agendas'. In a strongly worded resignation letter to party President Rajnath Singh, Advani wrote that BJP was no longer the same 'idealistic party' created by Shama Prasad Mukherjee, Deendayal Upadhyaya etc. The statement carries a huge weight, one can elaborate that when the Party is looked by suspicion by its senior most leaders, how come the party be able to maintain its position at the public place or when the party's decision making does not satisfy, rather, alienated its top leadership how can common man believe the decision making of the party would yield if voted to power.

Advani's letter bomb has badly shacked, not only the party but the whole alliance. His letter bomb has created wide cracks among the coalition partners. The Janta Dal (U) indicated that it would be difficult to remain in an alliance which was on 'ventilator support' following Advani's resignation, while the Shiv Sena said the NDA or the BJP without Advani was unthinkable. Terming Advani's resignation as a 'serious issue' and not good for NDA health, JD(U) President Sharad Yadav said that his party, an NDA ally, will meet to review the latest developments. Nitish Kumar, Chief Minister of Bihar also shares the same views regarding Modi's prime ministerial candidateship.

The critics often pointed out that Modi is projected before the people as the maker of Gujarat, a man behind its development or that Gujarat developed in Modian way. His third term is cited as an explanation or justification of his popularity. There is no doubt about Modi being the popular leader of Gujarat, but one needs to remind himself that Gujarat is a small part of India and not India. It is not only Modi's Gujarat that has shown development but Nitish Kumar's Bihar has showed more upward trend in the development than Gujarat. So on that account Modi is not rare. Imran Khan (Pakistani cricketer turned politician) was so impressed with Nitish's model of development that he said I want to rule on the line of Nitish Model. The fact was much earlier realized by Advani when he said, 'while Modi developed a healthy Gujarat into an excellent state, Madhya Pradesh Chief Minister Shivraj Singh Chouhan actually turned a BIMARU state into a developed one', thus puts Chouhan at number one.

One must not hoodwink the role Modi played in 2002 Gujarat massacre, where under a genocidal plan thousands of Muslims were brutally butchered. Recognizing his role in the planned massacre, various countries of the world, especially the USA didn't grant visa to Modi. To live down 2002 is not going to be easy, and anyone who aspires to be prime minister will definitely have to win the confidence of the 150 million minority community to be able to effectively rule the country.

Change is the law of nature, cycle of life but what is new in the present day change is that change in one part of the world brings changes in other parts of the world too _ what else represents a globalised world! Delhi is not far away from Kashmir; so any political change in Delhi may bring a political earthquake in Kashmir. The Modianisation of India or to say the Namo tide, has disturbed the tranquility of the ruling elites not only in India as a whole but also in Jammu and Kashmir. Since the arrival of two grand coalitions that is NDA and UPA, the Indian party system achieved a bi-nodal character. These umbrella type alliances are playing a seesaw type of power game; when one rules other remains in opposition. Stating otherwise, when one is up, the other is let down. The BJP is waiting for its turn to get up as it dipped down in 2004 when the situation drifted in favor of Congress. The elections of 2009 put huge question marks on the speculations made by political analysts and political pundits about the BJP's big show. BJP failed to make any ditch and the blame game within the party started. The saffron brigade started losing its colour, charm, health and even the leadership. But during the resent Lok Sabha elections it was not BJP VS Others but Modi VS Rest. The victory is not BJP's but Modi has won.

The million dollar question is why BJP high command went against the wishes of its senior most leaders? The reason perhaps is that the party wants a tough leadership, who is looked as pioneer of Hindutva by the Safron brigade. Modi has a tall image as a staunch profounder of Hindutva. Since L. K. Advani's Pakistan Yatra, where he suddenly discovered the virtues of Hindu-Muslim brotherhood in Jinnah and called him a secular, created a mismatch between Advani and his party. He earned a huge criticism for himself which forced his resignation and since then he is always dubbed to have softened his approach. This tilted the wave within the BJP towards Modi. The Indian voters have voted for "Change", but what kind of a change they voted for? Perhaps the most realistic answer is the people of India wanted democracy to be established over dynastic rule. But in the bottom of this change Modi's election as Prime Minister of India will surely bring a tussle between a Secular India and an India ruled according to Hindutva ideology. This change clearly represents the social mind set of Indian people, especially the youth who became the engine of this 'Hindu Nationalism.' This new brand of nationalism was so tactfully designated and articulated through mass media that 'Ab ki Bar Modi Sarkar' became the most popular phrase of 21 century India.

MAOISM OR NAXALISM

Background of the Movement: The movement began in 1967 as a peasant revolt in the Naxalbari police station area of Darjeeling district of West Bengal. Kanu Sanyal, the leader of the movement specified ten great tasks, which included distribution of land among the peasants, burning of all legal deeds and documents, arming of peasants by traditional weapons. The high point of the movement was reached in the month of May 1967 when forcible occupation of land by the peasants took place. The battle with the Maoists has raged since then. It intensified over the last few years following the formation of the CPI (Maoist), in 2004, through the merger of two prominent Naxilite groups, the People's War Group (PEG) and the Maoist Communist Centre (MCC). But who could have thought that a peasant movement, started in a small area of Naxalbari police station, in Dargeling district of West Bengal will pose a deadly threat to the unity and integrity of India. This movement has now engulfed in its fold as many as 16 states. Their capacity to kill and attack, rather massacre has reached to a deadliest height. It may be unwise to understand and approach the problem by linking it only with the left wing ideology, rather, it is movement for survival, an issue of India vs Bharat, Shining vs Backward and toiling, half naked, malnutritioned, modernity vs traditionalism, a few vs majority and at large state vs society. Ajai Sahni, Executive Director, Institute of Conflict Management, has related the problem with Indian demography. In an interview to *Frontline,* November 6, 2009, he said, "when you look at the Indian demography and its cumulative developmental deficits, 836 million people (77 per cent of the population) are living on less than Rs. 20 a day. More than half of them live on less than Rs. 10. They are living on the edge of survival." The paradox is that the Indian State is modern and the Society is traditional. The modern state is armed with a modern legal system, modern and sophisticated means to silence the voices coming from the society, demanding justice.

Expanding influence of Naxals: The expanding influence of Naxals has exposed the vulnerability of the Indian Political System. Naxalism has posed a great threat to the integrity of the nation. The Maoists, who operate in 231 of the 626 districts in the country and have 20,000 armed activists, apart from lakhs of supporters; is a serious challenge to reckon with. According to the Home Ministry's own figures, overall Maoist influence has spread from 56 districts in 2001 to 223 in 2009. The Maoists have waged a full-fledged war aimed at toppling India's democracy by 2050.

It took government of India 25 years to realize the magnitude of the movement. It was only in 2009 that the government woke up to the crisis at hand. P. Chidambaram, the then Home Minister, realized that the Maoists could not just be wiped away and sponsored a massive anti-Maoist offensive popularly known as "Green Hunt". A senior Home Ministry Official had explained then: "it is a comprehensive operational strategy that would first seek to clear an area of Maoists, occupy it militarily and follow it up with socio-economic developmental activity. The understanding is that it would take 18 to 24 months in each of the phase to operationalise the strategy and implement it successfully. (*Frontline*, November 6, 2009)

When mere uprising by people against Naxalite in the form of Salwa Judam (brainchild of Mahendra Karma), resulted in a massive destruction in the tribal areas, imagine what can arms offensive in conjunction with other states can do to the people, ask Human Rights activists. The violence has so far claimed over 1000 lives and led to a massive exodus of tribal people from over 644 villages. Of the 3.5 lakh displaced tribal people, around 70000 took shelter in the Salwa Judum camps of the government, while the rest went deeper into the jungle. But it is war that cannot be avoided, says Chhattisgarh police chief, Vishwa Ranjan. "For far too long we have been in a state of denial. Initially we did not even admit that there was a problem. Then, when the problem grew, we describe them {naxalite} as deviant tourists who had wandered in from other states. When the problem worsened, we described it as a law and order problem, and still later we described it as a political/ ideological problem, and now, when it has reached its climax, we realize that this is a national problem and a big threat to internal security.

However, even after the operation Green Hunt, it is evident that the strategy is not helping in minimizing Maoist activities. On the contrary, the Maoists have managed to stage counter attacks in different parts of the country, with the April 6, 2010 attack at Chintaland Dantewarda district of Chhattisgarh, in which 78 persons of Central Reserve Police Force CRPF were massacred, being the biggest yet. The other major attacks carried by the Maoists were in Koraput district (Orissa) on April 4, in which 11 security forces were killed; in Sidla (West Bengal) on February 15, in which 24 security forces were killed; and in Lahiri in Gadchiroli district (Maharastra), on October 8, 2009, in which 18 security men died. Overall, in the year 2009, 998 persons lost their lives in the Maoist related incidents. Out of 998, 392 were civilians, 312 were security personnel and 294 were believed to be the Naxals. Alone in the red corridor the number of Maoist related incidents went up. In West Bengal the incidents went up from 5 in 2008 to 255 in 2009, with Jharkhand 742 incidents, Chhattisgarh 529 incidents and Odisha 266 incidents. Similarly 2010 was the bloodiest year in terms of Maoist related deaths.

After a brief lull the Maoists have struck again, this time more mighty because the target were the giant political leaders of Congress. The audacious Maoist attack on May 25, 2013, which took the lives of 28 people has brought the spotlight back on a three-decade old internal conflict between the Maoists and the state. The attack killed Mahendra Karma, the architect of Salwa Judum, who had survived at least four attempts on his life by Maoists. The attack from one side highlighted the loopholes in the internal security establishment and on the other side it brought condemnation from across the nation. Prime Minister Manmohan Sing called the attack as a 'dastardly attack'. Omar Abdullah, the then Chief Minister of Jammu and Kashmir condemned the attack and called for strong anti-Maoist tactics be adopted. Professor Saifuddin Soz termed the attack as an attack on democracy.

The Government Failed to Curb Maoists: The highly planned and audaciously executed attacks of Maoists have exposed the failure of the

Government. There are various viewpoints being put forward to explain this failure. The most important reason is:

Lack of political will: Besides the superior planning and execution of the Maoists the single most important reason identified for the recent setbacks by large sections of bureaucracy and the security establishment is the lack of political will to tackle the Maoists. Shibu Soreen's comments which he commented in 2009, after Chintaland attack, underline this perception. A few days after taking over as Chief Minister of Jharkhand, Soreen described the Maoists as his brothers and asserted that the anti-Maoist operations were being carried out without his consent. Bihar's Chief Minister, Nitish Kumar followed the same line when he said that political and developmental work rather than military initiatives ought to be the priority in dealing with the Maoist issue.

No battle or war by underground forces can be sustained or succeeded without an above ground infrastructure to wage ideological war, provide recruits and most importantly supply guns and finance for the guerilla battalions. The above ground infrastructure of Maoists consists of those who are variously describing themselves as revolutionary writers, social justice protagonists, inclusive growth advocates and all those who describe the Maoists as 'misguided brothers', 'social justice seekers'.

Furthermore, the changed political landscape in Nepal has brought a historical change in the Foreign Policy as well as Domestic Policy of India. The Change of India from an anti-Maoist stance to pro-Maoism has far reaching effects on India's Foreign Policy. BJP warned New Delhi that pro-Maoist stance could encourage Maoist and Naxal rebels. The party leader said, 'if government could declare Indian Maoists and Naxalites as terrorists, why Maoists in Nepal are not treated alike'. They further held that accepting Nepal's Maoists as legitimate political organization would send mixed signals to India's rebels and weaken the government actions against them.

In communist terminology it can be stated that Maoists possess a strong base as well as a strong super-structure. The base constitutes the guerilla groups and armed militia while as the super-structure is constituted by intellectuals, elites, and all those who use soft power for hegemonising

Maoist ideology. If Indian government is serious to eliminate Maoism, it has to, first of all, eliminate the super-structure or the above ground infrastructure before digging the base and forcing the underground groups to lay down arms.

Two Movements, Two Responses: The Maoists, who operate in 231 of the 626 districts in the country, have 20,000 armed activists, apart from lakhs of supporters. But what is most surprising is the government's reluctance to deploy army in the Red Corridor. R.K. Singh, the Home Secretary pressed for intensifying anti-Maoist operations. But, when asked about the role of the Army against Maoists, he said, "there is no need to use Army in the region". Even the then Prime Minister and the Home Minister strongly negate the involvement of the Army against Maoists. Looking at the statement and the graph of casualties in the Maoist incidents compared with the situation in Jammu and Kashmir, one clearly can find the political will lagging to curb Maoists, plus a double standard Security Approach adopted by the Central Government. According to Director General of Jammu and Kashmir Police there are only 180 militants active in Jammu and Kashmir. In the light of this statement let us analyze the deployment of troops in the state of Jammu and Kashmir.

Jammu and Kashmir is one of the most militarized state in the world. By 1990, the first year of Kashmiri rebellion, there were approximately 150,000 soldiers in the valley- 17 for each square mile and one for every 25 civilians. In 1994 there were approximately 400,000 soldiers in Kashmir, representing just under half or 44 per cent of the total Indian army strength. A decade later, in 2004, the estimate ranged to 6,00000 soldiers with roughly one soldier for every ten civilians, making Kashmir the most heavily militarized place in the world. Muzaffar Hussain Beg, former deputy chief minister, told the Assembly on August 1, 2006 that there were more than 6,67,000 security forces in Jammu and Kashmir. Compare this with General Commanding in Chief of Indian army's Northern Command Lt. General H. S. Panag's statement that there are only 600 militants in the entire state. From time to time news reports, whose sources invariably are the defense officials, refer to the threat posed by infiltration of militants across the border. Actually, number of infiltration bids has fallen sharply:

in 2001 it was said to be 2417 but dropped to 537 in 2004, 597 in 2005, 573 in 2006, and 535 by 2007. In 2008 according to the army chief, there has been a 65 percent decline up to July 31, 2008, as compared to the same period in 2007. The Indian government also claimed more than 75 per cent decline in militancy- related incidents between 1990 and 2008, from 3500 to 709 incidents which is officially supposed to mean that situation is no longer considered critical. Firing incidents came down from 671 to 183. Bomb explosions declined from 914 to 69. Significantly, almost all the civilians killed in 2008, 2009 and 2010 were at the hands of forces. All this means that fighting armed resistance cannot be an over- riding motive for deployment of troops.

The point why the two movements are approached differently, treated differently, curbed differently, crushed differently and above all reacted differently is, perhaps, they are LEFT and we are RIGHT.

REGIONALISM

Regionalism has been widely used to indicate love for a particular region in preference to the country as a whole and in certain cases, in preference to the state of which the region forms a part. The Encyclopedia of the social sciences describes it as a manifestation of federalism and an intermediate stage between administrative decentralisation and federalism. A **region** is a defined territorial unit and the nucleus of a social aggregation for multiple purposes including particular language or languages, jatis, ethnic groups, tribes, particular social settings and cultural pattern, music, dance, folk arts etc. The region is characterized by a widely shared sentiment of togetherness and separateness from others.

> **Region**
> A region is a homogeneous area with physical and cultural characteristics distinct from those of neighbouring areas. As a part of national domain, a region is sufficiently unified to have a consciousness of its customs and ideals and thus possesses a sense of identity distinct from the rest of the country. A few examples of region in India are- Telengana, Vidharba in Maharastra, and Ladakh in J&K etc.

The term 'regionalism' has positive as well as negative meanings and usages. In the negative sense, it is used to imply excessive attachment to one's region in preference to the country or the state. In the positive sense it means the love for one's area of living or a particular region to which one belongs, one's culture, language, etc. It is something natural. While positive regionalism is encouraged through adopting a federal type of polity in which distribution of powers is made between Centre and different regions so as to maintain their regional identities. But on the other side the negative regionalism has threatened Indian nationalism and has become a great threat to the unity and integrity of the country.

Two factors foster regionalism, firstly due to the feelings of continuous neglect of a particular area by the government and secondly, it may arise because of increasing political awareness among the people of a particular area which was once backward. Regional feelings may give rise to secessionist demands and may prove dangerous for the unity of the country. Regionalism is regarded as one of the main barriers to the achievements of national integration in India. It may be added that quite often some political leaders encourage the feeling of regionalism to maintain their hold over a particular area or group of people. Negatively, regionalism 'reflects a psyche of relative deprivation' on the part of the people of an area. This deprivation psyche is exploited by the regional elite, who taking the benefit of the negative consciousness whip up the feelings of the people in the region and manufacture the ideology of regionalism.

Regionalism is not a new phenomenon in the Indian political system but its roots can be traced in the colonial period when the British imperialists deliberately fostered among the people of India a spirit of regionalism for their own imperialistic designs. After independence the leaders tried to foster a feeling among the people that they belonged to one single nation. The nation-building process in India was initiated soon after India achieved its independence. This was done under the dynamic leadership of PM Nehru and a galaxy of other national leaders. The goals for the nation-building were clearly laid and defined in the constitution. The Preamble of the constitution states that India should strive to achieve justice, liberty, equality and fraternity. The constitution defines India as a Sovereign, Democratic Republic based on Secularism and Socialism. Nehru showed India the model of development based on secularism, pluralism and welfarism and non-alignment. Analyzing the nature of nation-building process in India, Rajni Kothari refers to it as "the centre-periphery model" which seeks to secure socio-economic development through political development and modernization. This approach aimed to unite all regions of India in one single Indian Nationalism. Some other features of the Constitution like introducing single citizenship for all, a unified judiciary, all Indian Services, and a strong centre clearly reflect the agenda behind such features of the

Constitution. But in view of the vastness of the country and cultures regionalism soon made its appearance in India.

The first manifestation of regionalism was the demand for reorganization of states on linguistic basis which led to the formation of **State Reorganization Commission in 1953**. The reorganization of the states was a pressing problem then as now. The division of the states by the British was done on a highly irrational basis. Nehru on behalf of the govt. of India accepted the principle underlying the demand for linguistic provinces in the constituent assembly on 27 November 1947 and the Dar Commission was established to examine and report on the formation of the new provinces of Andra Pradesh, Kerala, Karnataka Maharashtra. Another committee known as JVP (Jawaher Lal Nehru, Vallabhai Patel and Pattabhi Sitara Maya Committee) was formed in 1948. Both considered the demand

State Reorganization Commission : *In December 1953, the government appointed the State Reorganization Commission for examining the issue of reorganization of states of the Indian Union in an objective and dispassionate manner and inorder to promote the welfare of the people of each constituent unit as well as of the nation as a whole. The Commission consisted of Justice Fazal Ali, Kavalam Madhava Panikkar and H. N. Kunzru. The Commission submitted its report in October 1955. For incorporating the recommendations of the Commission, the Parliament of India passed the State Reorganisation Act 1956.*

Some Recommendations:

1. *The Commission in its report recommended the reorganisation of states of Indian Union and suggested the creation of 16 states and 3 Union Territories.*
2. *Proper attention should be given to culture and communicative needs of other communities speaking different language in a monolingual state.*
3. *Linguistic miniroties should be well protected.*
4. *Attention should be paid to the development of other regional languages besides Hindi.*

for linguistic reorganization of states. However demands from various states led to the establishment of the States Reorganization Commission in 1953. The Commission in its report recommended reorganization of states of Indian union and suggested the creation of 16 states and three union territories. Andra Pradesh was the first state formed in 1953 on the lingual basis. The creation of Andra Pradesh further strengthened agitation for statehood. In 1960 the bilingual state of Bombay was also split into Gujrat and Maharastra. Punjab was extracted from Haryana in 1966. Later on various other states were formed on the same pattern. At present demands for separate statehood are raised from different regions of India.

Regionalism can be classified into three categories, suprastate regionalism, inter-state regionalism and intra-state regionalism.

The supra- state regionalism is formed by forming an identity by a group of states against other group of states or even against the Union. The group identity formed here is usually negative in character. Such type is also issue- specific. Its example can be cited by South India versus North India on language issue.

The inter-state regionalism is coterminous with state boundaries, here one state identity or group of states identities are juxtaposed against the identities of other states on certain issues that clash with the interest of one another. The Maharastra Karnataka boarder dispute and the river water dispute illustrate this.

The intra-state regionalism: Here part of a state develops the quest for self-identity and self- development positively, and negatively, it expresses a psyche of deprivation or exploitation in relation to the other parts of the same state. This phenomenon is also called as sub- regionalism. The main considerations behind sub- regional movements, however, are economic development and an anxiety for a proper sphere in political power. Vidharbha in Maharastra and Saurashtra in Gujarat explain this.

Regionalism has been a big hindrance in the process of national integration and nation building. The cries of Punjab for Punjabis, Assam for Assamese, Bengal for Bengalese etc, are often heard in India. In the words of N.D. Palmer, "one of the main barriers to the achievement of national integration in India is stronghold of regioal loyality". Factors like diversity of Indian society, over centralization, role of regional political parties, uneven development across the regions, communalization of politics etc. have helped the spirit of regionalism to grow stronger and stronger. Political parties, espicially the regional parties have played huge role in the growth of regionalism in India. The movements for greater autonomy by SAD in Punjab, DMK in Tamil Nadu, AGP in Assam, NC in Jammu and Kashmir etc. openly boosted the sprit of regionalism.

The growing menace of regionalism can be curbed by:

1. Decentralization of power.
2. Acquiring uniform kind of development across the regions.
3. Providing more safeguards for minorities.
4. Putting a restraint on communal parties.
5. Spreading right kind of education.

MAJOR FORMS OF REGIONALISM IN INDIA

1. **Demand for Separate Statehood**: The reorganization of the states was a pressing problem then as now. The division of the states by the British was done on a highly irrational basis. Nehru on behalf of the government of India accepted the principle underlying the demand for linguistic provinces in the constituent assembly on 27 November 1947. Dar Commission was established to examine and report on the formation of the new provinces of Andra Pradesh, Kerala, Karnataka and Maharashtra. Another committee known as JVP (Jawaher Lal Nehru, Vallabhai Patel and Pattabhi Sitara Maya Committee) was formed in 1948. Both considered the demand for linguistic reorganization of states. However demands from various states led to the establishment of the States Reorganization Commission in December 1953. The purpose of the commission was to examine the issue of reorganization of states of the Indian Union in an objective and dispassionate manner and to promote the welfare of the people of each constituent unit as well as of the nation as a whole. The Commission in its report recommended the reorganisation of states of Indian Union and suggested the creation of 16 states and 3 Union Territories. Some other recommendations of the commission were:

   a. Proper attention should be given to culture and communicative needs of other communities speaking different language in a monolingual state;
   b. Linguistic minorities should be well protected;
   c. Attention should be paid to the development of other regional languages besides Hindi.

The agitations for separate statehood for Telengana, Bodoland, Gorkhaland, and other areas have created hyper-tension at the centre and mental disorder in the states. It is no longer about language but regional aspirations, political as well as economic that define the behavior of such movements. The issue is not whether development has been taking place but the rate and equality or pattern of development is the core issue in the present agitations. Take Utter Pradesh where the demand is for the creation of Bundelkhand, Haritpradash and Poorvanchal. The unwieldy state, the sixth largest administrative unit in the world has 71 districts and if three more states are created, it would be reduced to just 15 which means that Utter Pradesh will mainly be the Awdh region with 31 MPs as against the current 80.

In Auronachal Pradesh there are demands from following regions for the separate statehood. Telengana with an area of 1,14,800 sq. km with a population of 3.2 crores consisting of 10 districts became the 29th state of Indian Union. In UP the demand is for Bundelkhand (population 7 crores, and area 60000 sq km, districts seven each from UP and MP), Harit Pradesh (consisting of 22 districts with a population of 5 crores and an area of 50000 sq km), Poorvanchal (having 27 districts with a population of 6.66 crores and an area of 86000sq km). In Assam, Bodoland comprising of 4 districts with a population of 30 lakh and an area of 8795 sq km, Mahakoshal (Orisa) with 10 districts and a population of 90 lakh and an area of 50,399 sq km, Gondwana (MP) comprising of 26 districts and population 2.65 crores and an area of 1.59 lakh sq km. In Maharastra Vidharba with a population of 2.63 crores and an area of 97321 sq km is demanding for separate statehood. In Gujarat Saurastra and in West Bengal Gorkhaland have intensified their demands for a separate statehood. Bimal Jalan, India's one of the leading economists, observes that the signs of the decline in the authority of the state are evident. These are to be found in the deteriorating law and order situation in several parts of the country, the increasing appeal of regionalism, tensions between the centre and its constituent parts, the decline in the quality of public services and the increasing failure of policies and plans to deliver what they promise.

4. **Secessionists Movements:** It is easier to meet the demands for separate statehood as these include using provisions of the Indian constitution to accommodate diversities. However, there are certain areas which are or were demanding a separate country. These demands put a huge question mark on the unity of India. Although, some demands have been pacified but here are some movements still going on against the Centre. These movements include:

   a. **Jammu and Kashmir:** Jammu and Kashmir, the land of contrasts, by virtue of its strategic position, literary balances the geo-politics of the region, covering an area of 2,22,236 square kilometers (the area includes the area under Pakistan and China) with a population of 1,25,48,926, larger than 68 sovereign countries of the world and is situated in the north of the subcontinent and in the heart of South Central Asia, it has borders with Pakistan, Afghanistan, China and India.

So sadly, when almost world over, the demand to safeguard the 'Rights of Man' was strengthening its ground, Kashmiris were intentionally and purposefully denied all kinds of rights. The white man's burden felt heavily on the dwarf people of the valley who were SOLD under the infamous Treaty of Amritsar (TOA), concluded between Maharaja Gulab Singh and the British Government on March 16, 1846, for a sum of seventy-five lakh rupees. Thus the Treaty of Amritsar is regarded as the originator of Jammu and Kashmir State. The time this inhuman treaty was conducted, Kashmir had a population of about three lacks. A simple statistical calculation shows that each person was sold for Rs. 25. Shocked by this inhuman practice, Dr. Sheikh Mohammad Iqbal expressed his sentiments in verses

    Their fields, their crops, their streams,
    Even the peasants in the vale
    They sold, they sold all, alas!
    How cheap was the sale.

Origins of the Conflict: At the time of independence there were 565 princely states ruled by the princes. On June 17, 1947 the Indian Independence Act was passed by the British Parliament providing for transfer of power to two newly created Dominions, viz., India and Pakistan; Section 7 of the said Act provided that the Indian princely states could choose to have had accession with either of the Dominions. But Kashmir did not accede to any one domain. The tribal invasion forced the Maharaja to enter into a conditional Accession with India on a condition that plebiscite will be held, which will finally determine the fate of Kashmiris. But this promise was never kept by the Indian Government and Kashmiris since then demand their Right to self determination.

The tribal invasion has divided Kashmir into two parts: Pakistan occupied Kashmir consisting of four districts while as twenty-two districts remain in the Indian occupied Kashmir. Of the total State population Muslims constitute 67.0 % followed by the Hindus (29.6%). According to Census 2001, Jammu and Kashmir, with a literacy rate of 55.5 % ranks low among the states and Union Territories. Male literacy rate is 66.6 % and female literacy rate is 43.0%. Ladakh is biggest region of the state area-wise, has a total population of 1,34,000. Of this Buddhists are in majority, constituting about 55% against 46% Muslims.

In this context of confusion and chaos, the panic stricken Maharaja acceded to the Union of India on the condition that New Delhi immediately sent its army to repel invaders. Lord Mountbatten accepted the accession on October 27, 1947 and made it conditional on the aspirations of the Kashmiri people. Sheikh Abdullah, who had been freed from prison a few weeks earlier assumed control of the collapsing administration. In 1948, when he (Sheikh Abdullah) became the Prime Minister of Jammu and Kashmir, he declared that he would accept the will of the people for the settlement of Kashmir issue and in May 1949, addressing himself in Srinagar to Pundit Nehru, he said 'I want you to believe that Kashmir is yours. No power in the world can separate us. Every Kashmiri feels that he is an Indian and India is his home land'. Kashmir was referred to the UNO by India which played its essential part in making a cease fire agreement between the two Countries (India and Pakistan) and opined that the dispute should be resolved in accordance with the wishes of the people. It was, however, made clear from the outset that the finality of the accession to India was strictly conditional on 'a reference to the people' of Jammu and Kashmir, as Mountbatten, governor-general of the Indian Dominion, put it while accepting the instrument of accession. On November 2, 1947 the Indian Prime Minister Jawaharlal Nehru declared his government's pledge to hold a referendum under international auspices to determine whether the people wished to join India or Pakistan. But unfortunately this promise was never kept and, rather became the base for the future conflict.

The demand, that Kashmiris should decide their fate themselves led to an arms uprising under the leadership of Mohammad Maqbool Bhat. The death of Maqbool Bhat was the birth of this new movement during 1990. Kashmir issue achieved new dimensions during 1990s. The armed uprising in Jammu and Kashmir and the conduction of nuclear tests by India and Pakistan in 1998 brought Kashmir issue back on international agenda. The United States and the other major powers soon recognized that the nuclear capabilities of the rival claimants made the issue more dangerous and its resolution more urgent. A widely shared perception is that these tests significantly raised the danger of another India-Pakistan confrontation, this time possibly sparking a nuclear war. As the American pressure was mounting on both the countries (India and Pakistan), the Prime Ministers of both countries (Atal Bihari Vajpaee and Nawaz Shareef) pledged to take immediate steps to reduce the risk of nuclear war and seek solution to their bilateral problems, including Kashmir. The mutual understanding between the two Prime Ministers lead to the signing of 'Lahore Declaration'.

Throughout the end of 1998 and early 1999, the world got the impression that India and Pakistan were coming closer. These hopes were soon dashed by the Kargil War of May 1999. The US blamed Pakistan for Kargil crisis and took a harsh stand against Pakistan's claim that the insurgents were Kashmiri freedom fighters. The American stand on

Kargil issue came as a pleasant surprise to India. Clinton while talking to Nawaz Shareef, bluntly asserted that the United States regards Pakistan as aggressor and demanded Pakistan withdrew its forces immediately. Frustrated with the turn of events Nawaz Shareef visited US to meet Clinton personally. At the end of the talks Shareef was forced to agree to the withdrawal of forces with a reservation that USA would take personal interest in enhancing or expediting talks between India and Pakistan once the sanctity of LOC is restored. President Clinton had won a major diplomatic victory, forging an agreement with Pakistan acceptable to India that headed off a possible catastrophe for both countries and the rest of the world. Washington's action during the Kargil crisis reflected the importance the nuclearization of South Asia had in shaping its approach to the Kashmir issue.

Kashmir issue has been lingering on for sixty two years and neither India nor Pakistan shows any positive approach to solve the issue. India treats Kashmir issue as a domestic problem but when the non-violent mass agitation took place in 2008 it shook the Indian state and society to its very core because it showed the alienation of the people to its utmost. Then the elections to State Assembly took place and a large number of voters, perhaps a record number of voters voted for which media jumped to the conclusion that people had rejected "Azadi". Then came the widespread protests against the rape and murder of Neelofar and Asiya in Shopian on May 29, 2009. Once again it became evident that whatever recovery was made vanished like fog and showed that anger against the government continues to simmer.

Contemporary Situation: Jammu and Kashmir is one of the most militarized state in the world. By 1990, the first year of Kashmiri rebellion, there were approximately 150,000 soldiers in the valley- 17 for each square mile and one for every 25 civilians. In 1994 there were approximately 400,000 soldiers in Kashmir, representing just under half or 44 per cent of the total Indian army strength. A decade later, in 2004, the estimate ranged to 6,00000 soldiers with roughly one soldier for every ten civilians, making Kashmir the most heavily militarized place in the world. Muzaffar Hussain Beg, former deputy chief minister, told the

Assembly on August 1, 2006 that there were more than 6,67,000 security forces in Jammu and Kashmir. Compare this with General Commanding in Chief of Indian army's Northern Command Lt. General H. S. Panag's statement that there are only 600 militants in the entire state. From time to time news reports, whose sources invariably are the defense officials, refer to the threat posed by infiltration of militants across the border. Actually, the number of infiltration bids has fallen sharply: in 2001 it was said to be 2417 but dropped to 537 in 2004, 597 in 2005, 573 in 2006, and 535 by 2007. In 2008 according to the army chief, there has been a 65 per cent decline up to July 31, 2008, as compared to the same period in 2007. Indian government also claimed more than 75 per cent decline in militancy- related incidents between 1990 and 2008, from 3500 to 709 incidents which is officially supposed to mean that the situation is no longer considered critical. Firing incidents came down from 671 to 183. Bomb explosions declined from 914 to 69. Significantly, almost all the civilians killed in 2008 were at the hands of Indian forces, 57 in Kashmir Valley alone during Amarnath Land agitation. All this means that fighting armed resistance cannot be an over- riding motive for deployment of troops.

Several questions erupt in the minds of all conscious minded people. Are Indian troops deployed here to defend the LoC and border, or are they instruments to alienate the people of Jammu and Kashmir by their subversive acts which cause human rights violations? India faces problems in many border states other than Kashmir, so the deployment of troops and other paramilitary forces in Kashmir has to be in the same proportion as to the deployment in border states facing Pakistan and China. India has to position seven lakh troops to defend the borders. For manning other states like Himachal Predash, Uttrakhand, UP, Bihar, Sikkim, Assam and Arunachal Predash, that share a long border (twice that of LoC) with the mighty China and which it perceives as another enemy, India has to raise a force of 14 lakh soldiers. India has 13 lakh active troops that constitute its Armed Forces. If 7 lakh troops are operating in Kashmir, the rest six lakh then should have to be on the border contiguous to Pakistan and China. If India's territorial integrity does not get undermined in placing a force strength of six lakh active troops facing the two nuclear-armed countries –though 'operational Standard' of Kashmir dictated it to have 7 lakh fighting soldiers there-how come Kashmir is threatened from Pakistan.

At the peak of conflict the Northern Ireland, the British government has deployed only twenty thousand troops to quell insurgency led by formidable Irish Republican Army (IRA). In Iraq, American and British troops had to wage deadly war against Al-Qaeda and other resistant groups. But even when they were fighting from house to house and carpet bombing them, the deployment of troops was less than two lakh. In Afghanistan, America and other NATO countries are receiving more and more body bags of their soldiers; still troop formation has not touched six- figures. India does not face such a situation in Kashmir.

Towards the end of the Amarnath Land row Syed Ali Shah Geelani (a prominent separatist leader) mentioned that the land issue is not confined to evacuation of 40 kanals of land allocated to the Amarnath Shrine Board but also related to other several lakh kanals under the illegal possession of Indian security agencies. The figure he gave was seven lakh kanals. The figure given in the State Legislative Assembly on August 24, 2009, however, reveals that the army grabs 10,54,721 lakh kanals of land out of which 8 lakh and 55 thousand kanals are held illegally and 1,99,314 kanals occupied by the agencies on the basis of lease, licenses and acquisitions under the provision of Land Acquisition Act. Kashmir Valley tops the list with 5,33455.78 kanals followed by Jammu with 3,21951.4 kanals.

These figures constitute only a fraction of the lands which have become out of bounds for farmers on account of border fencing. Kashmir has huge tracts of land which though not formally possessed have been mined both along Loc and International border and within the mainland for fear of *Fidayeen* attacks. People face problems in cultivation of those lands as well which fell in the vicinities of army camps. The figures do not include the lands which have been taken over by other Indian governmental departments other than the army. These figures remain inconclusive because the state has failed to clarify as to what type of land remains in army control.

Dissent and peaceful protest is the essence of democracy. But in Kashmir such is the height of growing intolerance that peaceful protests are labeled as 'agitation terrorism'. In the 2010 agitation more than 116 people, mostly young, fell to the bullets of soldiers. Furthermore, Public Safety Act (PSA) was slapped on more than 1600 Kashmiris aging from 15 years to 80 years. What else can reflect the Trust Deficit among Kashmiris than the three powerful agitations of 2008, 2009 and 2010? In one sentence it can be described as 'In Kashmir, 70000 are dead, over 10,000 have been disappeared, and 250,000 have been displaced since 1989.'

Here is a song from MC. Kash which explains why a Kashmiri protests: The Title of the Song is 'I Protest'.

> *I Protest, Against The Things You Done!*
> *I Protest, Fo' A Mother Who Lost Her Son!*
> *I Protest, I Will Throw Stones An' Never Run!*
> *I Protest, Until My Freedom Has Come!*

b. **Khalistan Movement in Punjab:** We know the composition of Punjab changed first with the partition and later on after the carving out of Haryana and Himachal Pradash. It was Akali leader Master Tara Singh who first launched the agitation for the Punjabi soba. The Sikh state was to consist of the Gurgaon district of Punjab and Patiala and the East Punjab State Union (PEPSU). The demand was conceded by the Centre and Punjab was made a separate state in 1966. The Akali leadres soon began to demand more and more powers for Punjab. The demand was reflected in famous "Anandpur Sahab Resolution" of 1973. The resolution wanted to redefine centre-state relations.

Since April 1981, the Akali extremists have been taking a hard-line approach for establishing a new all-Sikh nation called Khalistan. A well organized arms uprising was launched for achieving the goal of independent Sikh nation. The Bhindranwala group of Akalis established its centre in the Golden Temple and it became the seat for militants and militancy increased in the state. Once the movement became dangerous, the Indian Army launched "Operation Blue Star" against Sikh militants operating from the Golden Temple. This operation deeply hurt the religious sentiments of Sikhs. Though the militants in the Golden Temple were wiped off, the cause they were fighting for remained unresolved. The situation worsened when on October 31, 1984, Indira Gandhi was killed by her Sikh body guards. This tragic episode led to a wave of violence against Sikhs. Thousands of Sikhs were killed in different parts of the North India. Peace and normalcy returned to Punjab in 1985 when Rajiv Gandhi signed an agreement with the Akalis. This agreement is known as "The Punjab Accord". Elections to the Punjab State Assembly were held in September 1985, and the Akali Dal emerged as the winner and Surjit Singh Barnala became the Chief Minister.

c. **Secessionist Movements in North East:** The North East has been an area of strong regional sentiments. The area contains seven states, generally called as the seven sisters. Regionalism grew stronger during 80s and various secessionist movements were launched. Many militant organizations waged a war against Indian state. Although peace accords have been signed with different groups but the region is still volatile and disturbed.

Demand for Mizoram: The demand for separate Mizoram was first launched in the hill districts of Assam. The people of the Mizo Hill district of Assam demanded the formation of an independent Mizo State comprising the Mizos also of the contiguous areas of East Pakistan (now Bangladesh) and Burma. They formed the Mizo National Front to press their demands. The Mizo National Front(MNF) was the organisation who took up arms and commenced to guerrilla warfare. The union government responded by sending the army for crushing the movement, which led to a cycle of violence.

To bring normalcy in the region peace talks began between the MNF and the government of India in early 1971. The MNF demanded a referendum for a separate Mizoram and in 1972 the government decided to make Mizao Hill area a Union Territory. This new Union territory was named as Mizoram. This peace process did not satisfy all the MNF leaders. One faction led by **Laldenga** continued their militant activities till 1986. An agreement was signed between Rajiv Gandhi and Laldenga in 1986 in which Mizoram was granted a full-fledged statehood and MNF agreed to give up secessionist struggle. Today Mizoram is one of the peaceful regions of India and has made big strides in literacy and development.

Laldenga (1937-1990): *He was leader and creator of Mizo National Front. He led an armed struggle against India for over two decades. His group struggled to create an independent Mizoram. However, later he reached negotiated settlement with Prime Minister Rajiv Gandhi in 1986. He became the Chief Minister of Mizoram after peace was restored and Mizoram granted a statehood.*

Demand for Nagaland: Another tribe that demanded secession from the Indian union and agitated for an independent state was the Nagas of Assam. The Nagas formed the Nagas National Council under the leadership of **Zaphu Phizo** to carry on an agitation for the grant of independent status. In February 1950, Phizo held a plebiscite on the issue of Naga independence and 99 % of the Nagas were in favour of the independent state. Once the government of India denied Nagas a seperate state, they launched an arms movement against the government. However, after decades of fighting the peace process was initiated in 1957. The moderate Naga leadership came forward with a demand for integration of Naga areas into a single administrative unit to be governed by the Governor of Assam, on behalf of the President of India. This development was appericiated by the Government of India and in 1960, a decision was taken to grant statehood to Nagas within the framework of the Constitution.

On August 21, 1962, Jawaharlal Nehru introduced the State of Nagaland Bill and the Thirteenth Constitutional Amendment Bill in the Parliament, and after an easy passage, both the Bills received the President's assent. On September 4, 1962, Nagaland was given full-fledged statehood and became the sixteenth state of the Indian union. But this could not satisfy all the Nagas and they continued their militant tactics. Another agreement was reached between the Naga Rebels and the Government of India through which some peace was restored. However, some rebels have not accepted the settlement and a final resolution is still pending.

Conclusion:

It seems that India is not a "Unity in Diversity" but diversity forced to be united. From one side we hear Assamees making slogans like "Sons of the Soil" and from another side the Slogans of Azadi (freedom) are openly shouted in Kashmir. The identity crisis will make the conditions worse and the divide, which is till now felt in the Minds and Hearts of Indians, may divide India territorially. The community consciousness in every community is on rise which in turn has fastened communalization of politics and is leading towards an inevitable Clash of Identities. India did not become a nation when the system of parliamentary democracy was imposed. She is still struggling to become a nation. Even today, unity of the nation and national integration and an Indian identity are mere slogans for speeches from public platforms. It is difficult to pinpoint any issue on which there is national unanimity. Today, no national party has a monopolistic strength resulting in the organizational vacuum in the Indian political space.

Angami Zaphu Phizo (1904-1990): *He was the President of the Naga National Council which led an arms movement for independent Nagaland. He was forced to exile and was in exile for nearly three decades in U. K. during his last years of life.*

BIBLIOGRAPHY

1. Andrew Heywood, *Politics*, New Delhi: Palgrave Macmillan, 2003.
2. Andrew Heywood, *Political Theory*, New Delhi: Palgrave Macmillan, 2012.
3. O. P. Ghauba, *Introduction to Political Theory*, New Delhi: Macmillan India, 2006.
4. J. C. Johri, *Comparative Politics*, New Delhi: Sterling Publications, 2004.
5. D. D. Basu, *Introduction to the Constitution of India*, New Delhi: 2004.
6. Subash C. Kashyap, *Our Constitution*, New Delhi: National Book Trust India, 2007.
7. Subash C. Kashyap, *Our Parliament*, New Delhi: National Book Trust India, 2004
8. Subash C. Kashyap, *Our Political System*, New Delhi: National Book Trust India, 2009.
9. Gul Mohd Wani, *Kashmir: From Autonomy to Azadi*, Srinagar: Valley Book House, 1996.
10. Alastair Lamb, *Kashmir A Disputed Legacy 1846-1990*, Oxford, Karachi,
11. Ajit Bhattcharjea, *Kashmir the Wounded Valley*, New Delhi, USB Publishers, 1994.
12. Sumantra Bose, *Challenge in Kashmir*, New Delhi: Sage Publications, 1997.
13. Victoria Schofield, *Kashmir in Crossfire*, New Delhi: Viva Books Private Limited, 1997.
14. G. H. Khan, *Freedom Movement in Kashmir 1931-1940*, Srinagar: Gulshan Books, 2009.

15. Meera Verma, Mrinal Mehta, Rumki Basu, *Essays on Indian Government and Politics A Continuing Review*, New Delhi, Jawahar Publishers and Distributors, 2004.

16. W. H. Morris Jones, *The Government and Politics in India*, New Delhi: Universal Book Stall, 1989.

17. Atul Kohli, *State and Poverty in India*, Cambridge: Cambridge University Press, 1987.

18. Granville Austin, *The Indian Constitution: Cornerstone of Nation*, New York: Oxford Press, 1966.

19. Rajni Kothari, *State Against Democracy*, New Delhi: Aganta Publications, 1998.

20. Ghanshyam Shah, *Social Movements in India; A Review of the literature*, New Delhi: Sage, 1990.

21. J. C. Johri, *Principles of Modern Political Science*, New Delhi: Sterling Publishers Private Limited, 2002.

22. B. L. Fadia, *Indian Government and Politics*, Agra: Sahitya Bhawan Publications, 2010.

23. Ramachandra Guha, *Makers of Modern India*, New Delhi: Penguin, 2010.

24. Rajni Kothari, *Politics in India*, New Delhi: Oriental Longman, 2005.

25. M. N. Shriniwas, *Social Change in India*, New Delhi: Oriental Longman, 2004.

26. Gabriel A. Almond, G. Bingham Powell, Jr., Kaare Strom, Russall J. Dalton, *Comparative Politics Today: A World view*, New Delhi: Pearson Education, 2009.

27. Bipin Chandra, *India's Struggle for Freedom*, New Delhi: Penguin Books, 1989.

28. Bipin Chandra, Mridula Mukherjee, Aditya Mukherjee, *India since Independence*, New Delhi: Penguin Books, 2008.

29. Ernest Barker, *Principles of Social and Political Theory*, London: Oxford University Press, 1967.

30. Institute of Social Sciences, '*Status of Panchayati Raj in the States and Union Territories of India 2000*' New Delhi: Concept Publishing Company, 2000.

31. Justice A. S. Anand, *The Constitution of Jammu and Kashmir its Development & Comments*, New Delhi: Universal Law Publishing Company, 2013.

32. Mohan Ram, *Maoism in India,* New York: Barnes and Noble Inc, 1971.

33. D. Suba Chandran and P. R. Chari, *Armed Conflicts in South Asia: The Promises and Threat of Transformation* edited, London: Routledge, 2012.

34. Swamy Karan R., *Kashmir How Far Can Vajpayee and Musharraf Go,* New Delhi: Peace Publications, 2001.

35. Sanjay Kak, *Until My Freedom Has Come, the new intifada in Kashmir,* New Delhi: Penguin Books, 2011.

36. Mirza Waheed, *The Collaborator,* New Delhi: Penguin Viking, 2011.

37. Dipankar Sengupta and Sudhir Kumar Singh, *Terrorism in South Asia,* Delhi: Authors Press, 2004.

38. Ajay K. Mehra, D. D. Khanna, Gert. W. Kueck, *Political Parties and Party Systems, New Delhi: Sage Publications, 2003.*

39. D. C. Gupta, *Indian Government and Politics,* New Delhi: Vikas Publishing House, 1972.

40. Dr. R. N. Trivedi and Dr. Tripti Jain, *Indian Government and Politics,* Jaipur: College Book Depot, 2008.

Magazines

1. Economic and Political Weekly.
2. South Asia Politics.
3. India Today.
4. Frontline.
5. Pratiyogita Darpan.

News Papers

1. The Hindu.
2. Hindustan Times.
3. Times of India.
4. Greater Kashmir.
5. Rising Kashmir.
6. Tribune